THE SECRET WAR AGAINST HITLER

THE SECRET WA

TRANSLATED BY HILDA SIMON

NEW INTRODUCTION BY
BEATE RUHM VON OPPEN

WITH A FOREWORD BY
JOHN J. MCCLOY

GAINST HITLER

by Fabian von Schlabrendorff

Westview Press

BOULDER • SAN FRANCISCO • OXFORD

Der Widerstand: Dissent and Resistance in the Third Reich

Copyright © 1994 by Westview Press, Inc.

Published with new introduction in 1994 in the United States of America by Westview Press, Inc., 5500 Central Avenue, Boulder, Colorado 80301-2877, and in the United Kingdom by Westview Press, 36 Lonsdale Road, Summertown, Oxford OX2 7EW

First American edition published in 1965 by Pitman Publishing Corporation, New York

English translation published under the title *Revolt Against Hitler: The Personal Account of Fabian von Schlabrendorff,* edited by Gero v.S. Gaevernitz, in 1948 by Eyre and Spottiswoode, London.

First edition published in German under the title *Offiziere gegen Hitler.* Nach einem Erlebnisbericht von Fabian v. Schlabrendorff, edited by Gero v.S. Gaevernitz, in 1946 by Europa Verlag, Zurich.

Library of Congress Cataloging-in-Publication Data
Schlabrendorff, Fabian von, 1907–1980
   The secret war against Hitler / by Fabian von Schlabrendorff ;
(with a new introduction by Beate von Oppen).
     p. cm. — (Der Widerstand, dissent and resistance in the
Third Reich)
   Originally published: Zurich: Europa Verlag, 1946.
   Includes bibliographical references and index.
   ISBN 0-8133-2190-5
   1. Anti-Nazi movement. 2. Germany—Politics and
government—1933–1945. 3. National socialism—Germany.
4. Schlabrendorff, Fabian von, 1907–1980. 5. Hitler, Adolf,
1889–1945—Assassination attempt, 1944 (July 20)   I. Title.
II. Series.
DD256.3.S3273   1994
943.086—dc20   94-15065
                                                     CIP

Printed and bound in the United States of America

The paper used in this publication meets the requirements
of the American National Standard for Permanence of Paper
for Printed Library Materials Z39.48-1984.

10   9   8   7   6   5   4   3   2   1

"A ship may sink, but does not have to strike the flag."

Nikolaus von Halem,
on being sentenced to death
by the "People's Court."

Contents

vii

Illustrations

All portraits were drawn by Hilda Simon
from the best available photographs.

Introduction

When news of an attempt to kill Hitler
reached London in the afternoon of the
20th of July 1944, it came as a surprise and caused amazement. I still remember my excitement at the first fragments of information coming on the ticker tape with
British intercepts of German news agency material. (I was
working for the British Foreign Office in something called
Political Intelligence.) I also remember hearing Hitler's
midnight speech in which he assured his people that he
was alive and that his survival was an omen from Providence that he must carry on his work.

But I also remember what filtered down as expert and
official British reaction on the next day: There was relief at
the failure of the plot. Two reasons were given for it: one
reasonable, the other less so and, so it seemed to me, ex-
cessively cold-blooded. Success would have meant another
German "stab-in-the-back" legend and would have bedevilled a new German regime just as the legend that Germany was robbed of victory after the first world war had

bedevilled the Weimar Republic. That made some sense. The other, to my mind less respectable, reason was that these plotters were not the kind of people the Allies could work with, that they came from the very class that had let Hitler in: too many counts and barons.

The American President had no fondness for the "East-Elbian Junkers" either. The would-be assassin, Colonel Count Claus Schenk von Stauffenberg, came from west of the Elbe and was a Catholic Württemberger—and he was dead—but the other names that surfaced reeked of Prussia: and Prussia was widely taken to be the cause of German perdition and a peril to the world. A year later the Allies abolished the state at their Potsdam Conference. That Hitler could not by any stretch of the imagination be seen as a Prussian, that he was a stateless Austrian until naturalized in Germany less than a year before assuming power, that his cast of mind and speech—his way of being—was the very opposite of Prussian—such facts were rarely considered by those who saw the second world war as a reenactment and continuation of the first.

On 2 August 1944, in a parliamentary speech on the state of the war, Churchill had this to say about the affair:

> In Germany tremendous events have occurred which must shake to their foundations the confidence of the people and the loyalty of the troops. The highest personalities in the German Reich are murdering one another, or trying to, while the avenging Armies of the Allies close upon the doomed and ever-narrowing circle of their power. We have never based ourselves on the weakness of our enemy but only on the righteousness of our cause. Therefore, potent as may be these manifestations of internal disease, decisive as they may be one of these days, it is not in them that we

should put our trust, but in our own strong arms and the justice of our cause.[1]

It is worth noting that there was consistency in the British view of the German opposition to the Nazi regime as "internal disease," not as healthy antibodies.

There is a later, apocryphal Churchill quotation haunting some of the literature about the German resistance to Hitler. No source is given beyond "Churchill in the House of Commons 1946." That is quite a haystack; and it has never been possible to find this needle in it, despite diligent use of an adequate index appended to the Parliamentary Reports:

> In Germany there lived an opposition which grew weaker and weaker through its sacrifices and an unnerving international policy, but which belonged to the noblest and greatest that has ever been produced in the political history of any people. These men fought without help from within or without—driven only by the restlessness of their consciences. As long as they lived they were invisible and unrecognisable to us because they had to hide. But in their dead the resistance became visible. These dead do not have it in their power to justify everything that happened in Germany. But their deeds and sacrifices are the foundation of the reconstruction. We hope for the time when this heroic chapter of German domestic history will find its just valuation.[2]

These are sentiments that the magnanimous wartime leader of Britain may well have held after the war. But they need a proper source to be accepted by history.

This, however, is Fabian von Schlabrendorff's recollection of what Churchill said to him in 1949, ten years after their first meeting: "Reviewing the years that lay between our two meetings, he told me that he realized afterwards that during the war he had been misled by his assistants about the considerable strength and size of the German anti-Hitler resistance."[3]

Churchill's Foreign Secretary, Anthony Eden, in a memorandum of 23 February 1943 on "Morale in Germany" wrote, just days after the Stalingrad surrender, "There is still no evidence of organised opposition to the regime or of conscious and deliberate obstruction of the war effort."[4] In mid-June 1942 George Bell, the Anglican Bishop of Chichester, had asked Eden for an audience. He wanted to tell him about his meeting with Dietrich Bonhoeffer in Sweden, where he had learned of the opposition to Hitler inside Germany and its hope for British understanding and support. Eden had received him on 30 June, told him of his suspicion that such emissaries could unwittingly serve the Nazis' aim to put out "peace feelers" but promised to study the documents. On 17 July he wrote: "Without casting any reflections on the bona fides of your informants, I am satisfied that it would not be in the national interest for any reply whatever to be sent to them. I realise that this decision may cause you some disappointment, but in view of the delicacy of the issues involved I feel that I must ask you to accept it."[5]

The "delicacy" may in part have been the inability of the Western Allies to mount the Second Front for which Stalin was agitating and the desire, the need, to hold the Coalition together. This, of course, became even more delicate as time passed and the Russians continued to bear the chief burden of the war on land. The Anglo-Americans cleared North Africa, started their campaign in Italy, and eventually prevailed in the war at sea and in the air. George Bell continued not only to try to convince his government that there was "another Germany" plotting to overthrow Hitler but also that carpet bombing (the destruction of cities from the air) was both immoral and counterproductive. Inside the Foreign Office Eden was less polite about him than in public. There is a marginal note by Eden in an internal Foreign Office document in which he calls Bell "this pestilent priest."

Another adviser, John Wheeler-Bennett, was a historian who knew a lot about Germany, especially its Weimar and Nazi periods, and Churchill may have seen no reason not to trust him—though he may have been chilled by Wheeler-Bennett's comments on the trials and executions, Hitler's revenge after the miscarriage of the coup. On 25 July Wheeler-Bennett wrote:

> It may be said with some definiteness that we are better off with things as they are today than if the plot of July 20th had succeeded and Hitler had been assassinated. In this event the "Old Army" Generals would have taken over and, as may be deduced from the recent statement from the Vatican as to the Pope's readiness to mediate, would have put into operation through Baron von Weizsäcker a peace move, already prepared, in which Germany would admit herself defeated and would sue for terms other than those of Unconditional Surrender. By the failure of the plot we have been spared the embarrassments, both at home and in the United States, which might have resulted from such a move and, moreover, the present purge is presumably removing from the scene numerous individuals who might have caused us difficulty, not only had the plot succeeded, but also after the defeat of Nazi Germany.[6]

It is worth quoting this opinion verbatim, because it encapsulates most of the factors being weighed. The loss of lives was hardly a consideration, indeed the loss of plotters' lives evidently had its positive aspect. The subsequent enormous loss of Allied—and Jewish—lives in the eight and one-half months the war in Europe continued may have been regarded as a necessary price to pay for the elimination of the German menace. Continued Soviet co-operation was considered a necessity and brought the Russian army to Berlin and to the Elbe and resulted in the division of Europe. Among the Americans, as among the British, there were doubters of the policy of Unconditional Surrender, but they did not prevail.

American press comment on the plot and the punishment of the people involved in it indulged in bloodthirsty rejoicings. The *New York Times* instantly fell in with the assumption or suggestion that it was a "generals' plot" and headlined its comment on the first of the ghastly People's Court trials: "Hitler Hangs His Generals."[7] The *New York Herald Tribune* on the same day, 9 August 1944, opined: "Let the generals kill the corporal or vice-versa, preferably both."[8]

That first trial, of Field Marshal Erwin von Witzleben, three generals, and four other officers—all expelled from the Wehrmacht by a dishonorable "Court of Honor" and thereby surrendered to the jurisdiction of the "People's Court"—was a show trial. Subsequent trials were transacted more discreetly. It seemed inadvisable to allow public disproof of Hitler's claim that the plot had been the doing of a "tiny clique." Publicity of the trials would have revealed the wide ramifications of the plot and the true character of the accused. Access to them was severely restricted, and they were not reported on, though photographic and sound recordings were made, fragments of which can still be seen and heard, for example in Hava Kohav Beller's film *The Restless Conscience*.

Such, then, were some of the international circumstances and sentiments in which those opposed to the Nazi regime in Germany and willing to do something about it had to act. The internal conditions were no more propitious. The SS was immensely powerful, and despite the shock of Stalingrad most of the people remained loyal to Hitler. Any reappraisal after Stalingrad was hampered by the almost simultaneous Casablanca formula of Unconditional Surrender, which meant surrender not only to the Anglo-Americans but to Stalin.

Nevertheless, a determined man like Henning von Tresckow persevered in his efforts to eliminate Hitler. His faithful lieutenant, Fabian von Schlabrendorff, managed to convey explosives disguised as a package of two bottles of Cointreau onto Hitler's plane when the commander-in-chief had at last been lured to the headquarters of Army Group Center in Russia; he even managed to retrieve the package when it had failed to go off and to cover all traces of the attempt. That was in March 1943. A few days later, another attempt, this time in Berlin, by Colonel Baron Rudolf von Gersdorff failed because Hitler's sixth sense made him abridge the ceremony at which that officer was going to blow himself up with his commander-in-chief.

But it is time to say something about Schlabrendorff and his book. The first version of his account of the secret war against Hitler was entitled *Offiziere gegen Hitler*[9]—officers, not generals, against Hitler. The difficulties he and his friend and superior, Major General von Tresckow, had with their efforts to enlist generals in the enterprise of overturning the regime were recorded in that book. It was short and appeared under the name of the OSS officer who had discovered him among a group of prominent prisoners liberated by the Americans. It was published in 1946, in Switzerland, as were the other early books on the German opposition to the Nazis. The first publication of the letters Helmuth James von Moltke wrote to his wife, during and after his trial, took place in England. The Germans had to wait. But people who wanted to learn something about that secret war were deeply impressed by the early Schlabrendorff book when copies reached England; an English translation was published in London in 1948 under the title *Revolt Against Hitler.*[10] It was as short as the original German version and as moving in its immediacy.

That immediacy was lost in the later and much longer American version, which is republished here. In his Preface Schlabrendorff himself described what drove him to it: chiefly Wheeler-Bennett's interpretation in his *Nemesis of Power*[11] and the best-selling book by the American journalist William Shirer, *The Rise and Fall of the Third Reich.*[12] Readers must judge for themselves what has been gained and what may have been lost. They should make the imaginative effort to restore the spare original account by mentally subtracting later additions on the British attitude to the German resistance; the disappointment at the Munich Agreement; resistance activities on the Eastern front; and more about the military head of the conspiracy, Ludwig Beck. Lively criticism of the International Military Tribunal at Nuremberg is among other additions, and there is an interesting case of a German court foiling the knavish tricks of some Nazis in the early days of the regime. Later, of course, Special Courts and the infamous People's Court were added to carry out the intentions of the regime more faithfully.

Indeed Hitler appreciatively referred to the President of

the People's Court, Roland Freisler, as "our Vishinsky." Otherwise, with very few exceptions, Hitler hated the legal profession, and he probably had cause. It was Freisler who hurried to Munich in February 1943 to see to the swift beheading of the rebellious students of the White Rose and who presided over the trials after July 1944 until, in February 1945, he was killed in an Allied air raid—clutching the dossier of the accused—while Schlabrendorff's trial was in progress. It was one of the series of miracles that saved the life of the most persistent and intrepid enemy of the regime.

Schlabrendorff had not been arrested until the middle of August 1944. Tresckow's last service to the cause had been to disguise his suicide as a case of death in action. The police commissar later told the prisoner that four factors had pointed to his probable involvement in the plot: There was, first, theological literature in his luggage—a book on Catholic moral theology, a book on Protestant ethics, publications on the rapprochement between Catholics and Protestants, and a Bible. Second, he was a lawyer in civilian life, and the Third Reich had little use for lawyers. Third, he was an officer; in recent years the most troublesome opposition had come from officers, and the Gestapo was unable to suppress it. Fourth, he was a member of the nobility; that caste was by nature inimical to Adolf Hitler and National Socialism.[13]

It is worth examining these points—and interesting that the evidence of serious Christian convictions and concerns ranked first. The regime tried to hide its antagonism to the churches, especially during the war, most especially in the war against Bolshevism and the "atheistic" Soviet Union. The struggle continued, however, and indeed intensified. The secret morale and "public opinion" reports of the Security Service regularly included sections on opposition to the regime on the part of churches and their following or sympathizers. These might have even included a communist like Georg Elser, the man who planted the first bomb against Hitler in 1939 and who in the weeks of solitary and careful preparation often sought solace and strength by visiting churches. And it is altogether striking how many of the active opponents of the regime and particularly how many of the men involved in the successive conspiracies were serious and committed Christians who objected to the neo-paganism of the Nazis. Gestapo reports show this clearly and even show that Catholic objections to "neo-paganism" were objections to the idolatry of race and to anti-Semitic policies and that the ideological watchdogs of the regime understood this.

As for Schlabrendorff himself, he rarely travelled without theological reading matter, even after the war. It was probably the conflict with Hitler and National Socialism that had provoked this abiding interest. He once told me that German Protestantism had been somnolent and possibly moribund until the Nazi challenge roused it—or at least part of it. The wartime and postwar religious revival in Germany bore him out—even in communist East Germany. Martyrs like Dietrich Bonhoeffer may have helped, though his own official church disowned him for being "political." Catholics were less hamstrung by Romans 13 and its Lutheran interpretation.

That Schlabrendorff was a lawyer in peacetime was the second suspicious circumstance. In this book he may, by his account of an example of recalcitrance in the legal profession, give the impression that he was satisfied with its overall performance. He was not. He saw clearly that it had, to a large extent, gone along with the administration

of iniquitous laws and regulations. He deplored this slavish obedience to Positive Law; he had his doubts about
Natural Law, but his interest in moral theology and ethics
shows his concern with ethical and theological underpin-
nings of any system of law, however "historically" evolved.
That Hitler loathed the legal profession—despite its weaknesses and shortcomings—is made quite clear in public
and private utterances, in his speeches and *Table Talk*. That
speaks *for* the profession.

Third, there was a prima facie case for suspicion in
Schlabrendorff's status as officer, albeit a very junior one.
The title of his first book was no accident. Neither was the
Allied decision to treat the conspiracy as a "generals'
plot." It should be obvious that one cannot hope to overturn a government in wartime without an involvement of
generals. But both the first book and this one show clearly
how hard it was to enlist generals in the cause, how weak
and vacillating some possible candidates were, and how
morally obtuse most of them showed themselves to be in
their failure to respond to Hitler's revelations about the
mode of warfare to be adopted in the East. It was the junior officers who carried the main burden. Tresckow,
Witzleben, Beck, Stülpnagel, and a few others were exceptions. But colonels, captains, and lieutenants were willing
to stake their lives and lost them in large numbers in the
relentless proceedings after the failure of the coup. Yet it is
a noteworthy fact that even those not involved but who
knew something about the plotting did not denounce
their colleagues until it was all over and the tortures and
trials started.

The same goes for the aristocracy, the fourth "suspicious" category. There was enough solidarity in that caste
for denunciations to have been exceedingly rare, even

among those who had been approached about cooperation and had declined. This does not mean that there were
no Nazis in the aristocracy; indeed, many of the plotters
had been early supporters of National Socialism. But there
was a feeling of noblesse oblige among those who were not
Nazi careerists.

There were, of course, connections between the suspicious categories that led to the assumption of guilt in
Schlabrendorff's case. For instance, a divisional press on
the Eastern front printed copies of Bishop Galen's sermons against the "euthanasia" campaign to kill the inmates of institutions and disseminated them in the army.
Bishop Preysing of Berlin, the most consistent and determined opponent of the regime in the German hierarchy,
had studied law and was perfectly able to discuss the
maximal exploitation of the very narrow margin of ma-
noeuvre within legal limits of resistance with the lawyer
Helmuth James von Moltke.[14]

After the war Schlabrendorff went back to the practice
of law and especially concerned himself with looking after
the cases of the next of kin of the plotters. He was still doing it in 1960, when he turned up in Alexandria, Virginia,
to look for documentation among the captured German
records to substantiate the claims of these widows and orphans. He also fought for compensation for Ernst
Niekisch, a man of consistently Left and pro-Russian ori-
entation, who had lost his health and eyesight during years
of Nazi incarceration and was for many years denied compensation by the Berlin and Bonn authorities because after his liberation he had joined the Communist Party and
worked for the East German government while living in
West Berlin. Schlabrendorff went as far as Strasbourg to
invoke the European human rights convention against the

decisions of the German courts. He won, just in time, as he said, to provide for Niekisch's widow.[15]

For some years he served as judge on the Federal Constitutional Court, then went back to his law practice when his term was up. I only saw him in court once, in a case against a neo-Nazi who had maligned the memory of Dietrich Bonhoeffer by publicly accusing him of treason from base motives. Defamation of the dead is an indictable offense in Germany. The young prosecutor and judge were helpless against the insolence of the accused, who called in question the legitimacy of the Federal Republic and its right to try him. Schlabrendorff, appearing as counsel for the two surviving sisters of Bonhoeffer, reasserted the majesty of the law. For a moment he seemed to be its embodiment. The courtroom in Heilbronn was packed with the defendant's sympathizers. When it was over, there was a little demonstration by more neo-Nazis outside the court house, carrying placards denouncing the "Traitors' Republic." But they kept a respectful distance. Nonetheless it was an ugly scene and sad for the survivor, who had been Bonhoeffer's cell-neighbour in the Gestapo prison. The melancholy of the survivor never quite left him, and loyalty to his dead companions was a strong motive in all his postwar activities. It informed the first account he gave of their story and is still noticeable in the later version—which, however, lacks the "Totenliste," a first list of 126 names of people who perished after the failure of the attempt.

Anti-aristocratic resentment has been as harmful to a clear focus on the German resistance to the Nazis as proaristocratic snobbery, both in Germany and abroad. Naturally, sociological factors played their part in those catastrophic twelve years and in the history that led up to them. But the stark problems confronting Germans once

Hitler and his cohorts were in power and were supported or at least tolerated by the majority transcend class.

Men and women had to make individual decisions or made them by default by allowing themselves to be carried along. Resistance could take many forms, one of them being help to the persecuted and endangered. Protests could make such help harder to render by attracting attention and inviting punishment and prevention of further assistance. Even discreet help, such as that given by Dietrich Bonhoeffer and Hans von Dohnanyi to a group of Jews they managed to get to safety in Switzerland by having them declared agents of the intelligence service, led not only to the arrest of the helpers—and Dohnanyi had been a very active player in the conspiracy—but to the severe reduction in the radius of activity of Hans Oster and Wilhelm Canaris, the head of the Abwehr who had until then been able to support many resistance undertakings; and eventually it led to the execution of those four, just days before the end of the war.

This is another part of the context in which the story told here must be seen. The story concerns the endeavor to overturn an evil regime, first in order to prevent Hitler's war, then in order to end it. When Schlabrendorff spoke to Churchill, the conservative backbencher, in 1939 and pleaded for British firmness, he told him that he was not a Nazi but a patriot. The plotters were patriots—especially a man like Oster, who kept telling the Dutch and Belgians the dates fixed for the German offensive in the West.

Tresckow summed up the reason why the coup must be attempted even at a late stage when the chances of success were minimal. He said: "The assassination must be undertaken at any cost. Even should that fail, the coup d'état must be attempted. For it is no longer its practical purpose that matters, but the proof to the world and to history that the men of the German resistance movement dared to stake their lives and take the decisive step. Compared with this object nothing else matters."[16] On the 21st of July, before killing himself, Tresckow added: "Just as God once promised Abraham that he would spare Sodom if only ten just men could be found in the city, I hope that for our sake he will not destroy Germany."[17]

Fabian von Schlabrendorff died on the 3rd of September 1980, forty-one years after the beginning of Hitler's war.

Beate Ruhm von Oppen

Notes

1. Martin Gilbert, *Road to Victory: Winston S. Churchill 1941–1945* (London, 1986), p. 868.

2. Erich Zimmermann and Hans-Adolf Jacobsen, eds., *Germans Against Hitler: July 20, 1944* (Bonn, 1964), p. 64.

3. See p. 98 in this volume.

4. Armin Boyens, *Kirchenkampf und Oekumene 1939–1945* (Munich, 1973), p. 213.

5. Eberhard Bethge, *Dietrich Bonhoeffer: Man of Vision, Man of Courage* (London and New York, 1970), p. 670.

6. Gilbert, *Road to Victory*, p. 868.

7. Klemens von Klemperer, *German Resistance Against Hitler: The Search for Allies Abroad 1938–1945* (Oxford, 1992), p. 386.

8. Ibid.

9. Gero v.S. Gaevernitz, ed., *Offiziere gegen Hitler.* Nach einem Erlebnisbericht von Fabian von Schlabrendorff.

10. Gero v.S. Gaevernitz, ed., *Revolt Against Hitler: The Personal Account of Fabian von Schlabrendorff* (London, 1948).

11. John W. Wheeler-Bennett, *The Nemesis of Power: The German Army in Politics 1918–1945* (London and New York, 1954).

12. William L. Shirer, *The Rise and Fall of the Third Reich: A History of Nazi Germany* (New York, 1960).

13. Gaevernitz, *Offiziere,* pp. 168f. and Gaevernitz, *Revolt,* p. 157.

14. Beate Ruhm von Oppen, ed., *Helmuth James von Moltke: Letters to Freya 1939–1945* (New York, 1990), pp. 16, 23, 184f., 287, 334.

15. Joseph E. Drexel, ed., *Der Fall Niekisch: eine Dokumentation* (Cologne and Berlin, 1964). This book affords fascinating glimpses into the intricacies of the status of Berlin under Allied occupation and the legal consequences of the Cold War.

16. See p. 277 in this volume.

17. See p. 295 in this volume.

Foreword

It has been said that the character of a people is revealed in its heroes. During the Nazi period in Germany, heroism was largely obscured by the excesses of the regime. But on July 20, 1944, a culminating event took place at Rastenburg, East Prussia, which, though tragic in its outcome, gives the Germans, as it would any people, a noble and heroic standard. Slowly perhaps the German people are beginning to comprehend the full significance of the events of that day and the Resistance Movement which led to it.

Not only within Germany but without, an ever-widening circle of people is obtaining a deeper insight into the causes, the inspiration, and the extent of the Resistance. As more information becomes available it is apparent that the word "plot" is scarcely adequate to cover the urge on the part of a small but inspired group of Germans to restore decency to their nation by ridding it of the

1

leadership of Adolf Hitler. To be sure, there was a plot to kill Hitler, and the Resistance could not have had the significance it has attained without the attempt and the elements of destruction and martyrdom which flowed from it. But the Resistance was more than a plot. Just as Hitler's wrath after July 20 reached beyond the men directly involved, so the compelling urge to to defy Hitler and his regime reached far beyond the actual planning that placed Stauffenberg's bomb under Hitler's map table at Rastenburg.

I have attempted, since the first reports came in of the nature and extent of the Resistance Movement in Germany, to keep abreast of the materials and literature related to it. I have become increasingly impressed by the quality and faith of many of the small band of men and women who had the courage to undertake this effort against what was probably the most repressive police state of modern times. The Resistance was more than mere dissent; it was a solid determination, though not well-organized, to destroy the central authority of the Nazi state. It was, as Stauffenberg called it, a revolt against the "Evil Incarnate." Being human and therefore uneven in temperament and character, the men and women involved in the movement against Hitler were not all endowed with the same degree of spiritual and moral strength. They were not all cast in a heroic mold but many were; they were not all self-effacing martyrs but it is difficult to point to one among them whose motivation was personal advancement. They all had in common a determination to replace Hitler and what he stood for at the risk of their lives and fortunes.

The more I have learned of the *Widerstand*, the more

I have become convinced that the late President Heuss of Germany made the prophetic comment when he said of the July 20 attempt on Hitler's life that it was "the gift to Germany's future." Had there been no Resistance, had there not been the outright, dangerous and determined revolt, there would have been little for the new German nation to draw from the Nazi years and from World War II other than the memory of the aggression and madness of Hitler, the frightful persecutions, and the defeat—a dismal tradition for the future of Germany and mankind. The determined, even though unsuccessful, attempt gave the Germans an example of the high courage and purpose of a remarkable group of men and women who were prepared to go to the bitter end of their convictions. The courage and moral stature of men like Bonhoeffer, Tresckow, Leber, Dohnanyi, Kleist, Oster—how difficult it is to name any without naming a dozen more!—represent a pattern on which posterity can base its appraisal.

I venture to prophesy that in spite of attempts within and without Germany to disparage the importance of their sacrifice, those who did speak out and did act out their parts in the tragedy will be accepted, as time goes on, as national heroes and heroines. Inefficient, poorly organized as they were, they put their full personal responsibility on the line. They showed that there were men and women in Nazi Germany who, despite the organized pressure of a brutal police state, had the capacity to act, and in so many cases, to die, as moral human beings.

One of the authentic and persistent heroes of the *Widerstand* is Fabian von Schlabrendorff, the author of this book. He has written before of his part in the Resistance. He was in it from the beginning to the end. Owing his own escape from death to a succession of miracles, he saw and communed with most of the leaders of the Revolt, witnessing the last moments of many and sharing their tortures.

Fabian von Schlabrendorff now gives us a series of vignettes of the main participants, many of which shed new light on various aspects of the Resistance. Again there comes through with unmistakable emphasis the moral imperative which impelled so many of his band. It is a poignant story and it loses nothing in the retelling by this unassuming citizen and jurist who, when the challenge came, accepted every risk and endured every agony for the cause.

It is impossible today for serious students to contend that the Resistance was merely the move of a few ambitious, scheming officers and aristocrats seeking to save themselves and their country from the consequences of defeat. It may take a long time for the Germans to place the men and women of the Resistance in the shrines of their national heroes. Many of them deserve a place not only in a German shrine, but in all places devoted to the memory of those of whatever nationality or creed who have been prepared to perform their individual and personal responsibility to the furtherance of the right—even unto death.

John J. McCloy

Preface

The building was nothing but a bombed-out, burned-out, blackened shell. With some difficulty, my companion and I picked our way through the ruins, finally locating the entrance to the stairway that led to the cellars. At the bottom of the stairs, a long row of cells opened onto a corridor. The floor was strewn with rubble, the cells were empty, but on the doors the numbers were still clearly legible. Slowly I walked along, reading the numbers, until I finally came to a stop in front of cell No. 25.

A flood of memories assailed me as I stood looking at the small bare room in which I had been imprisoned for many interminable months. I thought of the desolate nights on the prison cot, when I had lain chained hand and foot and unable to move, at times exhausted after lengthy interrogations by the Gestapo. For the bombed-out building which my companion and I were exploring on that summer day in 1945 had been the most infamous Gestapo prison in Berlin, and within that long row of now empty cells had been confined, less than a year before, a very special group of prisoners: all members of the German anti-Hitler resistance who were apprehended after the abortive coup d'état of July 20, 1944.

As we walked from cell to cell, reading the numbers, name after name came to my lips—all friends and companions who had since died at the hands of the Gestapo and SS. Many of them had met their end in one of the numerous concentration camps through which I, too, had been dragged after we prisoners who had survived the first few months after July 20 were evacuated from Berlin early in 1945. During the following months, when I had to brace myself each morning anew for the end that seemed inevitable, the death that was always so close at hand, freedom and safety were a remote and unreal dream.

On that August day in 1945, the fact that I was exploring the ruins of my former prison still held a quality of unreality. It was only three months since I, together with a group of other political prisoners, had been liberated from the clutches of the SS by the American army. In the course of events following that liberation, I had become acquainted with Gero von Gaevernitz, special assistant to the regional chief of the OSS, Allan Dulles. It was Gaevernitz who had made possible, among other things, the trip to Berlin and our inspection of what was left of the Gestapo headquarters. The most important result of our association, however, was the book which forms the cornerstone of the present volume, and which was written during the summer months of 1945.

It all started in Capri where the liberated prisoners of

the group to which I belonged were quartered, by the American military authorities, in the Hotel Paradiso. Gaevernitz, who had been sent to Capri by General Lyman Lemnitzer with orders to investigate the background of the individual prisoners, became engaged in conversations with me, and finally suggested that I accompany him to Switzerland, where he wanted me to give an account of my activities in the German resistance movement.

I agreed to his proposal, and spent the following weeks dictating to his secretary some of my experiences as an active member of the anti-Hitler resistance in Germany. Gaevernitz, after editing the manuscript, published it under the title: *Offiziere gegen Hitler* (Officers Against Hitler). At that time the occupation authorities in Germany did not permit any publications by Germans, and therefore my story had to appear as one of the "based-upon-the-account-of" type of books. A number of other restrictions were also imposed upon the contents so that the scope of the book was severely limited and much of importance had to be left unsaid. The value of the original book lies mainly in the fact that some of my personal experiences —especially those dealing with details of my imprisonment and trial—were written down while they were still fresh and vivid in my mind, and before they became dulled by the passage of time and new impressions. To Gero von Gaevernitz must go the credit of having realized the importance of this, and of having made possible publication of an account of this kind at so early a date. I would like to take this opportunity to express my appreciation of his efforts in getting the original book published.

In the years that followed many changes took place. Occupation in the West ended, and the zones of Germany that had been occupied by the Western Powers became the Federal Republic of Germany. All restrictions on publications by Germans were dropped. It was then that many people urged me to revise and enlarge my original book and add all the parts that had never been published before, thus giving a more complete picture of the development and activities of the resistance so far as I had been involved in it.

Even though I realized that such a revision was called for, I could not bring myself to undertake the task, partly because, by that time, my career as a jurist was taking up an increasing amount of my time. The chief reason, however, was that I shied away from reopening old wounds that had never really healed. In addition, the post-war years had brought so bountiful a crop of books about the Nazi era, both by German and non-German authors, that it seemed to me the subject was being dealt with to saturation.

On reading some of these books, however, I began to realize that post-war appraisal of the Third Reich and of the role played by the German anti-Hitler resistance contained many errors and erroneous conclusions. This became especially clear when William L. Shirer's *The Rise and Fall of the Third Reich* was published, quickly made the best-seller lists, and was acclaimed as the authoritative source of information about the entire Hitler era. I then decided that, in the interests of historical accuracy, I must publish the facts which I knew from my own experience, and which in many cases shed a different light on the events of those years. It seemed all the more important because I am one of the handful of surviving active and early members of the German resistance, and probably the only one who knows from his own experience certain details of resistance activity within the military group.

I therefore dug out my old notes, added some new ones, and began the task of rewriting the story of the twelve years during which I was one of those who, opposed to the Nazi regime from the very beginning, became actively involved in the plans to assassinate Hitler.

This story is still basically a personal account, and does not at all pretend to be a complete history of the German resistance. I do, however, begin by offering a short historical analysis of the reasons and circumstances that led to the rise of Adolf Hitler in 1933. This seems important for a better understanding by the non-German reader of both the phenomenon of the Hitler rule and the growth of the resistance.

Of necessity I must take issue with some of Shirer's contentions and statements in the course of my book, although it is not my aim to criticize his impressive tome. Such a task is best left to the historians, and indeed has already been admirably dealt with by Professor Klaus Epstein, of Brown University, in his brilliant review of *The Rise and Fall of the Third Reich* (April 1961). Wherever I contradict Shirer it is done either because I find it impossible to agree with his interpretation of German history, or because the facts as I know them do not agree with his version. Personal knowledge and information often supply information that cannot be gained by the most diligent perusal of documents and statistics.

If my story contributes to a better understanding of the phenomenon of the Nazi era, and most especially to an appreciation of the reasons that compelled the members of the German resistance to risk and sacrifice their lives, their families, friends, and fortunes in the fight against Nazism, I shall feel that the purpose of this book has been accomplished.

I want to express my heartfelt appreciation to Hilda Simon, of New York City, without whom this book would not have been possible. In the first place, a translation of this kind of book calls for intimate personal knowledge of the conditions and atmosphere existing in the Third Reich as well as in the anti-Nazi circles of that time. Miss Simon has this knowledge. In the second place, it was not a question of simply translating an existing book or manuscript. My German book constitutes only part of this present volume; the other part is made up of numerous notes and records—all of them so far unpublished—which I had jotted down some time ago in an effort to complete my account of the years of anti-Nazi resistance activity. These notes were all in longhand, and Miss Simon had to decipher them—an achievement in itself—translate them, and insert them in the right places, tying them in with the rest of the book. She has handled this difficult job with great sensitivity and understanding. In addition, I am very much pleased with the fine portrait drawings she did for this book.

I also want to thank Jerome S. Ozer of Pitman Publishing Corporation for his great cooperation and assistance in getting this book published, and Stefan Salter for his dignified design and invaluable suggestions.

Fabian von Schlabrendorff

Wiesbaden
Spring, 1965

THE SECRET WAR AGAINST HITLER

CHAPTER ONE

How Could

Hitler Happen?

In spite of the two decades that have passed since the fall of the Third Reich and the mountains of material that have been published about the Nazi era, one question continues to puzzle many people: How was it possible for Hitler to grab power in Germany, and then proceed to implant National Socialism in the German people?

Beneath the more or less horrified fascination with which the Hitler era is commonly regarded outside of Germany, an alert observer can also frequently detect a feeling of uneasiness and apprehension on the part of the more thoughtful of those non-Germans who have studied the post-mortem findings about the Third Reich. Their apprehension seems to center mainly on the question—still largely unanswered despite many attempts—of how a man like Hitler, without a violent revolution, civil war, or similar such upheaval, was able to gain control of a modern republican government. Even more puzzling is the fact that, once he had taken over, he managed within a few short years to turn Germany into a barbarian totalitarian state. How could this happen? And since it could and did happen, not to some small, backward, illiterate nation but to an old European country with a history of great achievement in literature, the arts, and science, was there not the danger of something similar happening to other civilized nations? The theory that a high level of literacy and education is in itself a reliable safeguard against such dangers has proven invalid, for the Germans were without question one of the best-educated peoples in the world.

The thought that "it could happen elsewhere" can have most disturbing implications, and cause gnawing doubts about political institutions long considered impervious to attacks by usurpers of power. It is perhaps quite understandable that many non-German analysts of the Hitler era seek to allay such fears and doubts by attempting to prove that Nazism and its rule were peculiarly and exclusively German, and that other nations are exempt simply by virtue of not being German. This is a very comforting theory, for it automatically wipes out any lingering, nagging worry that a Hitler might conceivably happen at another time, in another country, to another people. Nothing, indeed, could be more reassuring to non-Germans than the statement by William L. Shirer, author of *The Rise and Fall of the Third Reich*, probably today's most widely-read book on Hitler and his time, that "Nazism and the Third Reich, in fact were but a logical continuation of German history" (p. 133). The question is whether this statement is valid.

Upon closer examination, we find that German history, as pictured by Shirer, seems to have been shaped largely by three events: the Protestant Reformation, and specifically the influence of Martin Luther on the German people; the Thirty Years' War (1618-1648); and Prussia's rise to power in the 18th and 19th centuries. Shirer claims that the demoralizing influence on the Germans of these three events led directly to Hitler and Nazism.

Martin Luther is held responsible not only for the rise of German nationalism but also for "ensuring a mindless absolutism," which, in Shirer's words, reduced the "vast majority of the German people to poverty, to a horrible torpor and demeaning subservience." (pp. 134-35). Then came the Thirty Years' War, causing large-scale devastation of the country. The Peace of Westphalia which ended this conflict was also disastrous, we learn, for it only strengthened the absolute rule of the local German princes. This was supposedly a blow from which Germany never recovered.

Matters went from bad to worse, according to Shirer, when Prussia rose to a powerful position. We hear that the Hohenzollern, the ruling princes of the state that was later to become Prussia, were "little more than military adventurers," and that under their rule the original Slavic population was "pushed back along the Baltic." (p. 136). The state of Prussia, Shirer claims, was "held together only by the absolute power of the ruler, by a narrow-minded bureaucracy, which did his bidding, and by a ruthlessly disciplined army." Thus, the state, which was "run with the efficiency and soullessness of a factory, became all; the people were little more than cogs in the machinery." (p. 137). And so, in Mr. Shirer's opinion, the Prussian state became the natural basis for Nazi dictatorship.

To anyone with even a fair knowledge of German history, the picture drawn in *The Rise and Fall of the Third Reich* must appear incredibly primitive, to say the very least, and typical of an attempt to make the actual facts fit a preconceived theory. It is undeniable that half-truths, precisely because they do contain an element of truth, are more misleading and harmful than actual falsehoods. Facts, events, and statements that are taken out of context, exaggerated, and invested with an importance they do not inherently possess cannot but present a lopsided, distorted picture.

Ever since publication of such books as *From Luther to Hitler* (Rohan D. O. Butler), it has become fashionable to place much of the blame for the rise of Nazism on Martin Luther. Erich Fromm's analyses of the Reformation also have advanced the idea that Lutheranism helped prepare German acceptance of a "Fuehrer." Although this theory may be interesting as an exercise in psychological speculation, it should never be made the basis for any serious historical analysis. "It has been said," declared Paul Tillich during lectures at the Washington Cathedral Library in the winter of 1950, "that Lutheran Protestantism especially has been the soil that fed National Socialism. This, of course, is a most primitive and unhistorical reasoning."

Martin Luther was a rebel, a reformer, and a challenger; symbol of rebellion against the excesses of an all-powerful, oppressive authority, of supreme courage of conviction in the face of all threats and dangers including that of death at the stake. He was also responsible for stressing the importance of the "individual conscience," and his lonely, stubborn "Here I stand, I cannot do otherwise, so help me God!" became the classical quotation for those engaged in struggles of conscience against oppression. This included many of those Germans who, four centuries after Luther, were locked in a struggle to the death with the Nazi tyranny.

Luther's political influence pales into insignificance when compared with his image as a towering figure of spiritual rebellion. In any case, only the northeastern and central regions of Germany were strongly affected by the Reformation, while large parts of the south, southwest, and west remained more or less solidly Catholic and under anti-Protestant rule. It is, therefore, somewhat difficult to see how the Protestant reformer could have influenced the "vast majority" of Germans.

The Thirty Years' War, which began as a Protestant-Catholic clash but later turned into a European power struggle, was most certainly a disaster for Germany. So, of course, is any long-drawn-out and bitter conflict for any country. At the end of the Thirty Years' War, Germany was devastated and exhausted and had suffered a setback in its entire economic, cultural, and political life which was to leave its mark for a long time to come. To put the blame for the resulting slowness of recovery solely upon the German princes and their autocratic rule is to oversimplify matters. And when Mr. Shirer goes on to state that "the pursuit of learning and the arts all but ceased" in these small principalities, he is so far out of step with the facts that even a casual student of German history can refute him. In fact it is difficult to find a period in which music, poetry, the theater, philosophy, and literature flourished to such a degree as under the reign of the German princes, especially in the 18th century when each one of these rulers vied with his neighbor in an effort to draw to his own court the best talents among actors, artists, poets, and philosophers, many of whom—Goethe, Schiller, Bach, Kant, to name only a few—achieved world fame.

To anyone with a fairly intimate knowledge of Prussian history, Shirer's short sketch of that country's development is a most astonishing piece of work. Far from being "military adventurers," the early Hohenzollern were able, down-to-earth administrators, who concerned themselves primarily with such problems as trade, reform of legal procedures, and cultural progress. Historians of all shades of opinion agree, for instance, that the Great Elector (1640-88) was undoubtedly one of the most outstanding figures among the rulers of that era. The gradual pushing back of the Slavic population toward the more eastern regions, for which Shirer blames the Hohenzollern, actually occurred in the centuries before the first Hohenzollern princes ever came to the province of Brandenburg, from which Prussia later developed.

In his entire discussion of Prussian history, Shirer does not even once mention the name of Frederick the Great. This is somewhat like writing a history of the United States without mentioning Abraham Lincoln. Prussian history was to a large extent shaped by Frederick the Great. Under his rule Prussia not only became an important European power but also a state based upon certain fundamental laws then unique in Europe, and, incidentally, the exact opposite, both in spirit and in practice, of those imposed upon the German people by Hitler two centuries later. Even a brief examination renders absurd any contention that the Nazi oppression was in any way a "logical continuation" of Prussian rule—on the contrary, it proves absolutely fatal to this theory, which is probably the reason why Shirer decided to pass over the great Prussian king.

Among the basic concepts of Prussia under Frederick the Great were equality before the law for all citizens, from the king down to the poorest inhabitant; complete religious freedom for all groups and individuals; and enlightened law enforcement, including abolition of torture, which at that time was still widely used in the rest of Europe as an instrument of official justice. It remained for Hitler's Gestapo to reinstitute torture two centuries later in Prussia—a point which I raised when I was on trial for my life before the "People's Court," after the abortive plot against Hitler in 1944.

The effects of Frederick's laws were immediate. Those persecuted on religious grounds, as for instance the Jews in Austro-Hungary, sought and found refuge and freedom in Prussia where they could become citizens, with all the rights enjoyed by the rest of the population. Although officially a Protestant state, Prussia allowed Catholics, Jews, and other religious groups to practice their faiths unmolested. The citizens, secure under laws that offered equal protection for all, openly voiced their opinions, which at times even included criticism of the king's policies. Books forbidden in other, especially Catholic, states could usually be obtained in Berlin. There can hardly be a greater contrast between the Prussian state, where the humblest citizen could bring suit against the king, and the Nazi state, where any kind of criticism of the ruling clique was considered high treason and punished as such.

Little wonder that the wisest of Frederick's contemporaries fully realized the outstanding qualities of the Prussian king. The fledgling United States of America had hardly attained its independence, when it sought—and got—a treaty with Prussia. In 1785 Franklin, Adams, and Jefferson came to Europe and signed the treaty, which concerned neutrality on the high seas, with the Prussian ambassador in The Hague. Thus the young United States owed its first acknowledgement as an independent power to the Prussian ruler who, in the words of the American leaders, was "cut out to be an example for all others." The impact of Frederick's rule on Germany was probably best formulated by Goethe, who once said that it was inevitable that a period of cultural flowering should follow in the wake of so great a king.

The successors of Frederick the Great kept intact his basic state concepts; and so, despite its faults and weaknesses, despite its large, rigid, and often narrow-minded bureaucracy and the excessive importance attached to all things military, Prussia remained a state based upon law. The equality of all citizens before the law was enforced with remarkable impartiality, as was the tolerance for all religions and confessions. Any kind of racial intolerance was, of course, totally unknown.

In view of all this it becomes clear that any attempt to explain Hitler as the logical consequence of German history, plausible as it may sound to non-Germans unacquainted with the facts, must be rejected. The background of Hitler's power grab and his success in instilling National Socialism in the German people is due to a pattern of facts and events so complex that it defies a simple explanation. Only the sum total of a number of factors—often quite unrelated but coinciding—could provide the basis necessary for the growth of Nazism. One may look at the centuries-old history of Germany: A Hitler is not only impossible to find but indeed quite inconceivable.

This does not mean, of course, that individuals with Hitler's mental and emotional make-up did not exist in other times. It means only that such persons remained either eccentrics without power or influence in public life, or that they spent their lives as objects of medical care, study, and observation. To make history, people like Hitler need a climate of chaos, upheaval, and dire material poverty as well as spiritual want.

When we examine the period immediately preceding Hitler's rise to power, we find that, on the material side, economic need was one of the chief causes contributing to the unstable and confused political situation in Germany in the years before 1933. The lost war of 1914-18, the inflation which followed and which wiped out the savings of millions of people, and the world economic crisis of 1929 had opened the door to economic chaos in Germany. Without this desperate material situation, without the six million unemployed—more than 40% of the total labor force—Hitler would never have succeeded in making himself the master of the German people.

Another reason for the ease with which Hitler demolished the existing government of the Weimar Republic, which had taken the place of the Monarchy after 1918, was the wide-spread popular disillusionment with the state of public affairs. This dissatisfaction with a government that seemed to rely more and more on "emergency measures" had mounted steadily as unemployment remained high. The blame for that sad state of affairs rested as much with the leading Social Democratic Party as it did with the right-wing opposition, which made little effort to find a solution to the country's problems. It is, however, a mistake to assume that the pre-1933 opponents of Hitler could have prevented his rise to power simply by working with and "strengthening" the Weimar Republic. One can often hear this theory expressed, especially in the United States; it is based on the erroneous assumption that there was anything left to work with in the Weimar Republic. It is best answered by an ancient oriental proverb: "Do not place your load on a dead camel." By the time Hitler's star was on the rise, the Weimar Republic was indeed a "dead camel."

The Treaty of Versailles, which unquestionably was designed more as an instrument of retribution than of peace, and which the Congress of the United States twice refused to ratify, had created deep-seated feelings of resentment in wide circles of the German population. The average German, who in the war of 1914-18 felt that he had simply done his duty, as had soldiers of the other countries, and had fought gallantly, could not understand why he should be punished so severely by the other participants in the war.

At the time, fear of Communism was also an important factor contributing to public uneasiness, for the Communist Party in Germany could muster several million votes, and the example of what had happened in neighboring Russia was fresh in everybody's mind.

All these fears and resentments were shrewdly exploited by Hitler, who promised to fight Communism, eliminate the "Shame of Versailles," and give "Work and Bread" to Germany's unemployed, thus striking the right note for a wide range of dissatisfied or apprehensive Germans. The importance of his emphasis on providing *work* as well as bread should not be underrated, for the German worker did not want welfare or to be the ward of the state: He wanted a *job* which would allow him to provide for himself and his family.

Hitler's diabolical talent for projecting exactly the kind of "futurama" his listeners were yearning for undoubtedly contributed heavily to his success. He did not even bother to keep secret his method for influencing his audience; it can be found in the second volume of his book *Mein Kampf*. Here he reveals the strategy he used to win over people of different ages, classes, and various parts of the country, all of whose hopes and wishes he managed to reduce to a common denominator.

His most amazing feat, however, was that he was able to persuade not only his followers but also many of his opponents of the impossibility of denying him some kind of participation in the government. The too-clever ones among his political adversaries finally came up with the idea of taking him into the government, giving him some semblance of power, and then slowly but surely undermining and choking him off through the activities of those government agencies not controlled by the Nazis. This astonishing theory led to talks between representatives of the Center (Catholic) Party and Hitler, during which a coalition government was discussed. Many other political leaders including Reichspresident von Hindenburg himself had the same idea, and even so natural an enemy of Hitler and Nazism as the Social Democrat Breitscheid fell victim to this fatal line of reasoning. When Breitscheid heard that Hitler had been appointed Chancellor he clapped his hands together in delight, exclaiming that now Hitler would soon be finished because he would never be able to cope with the difficulties of the Government!

But these gentlemen's expectations were not fulfilled. On the contrary, exactly the opposite occurred. Hitler's coalition partners and all the representatives of the Reichstag, from right to left, who had helped, against their inner convictions, to put him in control soon found out that their calculations contained some fatal errors. With a minimum of difficulty Hitler managed to render powerless Hindenburg, Franz von Papen, and the other political leaders, and to institute his totalitarian regime by breaking every parliamentary rule—in spite of the numerical strength of the other parties, in spite of large and well-organized Social Democratic labor unions, in spite of all the checks and balances of a republican government designed to insure against just such a takeover.

Once Hitler had *legally* become Chancellor of the Reich, he was aided in the consolidation of his power by the "other side of the coin"—the bad side of a normally good and typically German trait of civil obedience. It becomes apparent to any serious student of German history that one of the basic flaws in the character of the German people is a lack of feeling for form, poise, and balance. They are comparable to a torrent of water without a river bed to contain it and give it form and direction. This trait explains the tendency of the Germans to split up into a multitude of small factions; evidence of this tendency appears throughout the centuries, in the bewildering array of tiny German states, and in the equally bewildering number of political splinter parties—33 in all—in the German republic before Hitler. Several times in the course of German history these various currents have been gathered together by force into a single stream; each time this happened extraordinary feats were accomplished by a united German people. The proverbial excellence of the German soldier is based upon the same phenomenon.

Normal respect for authority is a necessary trait for any law-abiding citizen; but the average German's lack of natural poise led him to the other extreme: excessive civil and military obedience, with the inherent danger of accepting and obeying *any* law and *any* authority, whether good or bad. This trait was exploited to the hilt by Hitler; it explains why his *legal* assumption of power helped so much to strengthen his position. If he had taken over the government by means of a putsch or a revolution, he would have had a much more difficult time establishing himself with the German people, and opposition to his rule would have been much stiffer from the beginning. By giving him a place in the government, his opponents handed Hitler the perfect tool for the subjugation of the country. In effect Hindenburg, Papen, and all the other political leaders were cast in the roles of attendants holding the stirrups for Hitler against their own wishes—truly one of history's more vulgar jokes!

We now have a number of factors which all contributed to the establishment of the Third Reich. Singly, none of these factors would have been sufficient; but taken together they added up to a solid platform from which Hitler could launch his attack on government by law. And yet, in spite of everything that has been said so far, the heart of the matter has not been touched. Germany is, after all, a country that has given the world many people whose lives have contributed substantially to the prestige and fame of European culture and the progress of Western civilization. It would be futile to try and strike these names from the records of world history.

We must look deeper for the primary explanation of why Hitler was able to strangle all opposition in Germany at a time when the Gestapo, with all its means of coercion —the concentration camps, the tortures, and the executions without trial—was still in its infancy. And we find this explanation in the spiritual nihilism which had developed in Europe in the wake of the industrial revolution and the technical progress of the previous century; and which, spreading like a fast-growing weed, had choked off everything else in the process. I am not talking here about the anarchistic terrorist movement so well known from the history of Czarist Russia. In our case, the nihilism is a much deeper and broader current, not confined to any one country; it meant nothing less than the corrosion and disintegration of all ideologies, philosophies, and principles, until finally there remained nothing of the values of the Western world except meaningless fragments. This nihilism in Europe resulted in a spiritual climate which discouraged individual responsibility and nurtured the growth of organized mass pressure groups, the satisfaction of whose urges and demands produced a growing tendency toward totalitarianism. Thus, in 1917, a new totalitarian and Caesarean form of government was ushered into the modern world and quickly established itself in a number of European countries. Although this new political phenomenon took a relatively mild form in some countries, it proved extremely virulent and aggressive in others, depending upon prevailing circumstances.

Nations, like individuals, are organisms that can succumb to an illness. They pass through stages when an attacking virus or bacillus which, although easily repelled by a healthy body, takes advantage of a state of lowered resistance. This was the case when the Germans fell under the spell of Hitler, a man with a non-German, Austrian background; he has been called Austria's revenge on Germany for the lost battle of Sadowa, in 1866, which decided the Austrian-Prussian war in Prussia's favor. It may be well to remember this, as well as the fact that many of the influential men of the Third Reich, including leaders of the Gestapo, were Austrians. William Shirer, in his *The Rise and Fall of the Third Reich*, blames Prussia for providing the conditions in which National Socialism could grow and attain power, and claims that this process was accelerated by Prussia's victory over Austria in 1866. The historical facts, however, prove nothing of the kind. All they show is that in the 1860's, just one hundred years ago, both Europe and North America were going through a period of power struggles of great historical importance: the war between the North and the Southern Confederacy in America, and the war between Prussia and Austria in Europe. In both cases, what developments victory for the losing side would have produced must remain in the realm of historical speculation.

Bismarck, one of Germany's greatest statesmen, founded the German Reich in 1871. He was well aware, even then, of the dangers inherent in mass pressure groups led by demagogic orators, and feared that such a development would inevitably lead to dictatorship and absolutism, which he considered a disaster. Although Shirer does not hesitate to count Bismarck among Hitler's political ancestors, history shows that the great Chancellor's policies were distinguished by moderation, restraint, and efforts

27

to preserve a balance within the state; these qualities account for his conservatism as well as his suspicion of radical political movements. At the same time, he considered a free press and parliaments to be indispensable to criticism and control of the government.

Anyone who claims that Bismarck was one of Hitler's forerunners should read his memoirs entitled *Thoughts and Reminiscences*, in which he warns against orators who possess a great talent for misleading the masses. "The covetous element," he writes, "in the long run has the weight of the greater masses. It is to be hoped in the interests of those masses that their breakthrough comes without dangerous acceleration, and without destruction of the state vehicle. In case the latter happens, the historical cycle will inevitably and in a relatively short time return to dictatorship, rule of force, and absolutism, for even the masses finally succumb to the need for order."

When this happens, Bismarck maintains, the people will seek to buy order from dictatorship, and thus sacrifice that measure of freedom "which they can safely afford."

Bismarck's words, written more than half a century before Hitler appeared on the political scene, assume a prophetic quality when viewed in the light of the developments which took place in Germany after World War I.

It is idle to speculate on whether Hitler understood this process intellectually or whether he grasped it only by intuition. It really does not matter. What matters is that, in raising the banner of National Socialism, he seemed to create an Archimedean point in the chaotic whirlpool of political emotions which was sweeping across Germany and the entire Continent. In his speeches both before and after 1933, Hitler endlessly repeated identical statements and slogans, thereby earning the ridicule of his enemies both inside and outside Germany. From his own point of view, however, he was doing exactly the right thing in thus creating a new focal point, a central theme at which he hammered constantly; everything else developed quite naturally, so that his following was all of a piece, so to speak. In the end he defeated the multitude of his political enemies not only because they lacked this solidly united front, but also because they were all more or less infected by European nihilism. And so the German people, despite their proud history of so many great and humane thinkers, poets, artists, and statesmen, succumbed, together with their intellectual representatives, to Hitler and the ideas of National Socialism.

Anyone studying the world with any objectivity during the period of Hitler's rise to power must also come to the conclusion that even the non-German part of Europe was, to a certain extent, captivated by National Socialism. This is the only rational explanation of the reluctance on the part of Western leaders to deal firmly with Hitler during the first few years of his rule, when his military position was weak. It is also the only possible explanation for the fact that, when Hitler started the Second World War, his banners met with only token resistance, even in places and under circumstances where strong and effective resistance could have been offered.

In considering the question of why and how the majority of the German people came to accept with such docility National Socialism in all its odious aspects, it is necessary to bear in mind the tremendous power exercised by the combination of terror and habit. The effectiveness of this combination has, of course, long been recognized; its use is nothing new. We have to think only of the many cases on record where this system was used successfully to condition and indoctrinate children, for whatever purpose. In any nation, only a small minority of strong-willed, independent men and women will, over a long period of time, be able to withstand the enormous pressures created by the terror-habit combination; this is especially true if this system is imposed as gradually as it was in the Third Reich.

The theory and practice of National Socialism developed and grew, not all at once, but over the course of several years. If the German people in 1933 had known the National Socialism of 1943, their history of that period would have taken an entirely different turn. National Socialism unfolded slowly and injected its demonic teachings into the minds of the German people in small but ever-increasing doses; for this very reason, the masses grew accustomed to them, much as a dope addict can tolerate ever larger quantities of the poison that is killing him. In this way, the German people were slowly but inexorably pulled into Hitler's orbit.

Many of Hitler's opponents were destroyed in the same way. They believed that, by swallowing the small doses of National Socialism offered to them in the beginning, they would be able to avoid the greater evil later on. The result was, however, that the sum total of the "lesser evils" added up precisely to that greater evil they had hoped to escape. And so many people originally strongly opposed to Hitler found themselves on slippery ground. They could and should have known what would happen, but they ignored the teaching of the ancient Romans: *prin-*

cipiis obsta; because they did *not* "resist from the beginning," they helped consolidate Hitler's triumph, were caught up in the avalanche of Nazism, and carried with frightening speed along with the great mass of the German people, toward disaster and shame.

CHAPTER TWO

The Roots of the

Opposition

The origin of the German anti-Hitler resistance can be traced to the period during which National Socialism first emerged as an important factor in the German political scene. Even today this is not fully understood by many people, who continue to think that German anti-Nazi opposition was started by disgruntled generals during World War II, and only after the policies and strategies of the German dictator showed signs of heading for defeat. Many people who believe this theory were brainwashed by Hitler's own propaganda after the abortive coup of July 20, 1944. This propaganda —which has since been adopted by the Communists— reduced the entire German resistance to a "very small clique of ambitious officers," thereby hoping to obscure the real background and nature of the anti-Hitler movement as well as its extent. The truth is that our—the resistance movement's—battle against Hitler and National

Socialism was based not upon considerations of material or military success or failure, and not even primarily on political ideas, but upon the moral and ethical concepts taught by the Christian faith.

The Western world in its present form was developed and shaped largely by Christianity. In spite of all the quarrels among the various Christian churches, there can be no question that European culture rests solidly on Christian foundations. The teaching of the Christian religion centers upon man's submission to the will of God, and upon love for one's neighbor. Centuries of bickering about moral and ecclesiastical details often obscured this principle, reduced its effectiveness, and at times even set it aside altogether; but has never been able to destroy it.

Almost as though he were a part of that power which always wants to promote evil and in spite of itself accomplishes good instead, Hitler caused the ancient Christian concept to blossom forth with renewed vigor and influence. For, regardless of their individual beliefs, the foes of Hitler and Nazism all agreed in acknowledging the fundamental Christian truths. Much of what up to that time had seemed important lost its significance, and thus happened what had seemed impossible in the years before: Social Democrats, men of the Center Party, Conservatives and Liberals, Catholics and Protestants, civilians and soldiers found themselves united on the common ground of the old Christian foundations of the Western world. Each of us learned something from the rest, and for the first time there was the feeling that a serious attempt was being made to understand and appreciate others. True, it was only a beginning; but in the midst of spiritual enslavement and daily persecution this beginning held forth a new hope for the future. It was as though the first rays of sunlight were beginning to break through dark clouds. We wanted no power for ourselves; nor could mere material inducements have led us to incur the fearful risks of such a fight, or sustained us in the ordeals our course was destined to bring upon us. In any case, only the foolish measure the merit of an idea or course of action by its success or failure; the wise man weighs only the ethical worth of an idea or an action.

Opposition to Hitler began, then, not as an organized political movement but as the reaction of individuals with religious and moral convictions to the theories, and later to the practices, of National Socialism. Furthermore, Hitler's earliest opponents had enough foresight to imagine, at least to a certain extent, what would happen if this cancer of Nazism were allowed to spread and one day gain control of the country. This true patriotism roused in us the fervent wish to save our country and prevent the *Finis Germaniae,* which we felt certain would be the final result of Hitler's regime.

In 1928, when I was a student at the University of Halle, I acquired my first theoretical and practical knowledge of National Socialism. The former was based mainly on a thorough study of three books: Adolf Hitler's *Mein Kampf,* Alfred Rosenberg's *The Myth of the 20th Century,* and Gottfried Feder's *Breaking the Interest Slavery.*

I was an avid reader, with a special interest in historical and political subjects. To anyone accustomed to serious and objective writing in these fields, the above-mentioned Nazi books were an intellectual insult, and they turned me from the very beginning into an unequivocal and unconditional adversary of the National Socialist "ideology."

Later it constantly surprised me to find how very few people had bothered to carefully read the books in question, how few—within Germany as well as beyond her borders—had bothered to inform themselves sufficiently about the true nature of Nazism. As a result, at the beginning of Hitler's rule they adopted a neutral, wait-and-see attitude, which they began to change only after it was too late.

Not that it was difficult to understand why most people shied away from reading the books in question. Plowing through hundreds of pages of half-baked, half-digested ideas, many of which seemed to have originated in the brains of mentally retarded or even unbalanced people, is by no means a pleasant pastime. In addition, Hitler's book was written in poor German, and it took considerable will power on my part to stay with it to the end. However, the travail did pay off, for the reader wound up with a very clear picture of what National Socialism was about, and what kind of future the Nazis had in mind for Germany—a picture which was, in every single detail, repulsive and distasteful to me and to my friends.

Many people later claimed that Hitler had duped them; that is one charge that in fairness cannot be levelled against this man, for if there ever was a demagogue who spelled out his plans in clear and unmistakable terms, it was Hitler. Nobody who had carefully read *Mein Kampf* was left in the dark about the means and methods by which he intended to gain control of Germany, his plans for conquest, and his attitude toward the rights of others —individuals as well as nations.

Rosenberg's *Myth of the 20th Century* turned out to be an incredible hodge-podge of theories proclaiming the superiority of the so-called "Nordic" man, and at the same time launching an attack upon Christian beliefs and tenets. Because the ideas themselves are ludicrous, too many people at the time made the fatal mistake of dismissing not only the book but also the men backing this new "ideology" involving super- and sub-races. They did not realize that in not taking the authors seriously, they were making the prime mistake of underestimating the enemy, and that Hitler and his henchmen were perfectly capable, given the chance, of practicing what they preached.

Breaking the Interest Slavery was the third and last of the triology of books that provided the theoretical foundation of National Socialism. It was written by a man who considered himself an expert on economic matters. Although his basic ideas were socialistic, he proposed a "national" as opposed to an "international" socialism, thereby giving Hitler's party its name. Feder was one of the early authors of the program of the National Socialist Workers' Party, later nicknamed "Nazis."

Feder's ideas of how to "cure" the German economy were neither new nor original, but then Hitler knew next to nothing about economics, and cared less, since he was convinced that, if the political leadership was strong enough, everything else would somehow fall into line. The main premise of Feder's book was that what he called "speculative" capital—as opposed to "productive" capital —is responsible for practically all economic woes and therefore should be abolished. Later, when the program of the National Socialist Party was formulated, Feder and the other co-authors of the platform succeeded in including a number of radical ideas; one of these was the proposal to abolish all real estate speculation; another was the introduction of the death sentence for so-called "economic crimes," such as profiteering. That also, of course, was nothing new, for it had been, and still is, an established practice in the Soviet Union and other Communist countries.

These three books, then, represented the basic theories of National Socialism as advanced in the years of Hitler's struggle for power; Hitler's book covered the political, Rosenberg's the ideological, and Feder's treatise the economic field. Altogether National Socialism was an incredible mixture of totalitarian, communist, socialist, and anti-Christian ideas and sentiments, with the insane claim to racial superiority of the so-called "Aryan" man thrown in as a bonus.

If our study of the theory of Nazism had already turned my friends and myself into determined adversaries of Hitler and his ideas, the practical knowledge about the Nazis as individuals, which we gained through work in the student association, helped to confirm and strengthen in every way the impression we had received from the books. I must state here that for me, and others like me, there was no struggle or hesitation involved in the decision to reject Hitler and his followers from the very start. They went against everything my own upbringing represented, and the traditions, principles, and history of families such as mine. The conduct of the Nazi followers among the students showed a complete lack of good manners, a deliberate rejection of decorum and the proprieties, and a brutal, coarse vitality. That, together with their arrogantly paraded subjectivity on all questions and their confused ideas on political and economic matters, aroused first revulsion and then opposition. Confrontations with Baldur von

Schirach, who at that time was the leader of the National Socialist student association, did their share to harden our stand against the Nazis.

And so, quite naturally, my friends and I banded together in a group that was sharply opposed to National Socialism. We were still young, reckless, and adventurous enough to actually welcome crossing swords with followers of the Nazi Party. The older generation by that time had become somewhat cautious; but we did not hesitate to make life as difficult as possible for Jordan, the Nazi Gauleiter of Halle, during his large and turbulent mass meetings. The fact that we were outnumbered, and therefore always ran the risk of taking a sound beating at the hands of the Nazis, could not deter us.

I was especially exposed to the danger of attack by Nazi roughnecks during those years, for I had volunteered to take on their challenge and disprove their contention that the foes of National Socialism were too cowardly to stand up and publicly oppose them. In one mass meeting after another, I rose to contradict the Nazis' views, and speak for the opposition. In retrospect, I realize that I was lucky to survive these adventures. Despite the police protection which still existed in the years before 1933, the risk of being attacked and killed by Hitler's rowdy Storm Troopers was always present, and many a Nazi opponent in those days lost his life in just such a manner. Fortunately, the young are not inclined to take dangers too seriously, and so the risks I incurred did not cause me to lose much sleep, nor could they deflect me from my course. Once, after I had challenged a local Nazi leader to a duel after he had printed some slanderous material about me in a newspaper, I had the satisfaction of finding that he did not dare accept the challenge that I threw before him.

My studies, which included political economy as well as law at the universities of Halle and Berlin, took somewhat longer than normal, because I ran out of money before I was through. I left the university in 1929, and spent some time in Berlin; later, I returned to the University of Halle. There one of my teachers was Max Fleischmann, an eminent authority on the *law of nations*, noted for his work beyond the borders of Germany. As among intellectuals in general, opposition to Hitler within the ranks of the university professors was rather weak, refuting the belief that higher education alone provides sufficient protection against totalitarian ideas. Max Fleischmann, however, was one of the exceptions. He soon saw clearly what kind of an era had begun with Hitler's rise to political power. Attacked by the Nazis because of his Jewish ancestry, Fleischmann had to give up his teaching career soon after Hitler came to power. Although he could easily have obtained a teaching position at any of a number of foreign universities, he preferred to remain in Germany. Later he often placed his great knowledge at the disposal of the German resistance movement; and even during the early years of the war, he was working on constitutional drafts for a new Germany that would have rid itself of Hitler. Fleischmann suffered acutely from the ostracism he had to endure, and when he heard in 1943 that he was about to be transported to Poland he put an end to his life.

Toward the end of the year 1932, I found myself back in Berlin, where I started to work as a political assistant to the State Secretary of the Prussian Ministry of the Interior, Herbert von Bismarck, a great-nephew of the famous statesman. In that capacity, I witnessed the transfer of power in the German state to Hitler on January 30, 1933. On the basis of what we had learned during the years of our fight against the Nazis before 1933, my friends and I did not for one moment doubt where Hitler's rule would lead. If there had been any remaining doubts, they would soon have been dispelled by the wanton and illegal acts with which the Nazis proceeded to take over all power in Germany after January, 1933, and to institute their lawless rule. It took only a few months after Hitler's rise to power for this to be clearly demonstrated.

In an article written in March of 1933 for the *Information Bulletin of the Conservative Association,* I sounded the warning against the acts of terror that were so typical of the new regime. I quoted Goering, who had declared that it was not his business to "administer justice, but instead to destroy and extirpate," and that he would not be hindered in this aim by narrow "juristic doubts and bureaucracy." I stated in my article that by such acts the new Prussia had forever broken with the old Prussia, whose motto had been that "justice is the foundation of government."

It was inevitable that the early opponents of National Socialism, especially those of prominence, should, soon after Hitler's rise to power in 1933, become the targets of attacks by the Nazis. Towering far above us in our group was Ewald von Kleist, a conservative landowner from Pomerania. When I think back on the picture of Germany's future which this man painted for us at the very beginning of Hitler's rule, it seems hardly an exaggeration to call him a prophet. In judging Hitler and National Socialism, he

40

displayed an instinctive and unfailingly sure knowledge which very few of the German politicians of that era possessed. Shortly before 1933, Kleist wrote a paper in which he sounded the warning against Hitler. Published under the title "National Socialism—a Danger,"* it is a classic example of its author's perception and political farsightedness. Kleist belonged to that tiny minority which, openly and from the very beginning, showed itself as an unconditional and uncompromising foe of the Nazis. Kleist even went so far as to refuse to lift his arm in the required form of the Nazi salute. This man's accomplishments over a period of twelve years are worthy of a paean of praise.

Under the circumstances, it was only natural that Kleist soon should find himself in trouble. It began with his father-in-law, von Osten, who had a reputation for being an excellent administrator and politician in Prussia. Osten was also friendly with Reichspresident von Hindenburg, who trusted him. Trouble started when Osten, who owned an estate near a village in the province of Brandenburg, exercised his legal right as owner of the only inn in the village to deny the Nazis the use of the inn for their meetings. This was shortly before 1933. After Hitler's rise to power, the Nazis wanted to take their revenge on Osten, and tried to force their way into his estate with the intention of flying the swastika flag from his castle.

Osten declared that he would meet force with force. At that point I was asked to intervene by bringing the matter to the attention of Hindenburg. The result was that Hindenburg, in his capacity as Commander-in-Chief of the Armed Forces, ordered the garrison in nearby Kuestrin (a

---

* See Appendix II for excerpts from this essay.

EWALD VON KLEIST-SCHMENZIN

1890 — 1945

The conservative Pomeranian landowner was one of Hitler's earliest, most far-sighted, and most unbending enemies. In 1932, he published a pamphlet warning of the dangers of National Socialism. Deeply religious, Kleist had no fear of death, and continued his fight against Hitler throughout the years of the Third Reich. He was executed in April, 1945.

city in that part of Germany now under the jurisdiction of Poland) to get ready to move against the Brown Shirts if they should try to commit a breach of peace. That settled it. The Storm Troopers gave up their plan and limited themselves to a meaningless demonstration.

Now the Nazis dreamed up another idea. They requested Osten, because of his position as an honorary citizen of Kuestrin, to break off all relations with Jews. Osten's prompt answer to that challenge was to return to the city of Kuestrin the document proclaiming his honorary citizenship; he followed this by paying an official visit to a Jewish neighbor of his with whom, up until then, he had not been on very good terms.

On May 1, 1933, occurred the first major trouble for Osten's son-in-law, Ewald von Kleist. On that day the SA demanded that the pastor of the church whose patron Kleist was, fly the swastika flag from the church steeple. Pastor Reimer—who, by the way, is now pastor of the German congregation in London—refused to comply; Kleist forbade the flying of the flag outright. The Storm Troopers marched to Kleist's estate, had him arrested by the auxiliary police, and made preparations to force him to fly the swastika flag from his mansion. In spite of his arrest, Kleist remained adamant and did not give an inch. In the meantime, his friends got ready to defend the manor by force of arms. Faced with such determination, the SA again retreated.

This, however, was only the beginning. In the years that followed, Kleist was repeatedly arrested. His name, in fact, was among those heading the list of Hitler's enemies who were to be murdered on the bloody Sunday of June 30, 1934, the day of the so-called Roehm Putsch. Warned in time, Kleist managed to escape the Nazi agents sent out to get him; he was hidden in Berlin by Ernst Niekisch, editor of the outstanding publication *Resistance,* until the acute danger was past.

Finally, when all else had failed, the Nazi Kreisleiter of Belgard in Pomerania arranged a meeting with Kleist and tried persuasion. But Kleist remained firm. He told the Kreisleiter that he was an implacable foe of National Socialism, that he would never say "Heil Hitler," or fly the swastika flag, or contribute money to the Party. When the Kreisleiter tried the soft approach and proposed that Kleist give at least ten cents as a token to the Party, Kleist answered that he was a wealthy man; he would make either a sizable contribution, or nothing at all. Because he was determined not to aid the Party in any way, he would not contribute a penny. The Kreisleiter had to leave without having achieved anything.

Kleist was truly one of the few remaining knights "without fear and without reproach." That he would finally come to his end on one of Hitler's gallows was almost inevitable under the circumstances.

At Kleist's urging, in 1933 I wrote another article for the *Information Bulletin of the Conservative Association.* In this article, I stated in no uncertain terms our rejection of Hitler and National Socialism. That was the end of the conservative paper; from that time on publication was suspended.

The Nazis were especially incensed about that particular article because I had attacked the Hitler regime on its breach of the German constitution in removing the Communist delegates from the Reichstag, the German parliament. The unconstitutionality of that act was self-evident.

After Hitler had come to power, his party did not have the necessary numerical strength in the Reichstag to push through the changes he wanted in the constitution. He therefore proceeded to dissolve the Reichstag, and new elections took place in March, 1933. Again the results were negative from Hitler's point of view, for he still did not have the necessary majority. He then dissolved the Communist Party; it was this act which was a breach of the constitution. Had he dissolved the Communist Party *before* the elections, the Communists would have given their votes to some of the other parties, whose increase in strength would most certainly have denied Hitler the necessary majority. Through his trick of dissolving the Communist Party *after* the elections, the entire balance of Party strength within the Reichstag had been altered— against the rules of the constitution—to such a degree that Hitler finally won the majority of delegates that he had been seeking.

It was clear that in those early months before Hitler had begun to consolidate his power, he was eager to maintain— at least for public consumption—the illusion that his regime was a legal and constitutional authority. On the other hand, he feared nothing so much as honest elections, and from the start did not hesitate to order falsification of election results. A Ministry official told me in a private conversation that orders to falsify the election results had been issued by the regime. Simultaneously the Department of Justice directed the offices of the local state attorneys to refrain from prosecuting in cases of alleged election fraud. Through an oversight one of the district attorneys did not receive this directive, and indicted the chief of an election bureau who had been accused of fraud. In this way, at least one of these cases came to light, and the guilty party was punished.

In view of such danger signals, a few farsighted men made strenuous efforts to persuade President Hindenburg, Alfred Hugenberg, leader of the German National Party, and Franz Seldte, leader of the "Stahlhelm," an association of German veterans of World War I, to change their course and prevent the disastrous coalition which Hitler used to grab power. All efforts failed completely, defeated by the blindness of these basically unpolitical politicians. Kleist tried unsuccessfully to convince Hugenberg of the folly of his course, and predicted that if he persisted in it the result would be the end of his political career and the loss of his political honor. But Hugenberg could not be induced to change his mind.

The only persons with both influence and insight at that time were General Baron von Hammerstein, the chief of the Reichswehr, Germany's standing army, and General von Schleicher, the last Chancellor before Hitler. Both men believed they had Hindenburg's personal and political confidence; this proved to be an illusion that doomed both them and the German people. Hindenburg dropped Schleicher, and restricted Hammerstein to his military sphere of influence.

After Hammerstein's last effort to change Hindenburg's mind during a nighttime meeting ended in failure, he considered using the Reichswehr to stop Hitler's rise, but finally discarded that idea because it would have included acting against Hindenburg. That seemed too risky to Hammerstein in view of the great prestige enjoyed by Hindenburg not only among the German people, but also throughout the world. Much later, Hammerstein, in conversations with friends, admitted to grave doubts about the wisdom of his decision in 1933. Seen in the light of later developments he thought that it probably would have been better, in spite of the uproar it would have created, if he had moved forcibly against Hindenburg at that time.

Attempts by non-Nazis in the various government departments to frustrate Hitler's plans were doomed from the very start. Hitler was not satisfied to work through the departments that were in the hands of his party; instead, by breaking the law and using force through his Storm Troopers, he succeeded in grabbing power even in those departments where he had no constitutional right. Another good example of Nazi strategy was the manner in which the fire that destroyed the Reichstag building was exploited. I well remember the moment I first heard of that fire. My superior, State Secretary von Bismarck, immediately went to his office in the Prussian Ministry of the Interior, where he found Minister President Franz von Papen in the room of Hermann Goering, then Minister of the Interior in Prussia. Shortly afterwards Hitler arrived, and then Goering joined the company. While he reported the fire, he slapped his thighs in high good humor. Hitler sat stony-faced throughout the report, betraying no emotion whatever, nor even any interest. Bismarck received the impression that Hitler was already weighing the possible propaganda value of the fire. Goering succeeded in presenting the carefully prepared bill to the Communists; neither then nor later was it ever possible to unmask the Nazis as those responsible for the Reichstag fire.

And so, within a few short months after Hitler had become Chancellor, our fears and apprehensions were fully justified by the events. Badly outnumbered, we were faced with an unscrupulous, unprincipled, amoral enemy who could outmaneuver his opponents at every turn because he respected no law and no rules except force. Almost overnight, we had become involved in a bitter struggle whose growing dangers we realized only too well, but to which we as Christians and German patriots were unconditionally committed.

In the pages that follow, as I trace the growth and development of the German anti-Hitler resistance from its early beginnings to its bloody end, I am not doing so in an attempt to compete with the chroniclers of the Nazi era. Much less do I claim that my report is a complete history of those times and events; it is mainly a personal account, and therefore necessarily limited in scope. Its value is due to the very fact that it is a personal experience, with details that are not contained in official records. Hopefully, it has more life, color, and vividness than sober statistics and scientific analyses. It may perhaps awaken in the reader a sense of personal involvement in events that dealt with questions directly and urgently concerning all members of the human society.

CHAPTER THREE

The Battle Begins

After Hitler came to power in 1933, his foes began to form into the groups which eventually became the core of the future resistance movement. At this time, however, the terror apparatus of the Nazi regime was increased and perfected daily, so that the opposition found its efforts checkmated at every move. In addition, the very fact that our fight against Hitler was based upon Christian concepts and beliefs forbade us the use of the traditional instruments of revolutionaries: terror, violence, brutality, and anarchy. It is impossible to fight evil with its own methods without corrupting, and eventually destroying, the very principles one is fighting for. It is important for a clear understanding of the German resistance to realize how severely limited we were in the means we could employ to bring about the downfall of the Nazi regime. For the same reason, the assassination of Hitler was planned only as a last resort, and after all other methods of removing him from power had either failed or become unfeasible.

Because of the constantly increasing bitterness of the struggle against the Nazis in those early months of 1933 we began an urgent search for allies. This undertaking, marked by much disappointment and only limited success, placed us under severe nervous strain.

In our attempts to mobilize every possible spiritual and moral force for our battle, we were grateful for the echo we found in Martin Niemoeller, who, in the second year of Hitler's rule, had already focused much attention upon himself by his powerful sermons as pastor of Berlin-Dahlem. Later, Niemoeller, in his capacity as leader of the Confessional Church of Germany, gave new impetus to Protestantism, thereby dashing hopes of quickly eliminating the Protestant Church in Germany. In addition, Niemoeller supplied a good part of the ideological foundations of the German resistance. In this he was strongly supported by young Dietrich Bonhoeffer, son of the noted Berlin psychiatrist. In a settlement in Pomerania, Bonhoeffer taught and trained other young theologians. Furthermore, his activities in the Ecumenical Council gave him an opportunity to make contacts in non-German circles. Dietrich Bonhoeffer's sterling character and personality are the best evidence of the fact that, even during the war, Germans could communicate with the non-German world, including hostile nations, without betraying their country.

Another prominent Protestant in the resistance was Eugen Gerstenmaier. Forced to give up his teaching career at Berlin University because he had publicly criticized National Socialism, Gerstenmaier was not only active in the resistance, but also devoted himself to making life easier for the many foreign workers in Germany during the war. Gerstenmaier was one of the few to survive arrest and imprisonment after July 20, 1944, and now holds a high position in the German Federal Parliament.

In our efforts to broaden the base of the opposition, we did not limit ourselves to seeking the cooperation of Protestant leaders, but also sought to make contact with prominent Catholics. One of these with whom we met was Heinrich Bruening, Chancellor of Germany from 1930-32. At the time Bruening was living in St. Hedwig's Hospital in Berlin, where he was not so much exposed to surveillance by the Nazis. In contrast to the then rather vacillating position adopted by the Center Party, whose candidate he had been, Bruening left no doubt as to where he stood. Rejecting all customary avowals of loyalty to Hitler's regime, Bruening declared: "A man has to choose now whether he wants to stand under the swastika or under the cross of Christ. He can decide for only one of them."

At about this time, I made the acquaintance of other prominent Catholics, among them Baron Carl Ludwig von Guttenberg. As editor of the monthly publication "White Papers," he made it a rule never to print a single National Socialist word. In addition this magazine made untiring efforts to express as strongly as possible its anti-Nazi stand. The "White Papers" appeared right through the early months of the Second World War; and every issue is proof that, even under the Nazi regime, the truth could still be written—if not the whole truth at least a large part.

Another ally gained from the Catholic camp was Professor Sigismund Lauter, director of St. Gertrauden Hospital in Berlin. His great willingness to be of help to us, the broad scope of his intuitive mind, and his indomitable optimism were a tremendous boon to my friends and me. Many of our meetings took place in his spacious home, where his profession as well as his way of life made it possible for us to gather without attracting undue attention.

During our quest for aid, we also sought and made contact with a number of representatives of the German scientific world. We were especially grateful for our association with Rudolf Smend, whose reputation as a specialist in state law was no less distinguished than his achievements as one of the leading minds of the Evangelical (Protestant) Church. Hand in hand with a noble character, true kindness, and a Christian spirit, went an intellect broad enough to appreciate the wide polarity of human life. Although our collaboration with him suffered after he was transferred from Berlin to Goettingen University—a transfer which had to be considered a disciplinary measure—it was never broken off completely.

Another one of the professors from the University of Berlin who belonged in our camp was Eduard Spranger. His reputation as a philosopher and pedagogue are, of course, world-famous. In 1933, Lauter, Smend, and Spranger, representing the teaching college of the University, went to have a talk with Franz von Papen, who at the time was Vice Chancellor under Hitler. They wanted to obtain his help in securing freedom for the German universities, both in matters of instruction and of administration. After the meeting, Spranger wrote me a letter, in which he described the conversation with Papen in the following words: "It was worse than a failure, for we were not even understood."

In the continuing attempt to make contact with other groups and to try to work with them, I met Ernst Niekisch, whom I mentioned earlier. Niekisch had originally been a Social Democrat, and after the First World War had helped to found the "Old Socialists." Later he began to publish *Resistance,* a journal of high quality. He was a man of great steadfastness who said what he meant and meant what he said. In addition to this trait he possessed great knowledge, a keen mind, and an outstanding gift of expression both in speech and writing. His essay "Hitler, a German Catastrophe,"* written not long before 1933, showed that he foresaw the disaster which Hitler's rule would bring. There was a special bond between Niekisch and me because early in 1933 through intervention of friends of mine, we were able to liberate him, with other anti-Nazis, from a cellar in Berlin where they had been imprisoned by the SA.

Niekisch was able to present proof in a large number of cases that the SA, by breaking the law, had used force to terrorize and frequently to cause the disappearance of their non-Jewish as well as Jewish adversaries. Niekisch paid dearly for his activities, however. Involved in a high treason charge in 1937, he was sentenced to life in prison. Imprisoned in the penitentiary of Brandenburg, he miraculously escaped death, and was liberated in the spring of 1945. His resistance against Hitler cost him not only eight years in prison, but also his eyesight and the use of his legs, due to paralysis as a result of experiments for which he was used as a guinea pig.

State Secretary von Bismarck, my superior in 1933, added to the records of the Interior Ministry the cases which Niekisch had brought to his attention, thus making

---

* For excerpts from this essay, see Appendix III.

them official. Bismarck also tried to save the life and health of the victims. This was not always possible, but in the cases where we were successful, the knowledge that we had been able to help fellow human beings was no less a reward than the gratitude of those we had saved, Jews and non-Jews alike.

In time, the terror of the SA became a permanent part of life in the German state. This led to an important step by State Secretary von Bismarck. He made one last attempt to unite a number of non-Nazi officials against the lawlessness of the new regime by invoking the concept of the state—as opposed to that of the party represented by the Nazis—and in that way tried to stem the rising tide of terror.

Bismarck suffered agonies because during his tenure in office (and at a time when he was still in a position of political responsibility) people were being subjected to Nazi terror for their convictions or their racial ancestry. He therefore demanded that Goering, then Minister of Interior of Prussia, give orders to the police to act against anyone, regardless of position or party membership, who used force against a fellow human being unless he had been legally empowered to do so. Bismarck also suggested that the order be accompanied by a warning that disciplinary action would be taken against any policeman who failed to obey it.

To get this plan adopted by the cabinet, Bismarck needed help, but the other members of the cabinet refused to support him, and Goering himself expressed his own point of view in the remarkable statement: "I am proud of not knowing what justice is."

ERNST NIEKISCH

1 8 8 9 —

An early and courageous opponent of Hitler from Germany's political Left, Niekisch was condemned to life imprisonment in 1937. Treatment in prison caused him to become blind as well as partially paralyzed. He survived the Third Reich and was liberated in 1945.

Bismarck failed in all his attempts, which included a vain appeal to General von Blomberg, in the latter's capacity as War Minister. In a stormy session with Bismarck, Blomberg declared that he was a soldier whose first duty was obedience; he rejected Bismarck's plea that he accept political responsibility because of his cabinet post. When this last attempt failed, Bismarck decided that he could stay no longer, and resigned.

Outstanding among the earliest fighters against Hitler was one of my closest friends, Nikolaus von Halem. In the years from 1933 up to his arrest in 1942, this man waged an unrelenting war against National Socialism. Halem had a talent for quickly and adroitly formulating ideas and coining words. He dubbed Hitler the "mail carrier of chaos." His strong, genial personality was borne out by his appearance: Of an old Friesian family, he was tall, powerfully built, blond, and blue-eyed. Courage and intelligence, audacity and great poise, frankness and astuteness were foremost among the qualities of this remarkable young man. In addition he was soft-hearted, and his integrity, lofty sense of honor, and unswerving loyalty to his friends made him one of the most distinguished and valuable members of our group.

Past master of the art of winning people for himself and his ideas, Halem was able to draw a number of high Nazi officials over to our side by planting in them the seeds of doubt about National Socialism. In this way he won over Joseph Wagner, the Gauleiter of Silesia, who completely deserted the Nazi ranks.

When it was necessary to communicate with non-German circles, Halem again was one of the most active among us. His travels to Italy, Sweden, France, and Russia gave him the opportunity to establish the required contacts with important persons in those countries. There will be more about Halem in the chapters dealing with the later stages of the resistance.

Similar to the activities of Halem were those of Herbert Mumm von Schwarzenstein. He had been a diplomat, but had resigned from the Foreign Office after 1933 because of his political convictions. From that time on Mumm dedicated his life to the fight against Hitler. His good relations with foreign diplomats, especially Belgians and Americans, were of great importance to us. Up to the last moment before war was declared with the United States, he met and talked with Alexander Kirk, the last chargé d'affaires of the American Embassy. Mumm was well suited for this kind of work because of his discretion, his conscientious attention to detail, and his skill in conducting diplomatic discussions.

Although I soon realized that it would be impossible for me to remain an official under Hitler's dictatorship, I did not withdraw from the training prescribed for German jurists. Leaving Berlin in 1934, I spent several years in provincial towns. As had been the case with my studies, this training period also took a longer time than it would have normally because I refused to join the NSDAP or any of its organizations, despite all the pressures that were exerted to make me fall in line. Although every conceivable obstacle was placed in my way in the hope that time would wear me down, in the end I passed both state examinations without having become a member of the Nazi Party. Stubborn and determined passive resistance went a long way even in the Third Reich.

The extra time I had to spend on my training was not

wasted, for I used part of it to write the memoirs of Elard von Oldenburg-Januschau, a conservative leader from East Prussia. When the book was finished, the publisher in Leipzig insisted on a National Socialist preface. I refused, and the book was finally published without the addition of a single National Socialist word.

During those years, my political work did not cease altogether, but, removed from the mainstream of political life in Berlin, it was quieter and more limited in scope. It was possible, however, for me to create cells of resistance in Pomerania and Rhine-Hessen, and many valuable people were won to the cause of the resistance through long and painstaking efforts. In addition, a number of experiences in the legal field during that time supplied me with important knowledge and understanding of the aims and practices of the Nazi regime.

It is generally believed, outside Germany, that the entire judicial system of the country collapsed without a struggle after Hitler's take-over. This was not so, partly because any long-established, organically developed legal system has tremendous staying power and partly, of course, because the very character of such a system, based as it is upon justice and impartiality—the exact opposite of tyranny—offers passive resistance at the very least.

In 1935 I learned that Hans von Wedemeyer, a landowner I knew, had been brought to trial and found guilty of a charge of gross negligence of his "social duties" by not providing better living conditions for the tenant farmers on his estate. As a result, Wedemeyer lost his license as manager of the estate and the Nazis appeared as the champions of the "common man."

As was so often the case in the Third Reich, the accusation against Wedemeyer was only a smoke screen. The real reason the Nazis were out to "get" him was that he had refused to fly the swastika flag on his estate. At that time there was no way to legally force him to do so, and thus the best way to break him was to go after his license. The "Black Corps," organ of the SS, ran a long article about Wedemeyer's alleged criminal negligence of his workers' needs, illustrated liberally with photographs showing peasant dwellings in shocking disrepair.

Because the allegations were completely untrue—wherever the photographs came from, they certainly were not taken on Wedemeyer's estate—and because we knew quite well the motive behind the false charges, I suggested to Wedemeyer that he appeal the sentence. We needed a "big-name" lawyer as a front, for I was young and without courtroom experience. However, I worked behind the scenes, drew up all the necessary briefs, and collected the evidence.

During my efforts to unearth the real source of the photos which had appeared in the "Black Corps," I struck pay dirt. That the pictures did not represent the true conditions on Wedemeyer's estate, I had known all along; but I must admit that I was rather startled to find that they had been taken on an estate run by the Reichsbauern-fuehrer—the top Nazi official in charge of peasant affairs.

We were well prepared when the new trial started before a special department of the Supreme Court in Leipzig. As the case unfolded it became clear that the court was not only impressed but curious about the matter, for in the middle of the proceedings the eminent justices decided that they wanted to inspect the scene of the controversy. And so the Supreme Court judges packed up and moved to the estate—indeed a unique event in judicial history! There, the justices could—and did—see for themselves the actual conditions which proved that the accusations against Wedemeyer were completely false.

Wedemeyer was not only acquitted and his license as manager restored to him, but he was also commended by the court for the exemplary work he had done in improving the living conditions of the people working on his estate. Thus the entire affair, with the help of the highest court of the land, was turned into a resounding defeat for the Nazis at a time when they had been in power for several years—proof that Hitler's efforts to subvert and strangle the German judicial system were protracted and not uniformly successful.

During those years another case came to my attention which did not involve me directly but which nevertheless let me into one of the ugliest secrets of the Nazi regime, and left a deep and lasting impression on me and on my colleague, Karl Schultes, who witnessed the trial with me. Schultes was a convinced anti-Nazi, whose father had been a doctor and for many years the Independent Social Democratic delegate for the district of Nordhausen in the province of Saxony. Our mutual opposition to Hitler was a bond between us that led to close collaboration and a constant exchange of ideas.

At the time, Schultes and I were living in Magdeburg, a medium-sized city in the province of Saxony. We both worked at the local court. One day we discovered that a very unusual case was about to be tried, from which the public was to be excluded because of "danger to the security of the state." What had happened?

Under the Hitler regime each province of Germany had

its own concentration camp. A man who had been sentenced to a long term in prison for a criminal offense had been sent to the concentration camp at first, but had later been transferred to a penitentiary. The convict must have felt safe in the penitentiary, which was under the jurisdiction of the Department of Justice rather than that of the SS, because he wrote a letter to the district attorney at the Court of Appeals at Naumburg.

In his letter the prisoner described the conditions of life in the concentration camp. Whether by accident or because the bureaucratic machinery worked slowly but surely, the letter did indeed reach the district attorney who, convinced that the convict was a liar, indicted him on charges of slander. However, the man was able to describe the inhuman conditions in the concentration camp in such detail, and to support his charges by naming witnesses, that the district attorney asked the President of Saxony to inspect the concentration camp. To the consternation of the officials, who had known of the existence but not the nature of the camps, it turned out that the accusations of the convict were absolutely correct.

The district attorney dropped the charges against the convict and instead indicted the commandant of the camp on charges of sevenfold murder. The trial was held at the court in Magdeburg, thus giving Schultes and me a chance to get acquainted with the case. Only the court and the officials who were immediately involved knew what the trial was about, and every precaution was taken to prevent any information from leaking out.

The details that unfolded during the trial were, quite simply, horrifying. The commandant of the camp was a former policeman, who had been forced to quit the service because of irregularities. He had found his way to the SS, had been accepted as a member, and had successfully climbed from rank to rank until he was finally made commandant of a concentration camp. At the beginning of the trial this man was the personification of arrogance; but as the case unfolded, his attitude underwent a considerable change, until at the end he was nothing but a miserable, cowering creature.

It came out during the trial that every new prisoner who was brought to the camp was subjected to the so-called "welcome." This meant that he had to walk through two parallel lines of people who beat him with sticks and whips as he passed. This, however, was only the beginning, for in the camp proper the tortures reached their peak. It was proved, for instance—and on this the indictment against the commandant was based—that seven prisoners had died as a result of a special torture inflicted upon them by order of the commandant. This torture consisted of taking away all the prisoners' clothes. Then the SS smeared tar over parts of the victims' naked bodies, such as arms and legs. The fiendish procedure was completed by setting fire to the tar-covered parts, with the result that the prisoners died a horrible death.

The presiding judge of the court, shaken by this description, finally found his voice to ask the commandant what had induced him to do such things. "It was just a game of the SS," was the answer.

From the records it became clear that many other prisoners had met death as a result of other unspeakable bestialities inflicted upon them by the SS. But in those cases the guilty persons could not be apprehended because the SS, alarmed at the trial of the commandant, quickly changed the personnel at the concentration camp in an effort to thwart further investigations. These cases, which all bore the notation "murder charges against persons unknown," remained unpunished.

During the trial, the fact that the doctor attached to the concentration camp had certified in every case that heart failure had been the cause of death shocked everybody in the courtroom. One of these cases could be traced, for one body had been returned to the family for burial. The relatives had been suspicious, and had succeeded in having an autopsy performed at the Pathological Institute of the nearby University of Halle. In that way, the truth about the real cause of death had come out at least in this one case. Thereafter, camp officials received orders from the Gestapo forbidding them to return the bodies of prisoners to the families. Instead they were ordered to cremate the bodies and return only the ashes, thereby eliminating any possibility of establishing the cause of death.

Only the few people who had been involved in the investigation of these cases knew what really happened inside the concentration camps. The Gestapo constantly improved their system of keeping their deeds secret; besides this, threats of dire punishment for any leaks ensured that the few who knew anything would keep their mouths shut. Due to these preventive measures, a large majority of the people never learned the truth about the terrible things that were happening behind the walls and fences of the concentration camps.

As time went on, we came to realize that the German people could be divided into three groups: Nazis, non-Nazis, and anti-Nazis. The two groups at the opposite ends of the scale were each smaller than the large middle

FABIAN VON SCHLABRENDORFF

1907 —

The author of this book escaped with his life through a series of near-miracles, which included the death, in an Allied bombing raid on Berlin, of the president of the "People's Court" just as the author's trial was coming up.

group; active Nazis as well as anti-Nazis were far out-numbered by the mass of the people who were essentially non-Nazis. This, however, was of no help to us. On the contrary, we learned in the course of our fight against Hitler that some of the non-Nazis were worse than the Nazis themselves, for, although they frequently had the right ideas, their lack of backbone and moral courage was more difficult to cope with than the outright brutality and ruthlessness of the Nazis. With the latter, at least, we knew where we stood.

Even in those early years of Nazi rule the great issues involved were quite clear to us, and each successive day provided us with additional proof that our fears were justified. In retrospect the final goal of National Socialism was very clear: it was bent upon dethroning God and setting itself up in His stead. The annihilation campaign against the Jews, the racial madness, the policy of extermination in the occupied countries, especially in the East, the concentration camps with all their horrors—all these were means toward the same end. And if these were not enough, the suppression of justice and the ruthless confiscation of the rights of those who did not submit unconditionally to the dictates of National Socialism proved beyond doubt that the Nazi regime was willing to trample underfoot every commandment of humanity. In addition, the contempt for historical growth and evolution and the complete lack of respect for all other nations made it clear that the Nazi ideology included no understanding of the true concept of the Fatherland, which is based upon Christian beliefs. The campaign against all religions, especially the Christian faith, and the substitution of the hollow and shabby word "Providence" for the concept of God showed beyond doubt that National Socialism was engaged in a battle against God.

The fifty years before the arrival of National Socialism, not just in Germany alone, were a period of slow moral decay, a period which allowed spiritual Nihilism to become dominant. We might describe these years as an era *without* God. But when Nihilism was superseded by National Socialism, which claimed the total power of the deified Aryan man over all the provinces of life, then life *without* God had turned into life *against* God. Goethe once said that, in the final essence, the history of mankind is forever the story of the battle between God and the Devil. Many Europeans had never been able to understand the meaning of Goethe's words, because long years of peace, interrupted only by localized wars, had lulled the world before 1914 into a false sense of security. Hitler's story proves to us anew the depth of the great German poet's insight.

There can be no doubt that the German resistance against Hitler had a mission, through which the battle against him turned into a crusade—a crusade against the swastika and everything it had come to stand for. Our main goal was the reestablishment of the commands of humanity. At the same time, we wanted to free the true concept of the Fatherland, which rests upon respect for the life of other nations, from the errors of racial insanity. Reverence for God once again had to be made the basis of life. The total claim to power by National Socialism meant nothing less than that Hitler was attempting to set himself up as master of God, humanity, and country, and thereby to destroy the Christian religion. Through a coincidence, written proof of this ultimate Nazi goal was received by us during the war through Arthur Nebe, who was secretly a member of our group although he was also a high-ranking SS officer. In 1943, he gave me a document of truly historical importance. Early that year, Heinrich Himmler, chief of the SS, had delivered a report to a gathering of top SS officers in which he had described the military situation in rather bald terms. Nebe had taken down this report in shorthand. Himmler stated that the time had come when men with one eye and one arm would have to be drafted; he also said that although the ranks of the SS had been depleted by heavy casualties, the war would have to be fought through, nevertheless. Only on the surface, he declared, was this a war of conquest of territories and countries: actually the real goal of the SS was the extermination of Christianity in the entire world, but—Himmler warned—for the time being this aim must under no circumstances be made public.

And so the goals were set and the battle lines drawn. The swastika represented a fight to the finish against every law of God and humanity. On the banner of the German resistance were inscribed the words: "For God—Country —Humanity."

CHAPTER FOUR

Frustrated Efforts

Returning to Berlin from the provinces in 1938, I found a very different situation from the one I had left only a few years before. Then, the German resistance movement—if one could call it that at the time—had been no more than a loosely-knit group representative of the political currents from the years prior to 1933. Now, however, although it was not yet by any means a real organization, it had at least developed to the point where there was a definite measure of cooperation between the various people who represented the former political powers in Germany. Previously all these factions had exhausted themselves in fighting each other, but now they were beginning to work side by side. Thus a number of opposition groups had sprung up, many of them connected to each other. First one and then another of these groups would be at the center of activities and would take the lead. I knew quite a few people in all of these circles, but was not myself a member of any one of them. My activities were destined to take a different course.

Through my association with the former State Secretary of Prussia, Herbert von Bismarck, I became acquainted with Colonel—later General—Hans Oster, chief of the Central Office of the Counter-Intelligence in the Armed Forces High Command. Without at first realizing it, I had penetrated to the very core of the resistance organization. Oster brought about acceptance of the first practical principle of the resistance movement: the necessity of bridging the gap between the civilian and military opposition. By that time, 1938, it had become amply clear that any resistance to the Nazi rule could be effective and successful only if we managed to win over the top military leaders. We lived in a dictatorship where nothing could be accomplished by democratic means. Only the enlistment of help by the military could offer any hope at all for succeeding in our attempts to overthrow the Hitler regime.

Oster's main task had been to get this idea accepted and to initiate the first contacts between civilian and military leaders. He was, so to speak, the manager and clearinghouse of the resistance. That Oster was able to assume this important position is due to his superior, the Chief of the Counter-Intelligence, Admiral Canaris. Although Canaris hated Hitler and National Socialism, he himself did not feel capable of leading any decisive action against Hitler. Instead he protected Oster and allowed him to use the apparatus of the Counter-Intelligence, as far as it was under Oster's jurisdiction, to organize, strengthen, and enlarge the German resistance movement.

So far as military leadership was concerned, the hopes of the anti-Hitler opposition in the middle thirties centered on the person of General Baron Werner von Fritsch, Commander-in-Chief of the Armed Forces. In his antipathy to Nazism and all its aspects, Fritsch was strongly supported by General Ludwig Beck, at that time Chief of Staff. Both men were in close contact with Carl Goerdeler, until 1937 Lord Mayor of Leipzig.

Fate willed it that the personality of General von Fritsch was ill-suited to the role he would have had to play in order to outmaneuver the Nazis. Although an officer of the greatest personal and professional integrity, Fritsch was undiplomatic, unbending, somewhat narrow-minded, and limited in all except his outstanding military talents. In addition, he was much too straightforward to conceal his contempt for the Nazis, and especially his detestation of the SS.

Such a man was relatively easy prey for the amoral and unscrupulous manipulations of the Nazis. It is an irony of fate that Fritsch, broken in life by the most vicious kind of slander the Gestapo could devise, was subjected in death to a different kind of defamation by the victorious Allies. A look at the facts in both instances will help set the record straight and clear away some of the confusion that has arisen in connection with the Fritsch case.

By 1938 the Gestapo leadership was well aware of the fact that Fritsch was implacably hostile to them. Himmler and his top henchmen, who hated and feared the Commander-in-Chief, were looking for a chance to get rid of him. When such an opportunity finally presented itself, they were ready with a diabolical plan.

It all began when Field Marshal von Blomberg, at that time Minister of War, sought permission from Hitler, through Goering, to marry a young woman who worked as a typist-secretary in one of the ministries. Hitler, delighted to ignore the social prejudices of the past, gave his consent to the marriage. To emphasize the approval, both Hitler and Goering attended the wedding as witnesses.

Soon trouble started. It appeared that the young Mrs. von Blomberg had in the past been an object of interest to the vice squad of the Berlin Criminal Police. When it was established beyond doubt that the Field Marshal had married a woman of easy virtue, the storm broke. Hitler, furious at having been duped, demanded Blomberg's resignation. General von Fritsch would have been the logical successor to Blomberg. Such a move, however, did not fit into Hitler's plans, much less into those of Himmler and his SS leaders. They, in fact, thought the moment opportune to attack Fritsch in a way designed to destroy him once and for all. Himmler submitted to Hitler documents allegedly proving that the general, the highest-ranking officer in the German army, had been guilty of homosexual relations and had been paying blackmail to another homosexual over the course of several years.

Hitler's Chief Aide, Colonel Hossbach, was shocked when he heard these accusations. Against Hitler's strict orders, and unaware at the time that the whole affair was a frame-up engineered by the Gestapo, Hossbach informed Fritsch of the charges against him.

Consequently, when Hitler, with Goering present, confronted Fritsch with these charges, the accusations had at least lost the element of surprise. Fritsch categorically denied them all upon his word of honor. He was to find out, however, that this did not mean much to Hitler, who was not satisfied with Fritsch's declaration. There was now introduced into the meeting one of the most improbable witnesses ever to confront an officer of Fritsch's standing. This witness, a man by the name of Schmidt, was a creature from the shadowy depths of the underworld, a homosexual with a long criminal record including convictions for blackmail, fraud, and embezzlement. Speechless with rage, Fritsch had to listen as this man identified him as the officer whom he, Schmidt, had caught while committing homosexual acts, and who later had paid him thousands of marks to keep silent.

Hitler believed or pretended to believe the accusations of the ex-convict. In any case, he took advantage of a perfect opportunity to rid himself of the intractable general and demanded Fritsch's resignation. Fritsch at first refused; later on, however, in his bitterness, shock, and rage over the treatment accorded him, he wrote out the resignation. Himmler's plan thus had succeeded beyond the Gestapo chief's fondest expectations.

Hitler used the occasion as an excuse for a complete shake-up of the top army command. He eliminated the post of War Minister, declared himself "Supreme Commander," and appointed General Keitel, who was to prove one of Hitler's most slavish toadies, chief of the new OKW, the High Command of the Armed Forces. Brauchitsch was named successor to General von Fritsch, and sixteen other generals were retired. Thus, with one stroke, Hitler rid himself of most of his opposition within the army and established himself as its master.

In the meantime, however, the friends of Fritsch, especially Beck, had not been idle. With the help of Criminal Police Inspector Arthur Nebe and Dr. Carl Sack of the Military High Court, neither a friend of the Nazis, the charges against Fritsch were investigated. What came to light was a fantastic tissue of forgery, false evidence, and blackmail by the Gestapo. The witness Schmidt had once blackmailed an army captain by the name of von Frisch; the Gestapo had unearthed the old files on the case, utilized the similarity of names, and induced Schmidt to identify General von Fritsch as the man he had spied upon, and subsequently blackmailed.°

To clear the general's name, the case was brought before the Military High Court. During the interrogations Schmidt got entangled in contradictions; he finally broke down and admitted that the man in question had not been General von Fritsch. The court then acquitted the General of all charges, completely clearing his name. The Gestapo quickly got rid of the embarrassing false witness by shooting him without a trial.

Fritsch's friends had expected the General to be returned to his post after his rehabilitation, but were soon disillusioned. Hitler, having eliminated a man who, under certain circumstances, could have become a formidable threat to him and his aspirations, had no intention of returning him to a position of power.

Fritsch lived another year and a half, an embittered and broken man. When the war started, he went along as chief of a regiment. This was a courtesy title and did not involve a position of command. The death he sought found him during a battle in the Polish campaign.

False accusations, which had broken him during his life, continued to pursue Fritsch even after his death. At the

---

° For heretofore unpublished documents on the Fritsch affair, see Appendix IV.

beginning of the Nuremberg trials, Chief Prosecutor Robert Jackson quoted from a letter allegedly written by Fritsch to a friend. In this letter, Fritsch not only appears to be completely in favor of Hitler's aims, but strongly anti-Semitic, anti-Catholic, and anti-Labor as well. "It is very strange," the letter runs, "that so many people should regard the future with growing apprehension, in spite of the Fuehrer's indisputable successes in the past. . . . Soon after the War [World War I] I came to the conclusion that we should have to be victorious in three battles, if Germany was again to be powerful:

"1) the battle against the working class; Hitler has won this one;

"2) against the Catholic Church, perhaps better expressed Ultramontanism; and

"3) against the Jews.

"We are in the midst of these battles, and the one against the Jews is the most difficult."

Jackson, in his opening speech at Nuremberg, said that the Nazi aims had thus been summed up by "one of their own number." To anyone who knew Fritsch, however, it is clear that the contents of this letter are a complete contradiction of his attitude and opinions. The letter, widely quoted in non-German writings as evidence of Fritsch's unreliable and vacillating attitude, or, as Shirer calls it in *The Rise and Fall of the Third Reich,* his "pathetic confusion," deserves closer scrutiny. (It is interesting to note, by the way, that although this letter is quoted in the English edition of Shirer's book, p. 483, no mention of it can be found in the German edition.)

The letter in question purports to have been one of several written by Fritsch to the Baroness von Schutzbar-Milchlingen, and confiscated by the Allies after the war. Most of the letters were later returned to the Baroness. The original of the letter in which Fritsch allegedly made the anti-Semitic, pro-Hitler remarks, and whose authenticity was challenged by the defense at Nuremberg, was never at any time produced by the prosecution. Instead, they submitted a typewritten "copy," claiming that the document itself "could not be found." Neither then nor later did it turn up among the other documents of the Nuremberg trials. In addition, the Baroness von Schutzbar-Milchlingen testified under oath that she never received a letter of that or similar content from General von Fritsch. In the National Archives in Washington, D.C., are photocopies of all the Fritsch letters, with the sole exception of the one quoted by Chief Prosecutor Jackson.

The implications of this failure to produce the letter were clear; the International Court acknowledged that it fully understood its meaning by declaring, in the words of Lord Justice Lawrence, that a document that could not be produced would be ignored. Although the letter was disqualified from further use during the trial, the shabby, disgraceful incident had already caused considerable damage. The opening speech by Jackson remained in the trial records, and the non-existent letter is still quoted as an authentic document by some historians of the Hitler era, for example, Shirer.

Apart from everything else, the letter creates confusion and makes the background of the Fritsch case more difficult to understand. After all, there would have been no reason for Hitler and Himmler to eliminate Fritsch if the latter really had been so strongly in favor of the Nazi policies. Only by eliminating the possibility that Fritsch ever wrote the letter is it possible to appraise the facts correctly.

After the elimination of Fritsch, General Beck, the Chief of Staff, was the only man left in a high military position who was resolutely opposed to Hitler's aims. Beck had fought against the Gestapo in the Fritsch case with such tenacity that Hitler became apprehensive. "The only man I fear," he said in a conversation with Franz Guertner, the Minister of Justice, "is Beck. That man would be capable of acting against me."

The inevitable clash between Beck and Hitler soon occurred. After carefully watching and appraising the situation, Beck became convinced that Hitler was heading for a war. This, of course, was clear to any alert and critical observer who analyzed Hitler's fiscal policies. With the help of credit expansion, Hitler had been able to eliminate unemployment. Strict laws governing foreign exchange kept the currency stable: The amount of German currency that could be taken out of the country was limited to a few marks, and infractions against this law were punishable by death. Once started on this road, Hitler had to continue, for the resulting limitless credit expansion would have led to a situation which could have been resolved by nothing short of a war. Because he realized this, Hjalmar Schacht, President of the Reichsbank, refused to give Hitler more money. The only result of that refusal was that Schacht was removed from his position.

Convinced that any war started by Hitler would turn into a world-wide conflict, Beck was not willing to accept, before history and the German people, any part of the responsibility for these developments. When it became evident, during the summer of 1938, that Hitler was steering a course toward war, Beck made every effort to stop him, a task made more difficult by Hitler's easy and bloodless victory in the *Anschluss* of Austria. When signs of a Czech "crisis" began to appear on the German propaganda horizon, Beck decided to try to pin Hitler down and get him to spell out his future plans. Hitler admitted that an armed conflict could ensue in the course of the Czech affair, but denied that he was heading for a general war. Beck was not satisfied with such generalities, and demanded guarantees. These Hitler refused to give. "The army," he told Beck, "is an instrument of politics. I shall assign the army its task when the moment arrives, and the army will have to carry out this task without arguing whether it is right or wrong."

Undaunted, Beck declined to retreat from his position. Declaring that Hitler's viewpoint was not acceptable to him as Chief of Staff, he said that he could not be responsible for orders whose contents he could not approve.

Finally, when all else had failed, Beck made plans which were designed to force Hitler to change his course. These plans involved a démarche by the entire Army High Command, acting in unison. Beck's reasoning was simple and to the point: without generals there could be no war. But though he was thinking primarily in military terms, he also was considering the political aspects of such a move. In a conversation with Brauchitsch in July, 1938, Beck made it clear that he was convinced of the need for a political clean-up action at home. First and foremost would be a reckoning with the SS. Among the reforms he considered necessary were an end to the Cheka methods, the reinstitution of freedom of expression, the restoration of law and justice in the country, and a pledge against any war of aggression.

In his plans for a démarche, Beck was supported by such generals as Witzleben and Stuelpnagel. But when the time for action came, the new Commander-in-Chief, General Brauchitsch, was found wanting. "Brauchitsch," Beck later declared bitterly, "has deserted me."

After it became clear that all his efforts had been in vain, Beck decided to resign as Chief of Staff. Having failed to stop Hitler, he at least wanted no responsibility for Nazi war adventures. Hitler at first tried to dissuade Beck from resigning, but suddenly switched his tactics and dismissed him.

Thus, within the course of only a few months, the German resistance had been deprived of two of their hopes in the high military leadership. With Hitler now in control of the Army High Command, and with men such as Keitel and Brauchitsch in the top posts, the task of eliminating or even checking the German dictator had become much more difficult.

CHAPTER FIVE

Negotiations

with Britain

After the successful *Anschluss* of Austria in March, 1938, it became increasingly clear to the alert political observer that this latest easy victory had only whetted Hitler's appetite, and that he would continue to push for further territorial acquisitions —a course which would inevitably lead to a general war.

Because of this inescapable conclusion, the German opposition of that time considered it imperative to try to find ways of convincing the Western Powers, and particularly England, that unflinching firmness in the face of Hitler's demands was essential if the German dictator, who was threatening the peace of Europe and the world, was to be checked, and eventually removed from power. At the same time, we tried to persuade many influential but still undecided or vacillating Germans to actively participate in this attempt to stop Hitler before it became too late to save the peace.

This two-pronged effort found Goerdeler, the former Lord Mayor of Leipzig, in the very front line of action. Foreign relations had long been a field to which he had devoted his untiring efforts. Between 1937 and the outbreak of World War II, Goerdeler had made a number of trips to other countries, always widening the scope of his information on world affairs and his judgment of the international situation. During those years, he visited France, England, Canada, the United States, Belgium, Switzerland, Syria, Turkey, Yugoslavia, Bulgaria, and Rumania. He set down the impressions and insights gained on these journeys in long memoranda, which he sent to all the important German military and political departments in the hope of clipping Hitler's wings and preventing the outbreak of the war. On reading these memoranda today, one is inclined to consider them reports on past historical events, and to forget that they were prophesies of the future. For example, in December, 1938, Goerdeler sounds this warning:

"We are too easily inclined to judge as weakness that which is only natural. Anyone who has possessions will try almost anything to preserve them by peaceful means. Only the conqueror believes a war to be unavoidable. Behind England and France stand the United States of America. There can no longer be the slightest doubt that in a war the United States would from the first moment on stand at the side of England and France. They will protect a large part of the Atlantic Ocean; they will send planes, arms, and ammunition, even though they will try to avoid as long as possible the sending of troops. Thus the Axis has a clear-cut front against it, with the Nordic countries, Switzerland, and the Balkan countries being the cautious neutrals, while Bulgaria would be willing to support any successful action."

Later, Goerdeler adds:

"In my earlier reports, I have shown that the overwhelming mood of the peoples of the world today is a tremendous desire for peace. This still holds true. But now we slowly find a note of impatience creeping into the expressions of this peace longing, and even of open antagonism against certain events in Germany. This is an extremely grave symptom. Nerves all over the world are beginning to give. In my judgment we still have a chance to secure a sensible peace, and one that will be good for us as well. I have repeatedly stated that every single statesman in foreign countries today is convinced that the most expensive peace is cheaper than victory in war. This conviction still prevails."

Goerdeler ends on a note of prophetic warning:

"The span for any understanding, the limitations of which I already mentioned in April, is by all signs coming to an end. This end may not come today or tomorrow, but it cannot be too far in the future. One thing is certain: the happy lot of a just peace is even today lying on the table, and all we have to do is to pick it up."

As the Czech question began to loom larger, it became increasingly the concern of a number of members within the opposition that contacts with foreign countries be strengthened and relations with Britain improved in the hope of getting a chance to impress upon the British government the urgency of a firm stand against Hitler. Hans Oster, then a colonel and later a general in the German Counter-Intelligence, was particularly active in trying to bring this about.

But the task facing these people presented almost insurmountable difficulties. For the purposes of the German anti-Nazi resistance, there could hardly have been a less favorable combination of political power than that which existed in England, with Sir Neville Chamberlain as Prime Minister, Lord Halifax as Foreign Secretary, and Sir Nevile Henderson as the British Ambassador to Germany.

Many historians have minimized and downgraded the efforts of the German opposition to stiffen the prewar British government's attitude toward Hitler. This is just as much a mistake as the attempts by some Germans to blame the Western Powers for all that went wrong with the resistance against Hitler. The truth lies somewhere between.

J. W. Wheeler-Bennett, in his book *The Nemesis of Power*, dismisses our attempts as both unrealistic and fraught with grave risks to the British government. He states that, whatever the charges against Chamberlain and the other Western leaders may be, that of rejecting the warnings and proposals of the German resistance was "surely not among the most serious" (p. 414). William L. Shirer echoes this sentiment in *The Rise and Fall of the Third Reich*. Wheeler-Bennett goes on to claim that Chamberlain, Halifax, and the others were expected by the anti-Hitler Germans to "gamble with the fate of their countries," and that this "fantastic demand" was made "by men in Germany who themselves, in most cases, had been enthusiastic supporters of Hitler . . ." (p. 415). He concludes his argument with the remark that, even in the "very improbable eventuality of such a Putsch succeeding," there seemed to have been little indication that the anti-Hitler faction, once it had gained power, would not have continued Hitler's policies. In other words, to Wheeler-Bennett there seems to have been no basic difference between the aims of the Nazi regime and those of the anti-Hitler resistance.

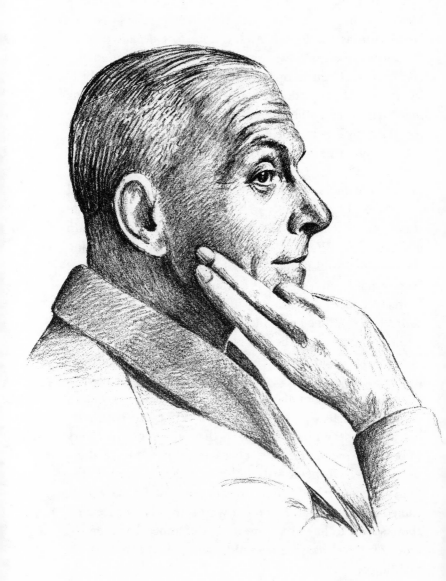

HANS OSTER

1 8 8 8 — 1 9 4 5

Chief of Staff of the Counter-Intelligence, Major-General Oster was one of the earliest and most determined of Hitler's opponents. His hatred of National Socialism led him to become one of the main organizers of the resistance, and author of early plans for the dictator's removal. Oster was hanged by the SS in April, 1945.

Here we have a classic example of how objectivity and clear judgment are impaired by basic dislike and suspicion, in this case of all Germans, Nazi and anti-Nazi alike. None of the above-mentioned arguments can stand up in the clear cold light of truth. First of all, there was no "gamble" whatsoever involved for the Western Powers in a firm and uncompromising stand against Hitler's demands during that summer of 1938. Any gamble was entirely on our side—our lives, after all, were at stake in this game. The British, on the other hand, would have incurred no risk by issuing a stiff "hands-off" warning to Hitler, for it had become clear during the occupation of Austria that the German army in 1938 was in no shape to fight a major war, especially if such a war meant military engagements on several fronts. Even an attack against Czechoslovakia alone could have presented serious difficulties, for the Czech frontier defenses were in excellent condition and, in the view of some of Germany's top generals, the German army in 1938 did not possess the means necessary to break through these fortifications. Had England and France come into the war while the Germans were engaged in fighting the Czechs, there can be no doubt that the defeat of Germany would have followed in short order. It seems hardly credible that this information should not have been in the possession of the British Military Intelligence, and this makes the attitude of the British government and the failure to adopt a tough stand against Hitler all the more difficult to explain. An uncompromising attitude by Britain and France in the summer of 1938 would have:

1) given pause to Hitler and his henchmen;

2) stiffened the backbone of those German generals who were still undecided and wavering;

3) instilled fear and apprehension in the German people, and thus lessened Hitler's prestige;

4) presented the ideal opportunity to those Germans who were prepared to accept great personal risks in an attempt to remove Hitler, and thus end with one stroke internal tyranny as well as the threat of war.

What if such a coup had failed? Wheeler-Bennett argues that in that case Britain, faced with a "belligerent" Hitler, would have found herself in a most dangerous situation. This argument is hardly valid. If the German army was in no position in 1938 to fight a major war under normal circumstances, it certainly would have been much less able to do so after an attempted coup involving many top military figures. If we had failed to remove Hitler, the dire consequences would have been borne by us alone, that is, by the people directly involved in the attempt inside Germany. England and France, far from being in danger, would have been in a much stronger position than before. A plot—even one that fails—is hardly a sign of internal strength and solidarity. An outward show of solidarity is vital to a totalitarian government, especially one about to embark on a war. The upheaval and unrest following an attempt to remove Hitler would have presented the Western Powers with the perfect opportunity to increase the pressure against him at a time when his internal weakness lay exposed. Such a course could conceivably have led to civil war in Germany, but hardly to war against the West. In the case of a civil war, the price in German blood would have been heavy, but any real danger to Britain and France in 1938 was non-existent.

The argument that a German government created after a successful coup against Hitler might have carried on his policies scarcely needs comment. Far from having at any time been "enthusiastic supporters" of Hitler, the men at the center of the German resistance were convinced and determined opponents of Nazism's ideological and political aims. A government controlled by such men would have been based upon concepts of law and justice, in both its internal and international relations.

The fact that we attached the greatest importance to obtaining support for our efforts through an uncompromising stand against Hitler by other countries, especially Britain, has been interpreted as a sign of the basic weakness and impotence of the German resistance by some chroniclers of the Nazi era. William Shirer, in *The Rise and Fall of the Third Reich*, wonders why we did not simply go ahead and act on our own, instead of waiting for others to help us and then blaming others for our failure to act. There is a grain of truth in this charge, but Shirer oversimplifies the situation, and disregards both the facts of today's international political life and the peculiar nature of the modern totalitarian state. Foreign support was vital because the hard core of resolute, determined men within the German resistance was hopelessly outnumbered, and besides was forced to push, pull, and carry along the many lukewarm, hesitant, and vacillating people at the edges of the conspiracy, who were nevertheless needed because of their influential positions.

A tough stand against Hitler by the Western Powers would have strengthened our position immeasurably, and would have brought many still undecided or wavering generals and other key figures into our camp. Strong outside opposition to the actions of a tyrannical regime has a tendency to consolidate and encourage internal resistance. Conversely, any relaxation or softening in attitude toward a totalitarian government is immediately followed by disintegration of the internal opposition. This relationship between internal opposition and foreign support was by no means typical only of the German resistance against Hitler. The same situation arises whenever internal resistance movements must operate within a ruthless dictatorship. The age of isolationism is past; the political life of the world of today is so closely interrelated that the policies of any great country cannot help but influence others. We find examples of this delicate interbalance between external pressure and internal resistance in the most recent history of Communist-controlled countries such as Cuba.

Those, then, were the reasons we sought so desperately to get the British in 1938-39 to adopt an uncompromising stand toward Hitler. A good opportunity to get in touch with leading English political circles came through Jan Colvin, an Englishman then living in Berlin. He was a member of the Casino Society, the most exclusive club in Berlin. Colvin had all the superior traits traditionally associated with the Englishman: He was intelligent, discreet, cautious, and at the same time daring. By arranging a visit to England by Ewald von Kleist, one of Hitler's most unbending adversaries, Colvin helped to establish a truly effective contact.

When Kleist visited Britain in the late summer of 1938,

he talked with Lord Lloyd, Lord Vansittart, and Winston Churchill, then leader of the Opposition. Kleist did his best to convince the British leaders that world peace could be maintained only if their country would stand firm against Hitler's demands. The least concession by England, Kleist warned, would irrevocably lead to a war with far-reaching consequences not only for Europe but for the entire world.

Kleist also assured his English hosts that a firm stand by the Western Powers would encourage the German generals in their opposition to Hitler's plans, for in whatever way these generals differed, they all agreed that they did not want war. Kleist also stressed that it would be a mistake for the Western Powers to equate National Socialism with the German people.

Vansittart considered Kleist's warnings and proposals important enough to pass on both to Chamberlain and to Halifax. However, the British Prime Minister was much too intent on his policy of securing "peace in our time" by appeasing the "Fuehrer" to pay much attention to Kleist's warnings. In a letter to Viscount Halifax, dated August 19, 1938, Chamberlain states:

". . . I take it that Von Kleist is violently anti-Hitler and extremely anxious to stir up his friends in Germany to make an attempt at his overthrow. He reminds me of the Jacobites at the Court of France in King William's time, and I think we must discount a good deal of what he says. Nevertheless I confess to some feeling of uneasiness and I am not sure that we ought not to do something. His (Kleist's) second remedy, that one of us should make a speech or give an interview in which we should, in Van's phrase, 'be more explicit,' I reject."

And so effective action by the British government was dismissed by Chamberlain as being too risky.

There can be no doubt that the reports and opinions voiced by the British Ambassador to Germany, Sir Nevile Henderson, played an important role in supporting the British government's conciliatory attitude toward Hitler. We all had the feeling during those years that Henderson was captivated by Hitler and National Socialism. Once, for instance, Henderson described to me in admiring terms his impression of what he had seen at the Party Day celebration in Nuremberg. The way in which the German Labor Service handled their spades evidently had struck him as being especially impressive.

We realized that the British Ambassador's attitude toward Nazism could not fail to influence his official reports. The extremes to which Henderson went to accomodate Hitler became painfully clear one day early in 1938, during a dinner in Berlin at the Hotel Kaiserhof. On that occasion, which was sponsored by the German-English Society, Henderson delivered a speech in which he said that he hoped to learn much for his own country from National Socialism. In its continuous efforts to influence the German people, the Nazi-controlled press in Germany naturally pounced upon this choice propaganda item. Small wonder that the average German, even though he may have had some doubts about Hitler, was impressed to find that so eminent a foreign diplomatic figure as His British Majesty's Ambassador publicly proclaimed himself an admirer of Nazism!

It came as no surprise to us, therefore, that Sir Nevile Henderson was quick to warn his government not only against the emissaries of the German opposition (he suggested, for instance, that Kleist should not be received in official quarters) but also against adopting a tough attitude toward Hitler. On the other hand he proved most eager to arrange a meeting between Chamberlain and the German dictator. In this he was successful. The result was the fateful Munich Pact, which led to the dismemberment and annexation of Czechoslovakia and later to World War II.

And so Kleist returned from England to Germany in the summer of 1938 without having achieved what he had hoped to do. He later gave me the details of his talks with the various British leaders, including the fact that he had proposed a plan for large-scale maneuvers by the British Navy in the "Wet Triangle"—a popular German term for the North Sea—which would show off to its best advantage the extent of British sea power. Kleist knew very well the respect and awe with which Germans, including Hitler himself, regarded the British Navy. This proposal, too, had been dismissed as too risky by the men in charge of British foreign policy. They feared that such a gesture— or, in fact, any strong gesture—would anger Hitler and provoke him into aggressive action. Here again it was Henderson who assured his government that no good could come of "upsetting" Hitler.

The only concrete achievement which Kleist could claim as a result of his talks in England was a letter written by Winston Churchill in his capacity as leader of the Opposition. In this letter to Kleist, Churchill stated that, regardless of differences in domestic policy, the English people were united in their decision not to accept without resistance any further unilateral action by Hitler.

Churchill's letter arrived by diplomatic pouch at the British Embassy in Berlin, where I picked it up and delivered it to Kleist, who passed it on to Admiral Canaris, Chief of the German Counter-Intelligence. Canaris in turn showed the letter to Hitler, hoping to influence him with this proof of Britain's stiffening attitude.

Any effect the letter might have had, however, was more than counteracted by the British government's continued efforts to appease the German dictator. Hitler was convinced that Ribbentrop, who had been assuring him all along that England was too "decadent" to fight, was right after all, and the Munich agreement strengthened this conviction as well as Hitler's mounting intransigence.

Other emissaries sent to England by the German opposition had no better luck than Kleist. In the summer of 1939, only a few months before the outbreak of World War II, my turn came.

The trip itself was arranged by Canaris. Among the reasons why I was picked for this assignment was the very special nature of the ties that existed between my family and the British Crown. My great-grandfather, Baron Stockmar, had for many years been the private physician and trusted confidential adviser of Britain's Queen Victoria. When some of the letters written by the Queen to my ancestor fell into the hands of the Gestapo, I managed to get them back with the help of friends, and then turned them over to the British Ambassador as a present to the Crown. As a result, I was invited to spend some time at Windsor Castle and look through the archives containing records about my great-grandfather. This invitation served as a convenient cover for the much more pressing purpose for which I had come to England:

to try to pick up the conversations with the British leaders where Kleist had left off the year before.

After arriving in London, I went to see Lord Lloyd. Throughout my meeting with him, I found him most sympathetic to our cause, but extremely pessimistic as far as his country was concerned. He told me that ever since 1926, he had harbored grave doubts about the strength and resolution of the English nation. When the conversation got around to Sir Nevile Henderson, whom he knew well from his time as High Commissioner in Egypt, Lord Lloyd made some scathing remarks about Henderson's abilities and qualifications.

During my conversation with Lloyd I told him that, according to our information, the outbreak of war was imminent, and would be started—regardless of all mediation efforts—by an attack on Poland. The only slim chance left to prevent war was for Britain to act quickly and forcefully so as to leave not the slightest doubt that action by Hitler against Poland would bring on a full-scale war. At that time Hitler did not consider this even a possibility.

I also told Lord Lloyd that his government's efforts to come to an agreement with the Soviet Union would be frustrated, because the signing of a treaty between Hitler and Stalin could be expected at any moment. On hearing this, Lord Lloyd asked me for authorization to transmit this information to the British Foreign Secretary, Lord Halifax. I did not hesitate to give my permission. The answer to my warning came quickly: I was informed that, in the opinion of competent experts within the Foreign Office, the willingness of the Russians to engage in further negotiations remained unchanged, which meant that a treaty between Hitler and Stalin was not to be feared! A few weeks later, the non-aggression pact between the Soviet Union and Nazi Germany was signed in Moscow.

Besides my conversation with Lord Lloyd, I also had a talk with Winston Churchill on the same subjects. The meeting took place at his country estate south of London. Churchill's appearance, his way of conducting the conversation, his rapid-fire questions and answers, all made a deep impression upon me. I had the feeling that I was in the presence of a statesman of historic stature. Unlike Lord Lloyd, Churchill avoided all personalities; and he also displayed none of Lloyd's doubts about the strength and determination of his country. On the contrary, Churchill seemed confident that the English nation was basically sound and fully capable of putting up a good fight.

Looking at him as he sat, compact and solid, on the sofa beneath the portrait of his famous ancestor, the Duke of Marlborough, he appeared to me the personification of England at the very height of her greatness.

I had no intention of letting any doubts arise about the fact that the men of the German resistance, although anti-Nazi, were unwilling to betray their country. I began the conversation with the sentence: "I am not a Nazi, but I am a good patriot." Churchill promptly retorted: "So am I!" A broad grin spreading over his face showed his delight at this quick rejoinder.

During the course of our conversation, he displayed great interest in the German opposition. Finally he asked whether I could guarantee a successful action by our group. The answer to that question was not easy for me, and I hesitated for a moment before replying in the negative, but I felt that it was most important to remain realistic and not give in to wishful thinking. In view of the

97

difficulties of living under a tyranny, and at the same time secretly working toward its overthrow, it seemed impossible to guarantee a successful coup d'état. I believe, by the way, that Churchill fully realized these problems, and that his question was meant to test my reaction.

Details of that conversation of 1939 vividly came back to me when, exactly ten years later, in 1949, I once again met with and talked to Churchill at his country estate. He showed me the entry of my name in the guest book of ten years before, and I was amazed at his keen memory. Later, while reviewing the years that lay between our two meetings, he told me that he afterwards realized that during the war he had been misled by his assistants about the considerable strength and size of the German anti-Hitler resistance.

The results of my journey to Britain in 1939 were as negative as those of the other emissaries sent by the opposition. Our warnings were dismissed, our information was met with doubt, or even with outright disbelief, as in the case of the Hitler-Stalin pact. Realizing the futility of further attempts, I turned down a request by some members of the German Counter-Intelligence that I make another trip to England in the fall of 1939, only a couple of weeks before the outbreak of the war. By that time, I knew that it would be in vain, that all chances to save the peace had been missed, and that fate would have to take its course.

CHAPTER SIX

Early Plans for a

Coup d'État

By late summer of 1938, when war against
Czechoslovakia seemed imminent, the first
concrete plans for Hitler's overthrow were drawn up. I
am frequently asked by foreigners why those within Germany who were opposed to Hitler waited so long before
attempting to get rid of him. One of the best answers to
that question is a quotation from the American Declaration of Independence: ". . . all experience hath shown,
that mankind are more disposed to suffer, while evils are
sufferable, than to right themselves by abolishing the forms
to which they are accustomed."

Most people, unless they are revolutionaries or fanatics
who want power for themselves, are slow to use force and
violence to solve political problems. They usually prefer
to wait in the hope that these problems will solve themselves, that somehow, given a little time, things will turn
out all right. This is especially true of the more slow-
tempered, patient populations of North European coun-

tries. Hitler's undeniable successes during the first few years of his regime encouraged a wait and see attitude and made it easy to defend. He did, after all, eliminate unemployment in Germany, and only relatively few people knew or cared that this was accomplished by highly questionable means. Successes in foreign policy, such as the Concordat with the Vatican in 1933 and the Naval Treaty with Britain in 1935, contributed to Hitler's prestige. The democracies of the West seemed almost pathetically eager to get along with Hitler. In view of these facts, it is not too surprising that even some of those Germans most strongly opposed to Hitler hoped that the leopard could be induced to change his spots and that the Nazi regime, after some reforms, would eventually turn into a more conventional type of government.

These hopes were shattered when it became clear, after the Fritsch affair and Hitler's shake-up of the military high command in 1938, that he was determined to make war. Now there was greater readiness within the opposition to listen to those voices which from the very beginning had claimed that the Nazis would lead Germany down the road to disaster. The opinion that only Hitler's elimination could stop such a development gained ascendancy.

Of the high-ranking army officers, Generals Witzleben and Hoepner were those most determined and ready to move against Hitler. From Oster we heard that Halder, who had succeeded Beck as Chief of Staff, also was close to agreeing to a coup. Even Brauchitsch seemed inclined to go along, but mainly because Witzleben and Hoepner exerted strong pressure upon him.

A detailed plan for seizing Berlin was worked out by

Witzleben and one of his subordinates, Major General Count Brockdorff-Ahlefeldt, who was commander of the 23rd Infantry Division. This division, whose staff was stationed in Potsdam, a suburb of Berlin, was to play a decisive role in the seizure of the city. The initial step in this plan called for the occupation of the Gestapo headquarters, and the arrest of Himmler, Heydrich, and their closest collaborators. After that had been done, Hitler was to be confronted with the fact, coupled with a demand that he immediately dismiss the top SS leaders. Upon Hitler's expected refusal, he was to be kidnaped from the Chancellery, and hidden in a place known only to the leaders of the plot.

Meanwhile, Witzleben's troops were to occupy the government quarters of Berlin and all the SS strongholds and take over all means of communication. The most important Party leaders and government members were to be placed under arrest.

Witzleben was optimistic about the plan, and believed that it could be executed successfully. During the crucial first ten hours the public would be given conflicting and confusing reports; then, proclamations charging that Hitler planned to drag Germany into a World War, and revealing the crimes committed by his regime would be issued, thus justifying the coup d'état to the German people.

Timing was of the utmost importance for the success of the coup. The plotters realized that, in order to make the accusation about Hitler's war plans valid, they would have to wait for the short period of time between the issuing of the order to attack Czechoslovakia and the beginning of the troop movements, and then move with lightning speed.

Once the attack on Czechoslovakia began, it would be all but impossible to stop it.

A strong stand by Britain against Hitler in the Czech question was essential to the success of the plan; it was for this reason that members of the resistance had been sent to Britain for talks with government leaders. Although these conversations turned out to be anything but encouraging, the men who stood ready to undertake the coup d'état in the fall of 1938 believed that, at the last minute, Britain and France would come forth with a strong declaration of support for Czechoslovakia against Hitler's continuing gamble with war.

As we waited with mounting anxiety in those tension-filled days of early September, 1938, we received the news that Britain's Prime Minister was coming to Germany, not to protest against Hitler's war-like tactics, but to talk peace with the German dictator!

Shattered though they were by this setback, the plotters did not give up all hope. The talks dragged on, and finally, on September 27, Hitler definitely rejected the British proposal concerning Czechoslovakia. Once again, the moment for action seemed to have come. Even the vacillating Brauchitsch was now willing to support the coup d'état. On the morning of the 28th, Witzleben went to his headquarters to wait for the telephone call which was to be the signal to start the insurrection.

The call never came. Brauchitsch learned on his way to the Chancellery that new mediation efforts, requested by Britain, were under way. A meeting of the heads of government of Great Britain, Germany, France, and Italy was being planned. Hitler had agreed to this meeting and called off the attack on Czechoslovakia.

The subsequent agreement of Munich gave Hitler one of the greatest foreign policy triumphs of his career, letting him appear in the role of a statesman who was fearless as well as moderate. In England Prime Minister Chamberlain was wildly applauded as the man who had secured "peace in our time."

There were those who did not agree. Beck, Goerdeler, and the others involved in the plan to overthrow Hitler knew that France and Great Britain had bought not peace but merely postponement of the inevitable conflict to a time when Hitler would be a much more dangerous and formidable antagonist. In addition, they had cut the ground out from under the German resistance and lessened any chance of Hitler's overthrow from within.

"The Munich agreement," wrote Goerdeler in a letter to friends in the United States only a few days after Munich,

"was nothing but capitulation, pure and simple, by Britain and France before bluffing tricksters. . . . By refusing to take a risk, Chamberlain now has made war inevitable. Both the English and French people now will have to defend their freedom by force of arms."

Later, after the war had broken out, Goerdeler added an epilogue to these reflections on Munich:

"Influential Americans and Englishmen were informed before this war that Hitler would start it, and bring a terrible catastrophe upon the world. . . . They considered us, the Germans who warned them, to be men without national feeling. They overlooked the fact that we love our country dearly, and want both its greatness and its honor; but that we, from the experience of our own suffering, knew which course would be chosen by the satanic and demonic Hitler. Despite our warnings, Chamberlain ran after Hitler in 1938. At that time, British firmness could have avoided the war, and unmasked Hitler. We do not wish to diminish the responsibility which we as Germans will have to bear; but the guilt for the tragic events rests not with the Germans alone, and the sacrifices we have made for our convictions are not among the least. If we succeed in liberating ourselves, the world will realize what decent Germans have suffered and borne, and how many of them have died a cruel death for German honor and the freedom of the world."

Across the Channel, Winston Churchill, one of the few dissenters from the general jubilant acceptance of "peace in our time," rose in the House of Commons and delivered a speech which echoed Goerdeler's sentiments, but which was much harsher in its condemnation of British action:

". . . the British people should know that we have passed an awful milestone in our history, when the whole equilibrium of Europe has been deranged, and that the terrible words have been pronounced against the Western democracies: 'Thou art weighed in the balance, and found wanting.' And do not suppose that this is the end. This is only the beginning of the reckoning. This is only the first sip, the first foretaste of a bitter cup. . . ."

The year following Munich was an almost unbroken period of triumph for Hitler, and a rude awakening for the West. The German dictator never intended to uphold the provisions of the Munich agreement. Only a bare six months after it had been signed, Czechoslovakia was forced to submit to German occupation, and became a "protectorate." Then in August, 1939, came the greatest triumph of all: the non-aggression pact between the Soviet Union and the Third Reich.

Now, in the fall of 1939 the climate for Hitler's overthrow was even less favorable than it had been a year before, but Hitler's determined opponents were still considering plans for a coup d'état, and continued to do so even after the outbreak of hostilities.

During the first days of September, my own personal task was to maintain daily contact with the British diplomats who still remained in Berlin, in order to carry on a continuous exchange of information about diplomatic and political events.

The climax of all this activity was reached on September 3, 1939. At about this time, General Baron von Hammerstein, one of the most resolute of Hitler's adversaries, emerged from the obscurity of retirement, and was given command of an army on the Rhine.

His appointment became the center of a far-reaching scheme, which involved an attempt to induce Hitler to visit Hammerstein's headquarters during the Polish campaign. In order to lure Hitler to the Rhine, Hammerstein advanced the theory that it would be good strategy to demonstrate the military might of the Third Reich in the West at the same time that the Polish campaign was being fought in the East. Hammerstein, with whom we kept in close contact through two of our collaborators, one of whom was my old friend Nikolaus von Halem, was determined to arrest Hitler during the proposed visit, thus overthrowing the Nazi regime.

Of all the generals, Hammerstein probably was most suited to move forcibly against the Nazis. A man of iron nerve, outstanding military talents, and a statesmanlike approach to political problems, he would have carried out the arrest of Hitler without any qualms or hesitation.

105

Despite last-minute efforts by Sir Nevile Henderson, war between Britain and the Third Reich was declared on September 3, 1939, at 11:15 A.M. It became my job to inform the British of Hammerstein's plan. The British Embassy had already been vacated, but I succeeded in reaching Sir George Ogilvy Forbes, the counselor of the British Embassy, around lunch time in the Hotel Adlon, and delivered my message.

While I was talking to Sir George in the hotel lounge, two SS officers appeared, spoke to the waiter, and were directed to our table. I had some most uncomfortable moments, for I thought they were after me, especially in view of the fact that I was having lunch with a high-ranking British diplomat hours after the outbreak of war between Germany and Britain. However, they paid no attention to me and after a short conversation with Sir George they left the hotel. The Englishman, who had not for one moment lost his presence of mind, told me that they had only wanted to find out details of the arrangements for the imminent departure of British Embassy personnel.

Once again, as so often in the past, our hopes of ridding Germany of Hitler were ruined. Hammerstein's scheme did not materialize. Hitler, who had a truly uncanny instinct for personal danger, suddenly cancelled his visit to Hammerstein's headquarters and shortly thereafter ordered a change in leadership; Hammerstein once more found himself in retirement.

I am sure that the failure of this plan—the last one which could have prevented the war—caused as keen disappointment to us as to the Englishmen who had been taken into our confidence.

In the late fall of 1939, after the close of the Polish campaign, Beck and Goerdeler attempted to win Brauchitsch
and Halder to a new attempt to remove Hitler. To influence them, it was decided to stress the military hope-
lessness of the imminent World War. With the help of
General Georg Thomas, chief of the Department for War
Economy, a correspondence between Beck and Halder
was arranged. On January 16, 1940, the two generals met.
During that meeting, Beck stated that Germany could not
possibly win the war. The United States, he declared,
would support the Western Powers. Germany, confronted
by the might of the world economy and production, would
inevitably be defeated. Beck further warned that initial
successes should blind no one to the fact that the war
would develop into one of attrition on a large scale, which
the powers with the greater resources were bound to win.
In Beck's opinion, the pact between Hitler and Stalin, far
from improving the situation, had in fact created an even
more dangerous one, for it had induced Russia to give up
its preoccupation with Far Eastern affairs. Now the danger
of a two-front war for Germany loomed large on the
horizon.

Halder replied that he was in full agreement with Beck's
arguments, and that he, too, believed that Hitler should be
stopped by force. But Brauchitsch, he said, was of a different opinion, and at this point seeemd incapable of deciding whether or not he should support a coup d'état.
He also feared that a large part of the officers' corps was
not reliable from an anti-Nazi point of view. In addition,
Brauchitsch claimed that Britain was fighting not only
Hitler, but also the German people.

In view of Brauchitsch's position, Halder felt that he by

107

himself could not adopt an opposing position, because to do so would split the army leadership in the middle of the war. It once more became clear that Brauchitsch and Halder, despite their basic disapproval of Hitler's policies, could not muster the firmness and resolve necessary to make so important a political decision.

Meanwhile, the resistance had made contact with non-German powers, this time through the Vatican, with the idea of creating a basis for foreign-policy negotiations which would remove the objections Halder and Brauchitsch had to a coup d'état. Canaris and Oster especially believed that this strategy had a good chance to succeed. Early in April, 1940, the resistance managed to get the Vatican to mediate a peace proposal between England and France and a German government resulting from a coup. The terms of this peace plan were acceptable to the resistance; the only condition was that Hitler and Ribbentrop be eliminated.

Now General Thomas made another attempt to get support from the army leadership. He approached General Halder with the so-called X-report, the Vatican-mediated peace plan. But while Halder stated in a letter to Goerdeler that "the German army will do its duty for the Fatherland even against the Hitler government if and when the situation should call for it," Brauchitsch, even now, could not be persuaded to change his opinion.

At this point, General Beck, who was determined to act, intervened and insisted on moving quickly against Hitler. He was strongly supported by several top officers, including Oster and Colonel Hans Groscurth, chief of a department in the Army High Command. Beck had made arrangements for taking over all government powers by force. For a short while after the takeover, the reins of the government would be placed in the hands of a three-man directorate with Beck at its head. Following a successful coup, Beck intended to inform the German people of Hitler's intention to attack Belgium and the Netherlands, and to state the reasons why this disastrous course had to be prevented by force.

The troops needed for such action were available; the prerequisite for the move was the assurance of cooperation by both Brauchitsch and Halder as chiefs of the Army Command. But when Brauchitsch remained adamant in his refusal to join the plot, this plan, too, had to be given up, and with it all hope of preventing Hitler's attack in the West.

CHAPTER SEVEN

The First Year

of the War

When, on September 1, 1939, Hitler started the campaign against Poland, it was clear to everybody with any political judgment that this attack would result in a world war. Hitler did not believe this, for he relied on information fed to him by his Foreign Minister, Joachim von Ribbentrop—information that ran contrary to all facts.

Shortly before the attack on Poland, General Thomas composed a memorandum in which he used information and statistics available to him as Chief of the Military Economic Staff. In this memorandum he emphasized two points: 1) that the war against Poland would bring about a world war; and 2) that Germany would not be capable of winning such a war. With this memorandum, Thomas went to see General Keitel, Chief of the High Command of the Armed Forces (OKW). Keitel did not even hear Thomas out, but cut him off with the statement that the danger of a world war did not exist, as the French were rotten with pacifism, and the British too decadent to come to the aid of Poland. The United States, Keitel declared, would not dream of sending even a single man to Europe to pull the chestnuts out of the fire for England or Poland. Undaunted by his initial failure, Thomas made one last attempt to stop the war. While discussing the situation with Admiral Canaris, Chief of German Counter-Intelligence, a few days before the date for which the attack on Poland had been scheduled, Thomas learned from Canaris that the date had been postponed. Once again he went to Keitel, and tried to convince him that the war against Poland would inevitably result in a world war. The conversation had the same negative result as the first one: Keitel rejected all of Thomas' arguments, and told him that Hitler had declared that no world war was to be feared because the pact between Russia and Germany constituted so great a political success that it had rendered a world conflict impossible. Other high officers of the army, especially Quarter Master General von Stuelpnagel, agreed with General Thomas, but it was clear that Hitler could not be stopped by reason and logic.

The Polish campaign ran its course. The world knows about the terror regime set up by the SS in Poland. When I asked Field Marshal von Bock a few years later about details of the atrocities in Poland, he told me that when Hitler had assembled the army leaders shortly before the start of the Polish campaign to tell them that he was determined to begin the war, he also informed them that the Poles would be dealt with unmercifully at the end of the campaign. In the course of action that was to be taken against the Poles, Hitler said, things would happen which

111

would not have the approval of the German generals. Because he did not want to burden the army with liquidations that were necessary for political reasons, he was going to entrust the extermination of the Polish upper classes, particularly the clergy, to the SS. All he asked was that the generals not interfere with these matters, but concentrate exclusively on their military tasks.

Hitler's statement, Bock told me, was received in icy silence by the generals; and after the campaign in Poland serious differences arose between General Blaskowitz, then military Commander-in-Chief in Poland, and the SS because of the atrocities committed by the latter.

During the Polish campaign I heard from Oster that the German General Staff feared a French offensive on the Rhine. In the opinion of the German General Staff, General Maurice Gamelin could have made a breakthrough on the Rhine during the Polish campaign. Such a breakthrough, although not easy, would have been feasible if a determined effort had been made by the French. Why Gamelin, who was then the French Generalissimo, did not take advantage of the favorable opportunity to attack in the fall of 1939 remains inexplicable, for his high military qualifications were unquestionable.

During the first months of the war, the German resistance once more felt hopeful, for now three prerequisites for a coup against Hitler had been fulfilled:

1) We had made contact with a number of non-German circles. This was a step forward which had brought within the realm of the possible a world-wide collaboration among all the forces fighting National Socialism.

2) The civilian resistance movement, based on and nurtured by Christian concepts, had established contact with the military leadership, thereby reaching out for the one and only instrument capable of dealing the death blow to National Socialism.

3) With the outbreak of the war, our chosen instrument, the army, had been freed from peace-time restrictions and was in a position to increase its power and influence.

With this in mind, many high-ranking members of the officer corps believed that the hour of liberation from Hitler's yoke would come at the moment of a German offensive against France. These officers were convinced of—and hoped for—a failure of this offensive, for they still bore in mind the military performance of the French in the First World War. Early in 1940, Henning von Tresckow, then staff officer in the Army Group Rundstedt, explained to me in detail his theory that the planned German offensive against France would get bogged down after short-lived initial successes. This was also the opinion of the majority of the German General Staff. The officers who were looking for a chance to overthrow Hitler thought that failure of the campaign against France would provide the right psychological moment for such a coup. It was a paradoxical situation: High-ranking, patriotic German officers hoped for a German military setback, because they believed this would give them a chance to try to save Germany from ultimate total disaster.

With this in mind, Colonel Oster of the Abwehr decided to commit what was technically high treason and warn the Dutch that Hitler planned to attack their country. Oster's decision was not made lightly, for he realized that it might cost thousands of German lives if the Dutch army was prepared to meet the German attack. He nevertheless informed a Dutch friend of his, Colonel J. G. Sas, of the date set for Hitler's move against the Low Countries. Oster knew that his act would be considered treason by many of his comrades-in-arms, but that did not deter him. "There are those who will say," he remarked at the time, "that I am a traitor, but I truly am not. I consider myself a better German than all those who run after Hitler. My plan and my duty is to free Germany, and with it the world, of this pestilence."

Shortly before the German occupation of Denmark, Oster issued the same kind of warning, but the Danes rejected the information as being most unlikely. Because the date for the attack on Belgium and the Netherlands was postponed several times by Hitler, the governments of those countries paid little attention to the news that came to them from Oster via Sas. Early in May, 1940, Oster gave Sas a final warning, which was finally heeded—too late— by the Dutch and Belgians. The French and British, on the other hand, were caught completely by surprise.

In the months between the end of the Polish campaign and the spring of 1940, the General Staff somewhat revised their opinion of the state of French military preparedness. A former Austrian Pioneer officer had developed an almost incredible skill in interpreting aerial photographs. He was capable of examining photographs taken, in many cases, from heights of 30,000 feet and picking out every single fortification and every piece of artillery. On the strength of his findings, the General Staff concluded that the Maginot Line had been vastly overrated. It was only half as valuable as French propaganda had purported it to be, especially in view of the offensive weapons the Germans had developed. In addition, France's fortifications on her northern borders were mere field defenses which did not offer any serious resistance to attack. To the surprise of the General Staff, repeated aerial surveys showed that the work on these fortifications was proceeding at an incredibly slow pace. The Dutch-Belgian border defenses did not seem to be serious obstacles either.

In spite of this, Tresckow told me he still believed that the German offensive against France would not be successful. Even though French fortifications were weak, the French army, he said, was a past master of defensive warfare. If the French soldiers would fight as well as they had fought in World War I, the German attack would get bogged down despite German superiority in air and tank equipment.

But Tresckow and most other German General Staff officers had overestimated the France of 1940. When, in May of that year, the offensive against France began, the advancing German armies found a soft adversary. The great majority of the French troops fought half-heartedly, and so, to the great surprise of the German General Staff, the offensive was a tremendous operational success. As soon as Holland, most of Belgium, and a great part of northern France were in German hands, the General Staff was faced by a problem: Would it be better to disregard the British army in western Belgium and instead turn south and completely defeat France, or would it be better to destroy the British forces and then complete the occupation of France? Hitler was in favor of the former plan; an overwhelming majority of the General Staff favored the latter. After considerable argument, Hitler's view prevailed because Goering promised that his air force would prevent the British army from retreating across the Channel. The consequence of this strategy was the failure of Hitler's plan, for in sharp contrast to the half-hearted French, the fighting spirit of the British soldier was first rate, and the German air force was *not* capable of preventing the withdrawal of the British forces across the Channel. However, in the opinion of the General Staff the British success was merely a tactical one. From an overall operational viewpoint, the success would have been greater had Lord Gort, the British Commander-in-Chief, pushed south with his united forces and joined the French army. In the mean time, General Gamelin had been replaced by General Maxime Weygand, who was expected to offer stiff resistance. Had Lord Gort adopted the above-mentioned strategy, the Allied forces would have been able, in the judgment of the German General Staff, to stop the German offensive at the crucial moment, and France would have been preserved as a military and political power for the allies. But the British preferred to withdraw across the Channel, and thus paid for the rescue of their land army by sacrificing the holding of the Weygand Line in the south.

To the resistance movement in Germany, all these military considerations were of prime political importance. As Tresckow stated clearly, a coup against Hitler could be attempted, with hope of success, only after the failure of the German offensive. It was obvious to all of us that to lead the victorious German army against a Hitler appearing as a successful military leader would be psychologically impossible, just as it had been impossible before the war to act against Hitler while he appeared as a successful statesman. The situation would have been entirely different at that early stage of the hostilities, if the 1940 offensive, started by Hitler against the advice of his generals, had ended in failure. Only such a defeat could break the spell under which Hitler, with the help of Goebbels' propaganda and Himmler's Gestapo, held the German people. A military reverse would also increase our chances of getting important military leaders who so far had kept aloof, such as General von Rundstedt, to come over to our side. There cannot be the slightest doubt that a coup by the army against Hitler after the victorious campaign in France would have been unfeasible. The fact that France had collapsed morally as well as materially was plain for all to see and made a deep impression on the German people, especially in view of earlier Nazi predictions of French "decadence."

When France, after signing the truce, had to surrender her large air force, a large number of fighter planes were among the aircraft turned over to the Germans. The victors were astonished to find that a great many of these planes were not only still intact, but were actually factory-new. They had never been used against the invading German army. In the opinion of the German General Staff, the offensive would have taken a different course if the French had not decided to spare their air force so completely.

It is well known that Hitler extended peace feelers to Britain in July and August of 1940. After these proposals were rejected, he started to draw up plans for an invasion of England under the code name "Sea Lion." We were convinced that a successful invasion of England would have meant Hitler's ascendancy over all of Europe. With the disappointing performance of the French army fresh in our minds, we therefore apprehensively followed the preparations and anxiously asked ourselves whether fate would once again favor Hitler.

An invasion of England directly after the collapse of France, before the British had had a chance to recover from Dunkirk, seemed to promise the best chance of success. But a tremendous amount of tonnage would have had to be instantly available, and this the German navy could not supply. So the invasion was advanced in another way: While ships were being built, Goering started his notorious air offensive against Britain. We knew that Hitler himself had ordered the air force to attack not only military centers, but also residential areas, and to destroy historical sites, especially old churches. Hitler justified this order by stating that it was necessary to deal a blow to English national pride and thoroughly humiliate the English people.

At the same time, preparations for the invasion were stepped up. The above-mentioned Austrian Pioneer officer examined and interpreted aerial photographs of the British coastal fortifications. But in sharp contrast to that of the French, work on the English defensive installations progressed at such a rapid pace that with each passing day it became more dangerous to attempt the invasion. In addition, the British Royal Air Force showed their mettle in those critical days by engaging in one air battle after another with the Germans. When one day more than 100 German bombers failed to return from an attack against England, the order was given to cease the air offensive, and from then on only nighttime bombardments were undertaken.

Our worries about a possible successful invasion of England, and the resulting hegemony by Hitler over all of Europe, were eased. With a new campaign in the East now looming on the horizon, we turned our attention to that front. Although we realized that Hitler's victory in the West had made matters more difficult for us, we were determined to do everything in our power to advance our ultimate goal of overthrowing Hitler and his regime.

CHAPTER EIGHT

The Early Years

of the Russian Campaign

Early in 1941, Tresckow managed to get me transferred from the West to the Army Group Center in the East, where he had just been appointed senior staff officer. I became his A.D.C., and from then on we remained in close daily contact.

There were several reasons why Tresckow selected me to be his aide and confidant, and for my subsequent role in the inner circles of the resistance—a role greatly out of proportion to my low military rank. Foremost among these reasons was Tresckow's need, once he had made up his mind to play a decisive part in the military resistance in the East, for an aide whom he could trust implicitly, and preferably one whose background, traditions, and upbringing was similar to his own. Our social and family ties—my wife was one of Tresckow's cousins—formed a solid basis of effortless understanding and complete trust which facilitated our cooperating in the delicate and dangerous activities in which we were soon to engage. His second reason for choosing me was that he realized I had gained invaluable inside knowledge of the Nazis and political experience--both of which he lacked—through my career and my early involvement in the anti-Hitler opposition. He could rely on me to advise and counsel him on political matters. Furthermore, I fulfilled the requirements and could handle the tasks of an assistant to a ranking staff officer. This made it easy for Tresckow to pick me for the job, for it is clear that all my personal qualifications could hardly have justified my being selected as his A.D.C. if I had been incapable of performing the necessary military duties.

My first meeting with Tresckow took place shortly before the war, just after I had returned from talks with British leaders. He and I had a long and soul-searching conversation during which we discussed all the aspects of resistance to Hitler. It ended with both of us reaffirming our conviction that duty and honor demanded that we do everything in our power to overthrow Hitler and National Socialism in order to save Germany and Europe from the danger of barbarism. This conversation was the beginning and the basis of our subsequent close cooperation, which lasted until Tresckow's death by his own hand after the abortive coup of 1944.

In the spring of 1941 the plan for the conquest of Russia was completed. Maps and orders for "Operation Barbarossa," as the attack on Russia was called, were already in the safes of the Army Group Center, while outwardly at least, the Third Reich was still on friendly terms with the Soviet Union. Hitler assembled his generals, as he had before the Polish campaign. We later heard from Bock,

HENNING VON TRESCKOW

1 9 0 1 — 1 9 4 4

By character, tradition, and upbringing, Major-General Tresckow was one of National Socialism's natural enemies. His unflagging zeal in his fight against Hitler made him one of the
outstanding figures of the resistance. His struggle against the
Nazis came to an end only with his death by suicide in 1944.

Commander-in-Chief of the Army Group Center, that Hitler had allowed a period of six weeks for the conquest of Russia. During the first three weeks, he warned, there would be some heavy fighting, but thereafter the German tank armies would thunder across the vast Russian plains without encountering more than negligible resistance. Amazingly enough, Hitler's view was supported by Brauchitsch, who also thought that six to eight weeks would suffice to conquer Russia. Bock, however, was of a different opinion. Already at that early date he remarked—if only to fellow officers—that he could not see how the war against Russia was going to be won.

During the briefing Hitler again told his generals that the SS would follow in the wake of the advancing German armies and would establish in the occupied Russian territories a regime of blood and terror similar to that in Poland. Again, this declaration was met with silence by the generals. Only when Hitler ordered that all Russian officers and commissars were to be shot did Brauchitsch object. The order thereupon was changed to apply to commissars only. We managed to get Bock, supported by his army commanders, to protest this order. All our efforts were in vain, however, and the order remained in force, even though we did everything in our power to draw wide attention to its inhuman and illegal content. Shortly after the hostilities against Russia had begun, the first Russian commissar was taken prisoner. Colonel Baron von Gersdorff, who belonged to our side, informed Tresckow, who without hesitation decided to let the man live. This incident illustrates that, risky though it was, Hitler's orders occasionally could be, and were, successfully defied.

Among the preparations for the Russian campaign were

lectures of an economic nature, given on Hitler's instructions to the staff members of the Army Group. These lectures, delivered by so-called "experts" on Russia, claimed that Russia's main sources of agricultural and industrial raw material were located west of the Ural mountains, and that the productive capacity of the Russian economy was very low. It therefore was to be hoped that the Russians would be unable to produce really good arms—especially tanks—in sufficiently great numbers, and even more important, would not be capable of replacing lost matériel.

Ridiculous as these statements may sound today, they were repeated, with certain modifications, year after year during the Russian campaign, each time with the assurance that "now, finally," the Russians were at the end of their tether. One of these lectures was attended by Admiral Canaris. Afterwards, the officers who had made up the audience stayed together for the customary drinks. Canaris, the old seaman, could outdrink most of the others, and was still around late at night when the company had thinned out considerably. During a lull in the conversation, Canaris suddenly asked: "Gentlemen, do you really believe all the nonsense you heard here today? To the best knowledge of the experts in my department, the entire situation is quite different. So far, no one ever has succeeded in defeating and conquering Russia!" During the subsequent months, the number of those who believed in the lectures diminished rapidly, while the viewpoint of Canaris just as rapidly gained new adherents.

When the German offensive started, the mass of the European Russian army, to the great surprise of the German General Staff, was concentrated close to the country's western borders. This went contrary to everything General von Clausewitz had so successfully taught the Russians in 1812, which was to exploit the strategic advantages of the vast Russian territory, and, in case of attack, to pull their armies back toward the east. This time, the Russians at first did exactly the opposite. Consequently, most of the Russian European army was defeated and destroyed west of Moscow in a relatively short period of time. One must keep this in mind in order to realize the extent of Russia's achievement. Not only did the Russians halt the German advance just before it reached Moscow, but they also, aided by the terrible Russian winter, defeated the German armies and, in the years that followed, slowly but surely forced them back. In the fall of 1941 the staff of the Army Group Center was located in Borisov, not far from the historic Berezina where the Russians had won a victory over Napoleon's armies in 1812. Bock one day visited the spot where Napoleon had been defeated. There we found a sign which read: "At this point, Napoleon's army crossed the Berezina in 1812. At the same spot, the German 10th Division crossed the river and headed for Moscow." Bock read the inscription, and remarked sarcastically: "Two unlucky war lords!"

As winter approached, Bock realized that rather than trying to advance any farther it would be better to dig in and spend the winter in positions protected by field fortifications. Bock's plan, however, was rejected by Hitler. Consequently, the German troops, while close to Moscow, were not able to take the city; the German army was destined to get bogged down not far from the Russian capital, and then find itself in danger of being strangled in the deadly embrace of newly-mobilized Russian armies.

Hitler wanted to give the offensive against Moscow an

added impetus by personally visiting the Army Group Center headquarters. Again and again he announced his visit, only to cancel it each time—an unfailing habit of his. Finally he arrived by plane. The airstrip was only four kilometers away from headquarters by road. But Hitler refused to travel this short distance in a car provided by the Army Group. Instead, days before his visit, he had sent a long motorcade to the air strip from his headquarters in East Prussia, so that he could be escorted by his own cars from the air field near Borisov to Bock's headquarters and back again. Incredible security measures were taken to prevent an incident.

During the talks at Bock's headquarters Hitler went into one of his frequent fits of rage at his own General Staff, which he accused of chronic vaccillation. This was one of his favorite themes, and even before the Russian campaign he enjoyed characterizing the German General Staff as follows:

"Before I became Chancellor, I believed that the General Staff was somewhat like a butcher's dog, whom you had to hold tight by the collar to prevent its attacking all other people. After I became Chancellor, however, I realized that the General Staff is anything but a ferocious dog. This General Staff, in fact, has constantly impeded every action I deemed necessary. It objected to rearmament; to the occupation of the Rhineland; to the march into Austria; the occupation of Czechoslovakia, and, finally, even the campaign against Poland. The General Staff warned me against an offensive in France, and counseled against war with Russia. It is I who at all times had to goad on this 'ferocious dog'."

During his visit in Borisov, Hitler told Tresckow his plans with regard to Moscow. No German soldier, he said, was to set foot within the city. Instead, it was to be surrounded in a wide circle, and no inhabitant, whether soldier or civilian—man, woman, or child—was to be allowed to leave. Any attempt to do so was to be repulsed by force of arms. Hitler had ordered arrangements made so that, with the help of gigantic installations, Moscow and the surrounding areas could be flooded and completely submerged in water. A vast lake would appear where Moscow had been, and the metropolis of the Russian people would forever be concealed from the eyes of the civilized world.

I vividly remember an incident which happened when the defeat of Moscow was imminent. Brauchitsch went to visit Bock at the headquarters of the Army Group Center. It was bitterly cold, and the ground was icy. Count Hardenberg and I were the accompanying officers. As we were getting out of the car, Brauchitsch slipped and fell on the ice. Bock, attempting to help him up, slipped and also fell, while both Hardenberg and I managed to stay on our feet. The incident was like an omen. Only a few days later, both field marshals lost their posts of command, for when, in November, 1941, as had been expected, the German defeat in the East took place, Hitler blamed Brauchitsch, and promptly dismissed him. Bock had the foresight to ask for his transfer to the "leadership reserve" for reasons of poor health. Against all expectations, Halder remained as Chief of Staff.

Just before all this happened, Bock sent one of his generals to Hitler with instructions to inform the "Fuehrer" that practically all the generals were against continuing the war during the winter, especially the simultaneous push against Moscow and the Crimea. Before the general had even returned to Bock's headquarters, Bock got a call from Halder, who asked angrily why that particular general had been sent to Hitler. Instead of trying to dissuade the dictator from further winter offensives, he had done just the opposite. When the general returned, Bock asked him to explain his actions. The general answered that he had gone to Hitler resolved to try and talk him out of the winter war, but that Hitler's personality had so impressed him that he had ended up agreeing with everything Hitler had said!

Bock's successor as Commander-in-Chief of the Army Group Center was Field Marshal Guenther von Kluge. Immediately after taking over the command, Kluge began to fight both the Russians and Hitler. The latter kept himself informed about the military situation by demanding long and detailed daily telephone reports from Kluge. To our surprise, Kluge quickly managed to get the upper hand. He talked rapidly and volubly on the phone, introducing a wealth of detail. This volubility made Hitler uncertain, especially because he could not match Kluge's knowledge of military terminology. Whenever Hitler, citing his own personal experience from World War I, criticized the alleged unsatisfactory performance of the German troops, Kluge was quick to counter, pointing to the special circumstances of war in Russia. Once, when Hitler denounced the retreat of a German infantry division and demanded that they recover the lost terrain, Kluge defended the division. Rejecting Hitler's accusations, he managed to get Hitler not only to retract his order, but even to apologize. During those days of the battle for Moscow, one could clearly feel that Hitler was beginning to have some doubts about his invincibility.

Then all of a sudden the situation changed. On New

Year's Eve of 1941, Kluge requested Hitler's permission to carry out far-reaching plans of retreat. Hitler refused, maintaining that for political reasons the lines must be held without consideration for military necessities. At that moment Kluge said nothing, and by his silence acknowledged the priority of political over military considerations. The die had been cast, and from then on Hitler's will rather than the insight of the field marshals became dominant in the East.

Kluge's defeat was compounded by an incident involving Colonel General Hoepner. Hoepner, at that time Commander-in-Chief of the Third Tank Army, pulled back his front lines, obeying a generally acknowledged military necessity, but going against Hitler's express orders. Hitler ordered Hoepner expelled from the Armed Forces and charged Kluge with carrying out the order. We of the resistance used that opportunity to impress upon Kluge that Hoepner's expulsion from the Armed Forces was illegal, for the Military Code of Law did not allow any such act. Cases of disobedience had to be investigated according to an orderly procedure. We made it clear to Kluge that the decisive moment had arrived. If the army were to tolerate such an illegal measure, the prestige and political power of the officer corps would be ruined once and for all. If, on the other hand, Kluge were to refuse to execute the order, the army would win a decisive victory over Hitler and the Party.

Kluge at first seemed to understand this. He did nothing about expelling Hoepner; instead, he telephoned Hitler a few hours later, and told him that he had misgivings about the order. Hitler was furious and told Kluge that although he greatly honored his military leaders, he expected unconditional obedience from them. He brushed aside the legal aspect of the question with the remark that he was the supreme judge and legislator of the German people. Kluge did not argue that point, but protested that expulsion would mean untold misery to Hoepner and his family. Hitler shrugged that off by saying that he would financially compensate Hoepner's family. When Kluge insisted that he was seriously considering not carrying out the order and instead resigning from his command, Hitler retorted sharply that nothing could make him change his mind, and that he would transfer the command of the Army Group Center to someone else if it became necessary. The very next day, Kluge asked to see Hoepner at his headquarters, and informed him of Hitler's expulsion order. No witnesses were present at their two-hour-long meeting.

Shortly after the Hoepner affair, a sensational Reichstag decision gave Hitler the power to institute retroactive measures against anyone.

Kluge could not prevent the battle of Moscow from ending in defeat. This defeat, however, was more than just another lost battle. With it went the myth of the invincibility of the German soldier. It was the beginning of the end. The German army never completely recovered from that defeat. On the other hand, a new attitude became apparent among the troops. In the thunder of the battle, the German soldier had found his God. After losing everything he had, and with nothing but violent death before his eyes, he sought and found solace in religion. Soldiers partook in communion in unprecedented numbers during those days.

In 1942, the German armies in Russia could still point

to several great military successes. By the end of that year, however, the situation was changing, not just in the East, but on all fronts. The landing of the Americans and British in Northwest Africa was a forewarning of future invasions. The German military leadership had considered the landing impossible, on the grounds that the Americans and British did not have the experience for such an operation. After the landing had been successfully carried out, it became clear that the war in Africa was lost for Hitler. The outlook in the Mediterranean was also gloomy, for the collapse of Italy loomed on the horizon. The battle for Western Europe, seemingly ended in 1940, was beginning again.

One of the reasons for the change of fortunes in Africa was British General Montgomery's order for total radio silence. The American liaison officer in the British camp had made regular and detailed reports to his superior officer. Even though these reports were made in code, that code—like all others except the one used by the Vatican—was cracked by the Germans. Because the American reports were very accurate, and gave details about the position and equipment of each British battalion, the Germans found out all they needed to know.

At the end of each of these reports, the American liaison officer added a few critical and frequently quite biting remarks of his own. I remember for instance that he once criticized the lack of cooperation between British air and ground forces. He also had some disapproving comments on the British officers' habit of spending the weekend in Cairo and leaving the training of the troops to non-commissioned officers.

At the beginning of 1943, two of Hitler's mistakes began

taking their toll. The first one was underestimating Russia's strength, and the other was the attempt to force through two gigantic operations at the same time: the occupation of Stalingrad and the conquest of the Caucasus. Hitler shot at two hares simultaneously and got neither one. The strategic law that diminishing military strength follows as a result of advancing attack was once again mercilessly demonstrated. For the first time in the war an entire German army was surrounded and destroyed.

Against the advice of his generals, Hitler believed that by ordering resistance to the last man, he could induce the trapped army in Stalingrad to stand its ground until it could be relieved by fresh troops. Thousands of young men believed in Hitler's promise to liberate them, but soon the ceaseless Russian attacks and the harshness of the Russian winter showed their faith in Hitler to be an illusion. Vanquished by the icy cold, hunger, and the might of the Russian arms, tens of thousands of German soldiers perished cruelly.

Stalingrad was a loss that could not be repaired, a loss the likes of which German military history had never before seen, a loss that was solely the result of a megalomaniac's amateurish attempt to play the role of a great military leader.

As for the German resistance, the military setbacks in Russia lent an added urgency to our persistent efforts to eliminate Hitler before it was too late to salvage anything from the ruins of the Nazi war.

CHAPTER NINE

Resistance on the

Eastern Front

When I joined Tresckow in 1941, I received from him a thorough briefing on the military situation. He told me that Hitler for the time being had given up his plan to invade England. Instead, he had ordered the High Command of the Army Group Center—then stationed in Posen under the command of Field Marshal Fedor von Bock—to work out a plan for the military conquest of Russia. At first, Tresckow said, he had thought that Hitler's war plans against Russia indicated only the conqueror's insatiable greed. But on second thought he had come to a different conclusion. Hitler evidently had realized that England, through its pact with the United States, had acquired a "hinterland" with so great a reservoir of resources, both human and material, that the German war machine was bound to run dry much sooner than that of the Allies. To counterbalance this Allied advantage, Hitler wanted to conquer Russia and thus acquire control over a country whose manpower as well as its industrial and agricultural resources would make him economically independent.

Tresckow did not believe that the plan to subjugate Russia would be successful. Not only, he said, did historical precedents argue against such a success, but also there were simply not enough German troops available to get even the European part of Russia under control. Tresckow's one fear was that—contrary to all expectations—the Russians would fight as poorly as the French had in 1940. If they should, any attempt to overthrow Hitler would become infinitely more difficult. Tresckow considered it most important to exploit the first German defeat in Russia for our purposes. Such a defeat could be expected in the course of the Russian campaign, and might offer the psychologically opportune moment to induce the army to act against Hitler. Tresckow did not, however, harbor any illusions about the difficulty of such a strategy; he realized that it probably would be a protracted affair and plagued by discouraging setbacks.

Halder's plans ran along similar lines at that time. He wanted to use the imminent crisis in the East to move against Hitler in the spring of 1941. But this plan was frustrated, as had been earlier ones, by Brauchitsch's lethargy and indecision. Halder was under such tension in those days that, with tears in his eyes, he told Tresckow he saw no chance for a decision which would help rid Germany of Hitler, since the conditions existing in the Army High Command were not favorable.

One basic requirement for action against the Nazis was to have the right people in the right places. Tresckow, therefore, made every effort to place into key positions within his sphere of authority officers who were thoroughly honorable, had the correct political attitude, and were sufficiently resolute.

At the beginning of the Russian campaign, Field Marshal Fedor von Bock was the Commander-in-Chief of the Army Group Center. Although no military genius, he had great operational talents. Politically Bock was non-Nazi, for National Socialism was not his cup of tea. But deep in his heart Bock was determined—as was Field Marshal von Runstedt—never to lift a hand against Hitler. Prominent features of Bock's personality were vanity and egotism, which did not leave much room for anything else.

To make sure that no stone was left unturned in the effort to draw Bock over to our side, we supplied him with two aides who belonged to our group. One of these was Count Carl Hans von Hardenberg, the other, Count Heinrich von Lehndorff. It most certainly was not the fault of those two if the attempt to convert Bock to our cause failed completely.

After initial successes, the defeat of the German armies before Moscow daily became more and more certain. We decided that the imminent defeat had to be exploited for our political aims. Judging the time to be ripe for a frank talk with Bock, Tresckow, in a lengthy discourse with the Marshal, appraised the grave military situation, and claimed Hitler to be responsible. But before Tresckow could finish, Bock interrupted him. Trembling with rage, he sprang to his feet and stormed from the room shouting, "I shall not tolerate any attack upon the Fuehrer. I shall stand before the Fuehrer and defend him against anyone who dares attack him." After that outburst we wrote off our efforts to win over Bock as a total failure.

While the Army Group Center was halted at Smolensk, west of Moscow, our attention was drawn to our hinterland. SS terrorism in that part of occupied Russia had been cut down to a minimum. Credit for this achievement was not due so much to our efforts as to those of the SS-Gruppenfuehrer Arthur Nebe, about whom there will be more in a later chapter. Nebe was, so to speak, a "sheep in wolf's clothing," a determined anti-Nazi in the uniform of an SS officer. With Nebe's help, it was possible for us to save many Russian lives—a fact which soon became known and was gratefully acknowledged by the Russian people of that area.

Tresckow had already decided to ignore Hitler's order to murder any Russian commissars who were taken prisoner; he also made it a point to treat other Russian prisoners decently. I still remember the day the first Russian general was taken prisoner by our Army Group. The poor man, who evidently thought his last hour had come, was visibly bewildered to find that he was accorded every courtesy, even to receiving a German general's ration of food, liquor, and cigarettes.

When Stalin's elder son was taken prisoner, the Gestapo immediately wanted to get their hands on him. Tresckow thwarted their efforts, however, and only allowed them to interrogate the prisoner—in our presence. Young Stalin conducted himself well and with dignity, and the Gestapo came out second-best in that encounter. Unfortunately we could not hold on to our prisoners forever. Stalin's son was eventually taken to a concentration camp, where he was shot by the SS at the end of the war.

During the first year of the Russian campaign, the influence of the army in the East increased considerably. It

137

was so far from its home base that it became an independent power. If ever during the war the army had possessed the strength necessary to move decisively against Hitler, it was during the period from 1941 to 1942. Whatever the difficulties of a coup d'état had been before—and they were far more formidable than foreign critics of the German resistance can appreciate—in 1941 the army *did* have the power. Blame for the failure to overthrow Hitler at that time rests squarely on the weak and vacillating army leadership. There can be no doubt that, had resolute and farsighted men occupied the top military posts in 1941, the end of both the war and the Third Reich would have come no later than the summer of 1942.

The way things were, however, all we could do was work and hope. To understand the situation, one must keep in mind that our everyday military duties had to be taken care of before we could even think of tackling our political tasks. Many people seem to have rather foggy and erroneous notions of what was involved in taking on the dual role of officer and active resistance member. Our military duties had to be carried out meticulously because they supplied indispensable cover for our clandestine activities. However, that was not all; for patriotic officers such as Tresckow, it was a matter of greatest concern to try to save as many German soldiers' lives as possible from a situation whose dangers we had realized from the beginning.

Resistance work was an addition to, not a substitute for, our military chores. Only by appreciating this can the outsider get some idea of the work load as well as the nervous strain which our double life imposed upon us. This was especially true because, in addition to the purely political side of our work, we took advantage of every opportunity to thwart and check the SS and their reign of terror.

One incident I recall was not without its humorous side, even though it started out grimly enough. One day we were informed that the local SS commandant had arrested a number of Russians from a nearby kolkhoz, or collective farm, and that he was planning to have them all shot. Nebe, our confederate in the SS, was not with us at the time, but when we contacted him he gave us permission to do whatever we thought best. Tresckow thereupon asked me to go and take the Russians away from the SS. I picked out some of our men, and we all drove to the SS quarters.

My request to the SS commandant was simple and to the point: let us have the Russians—without delay and alive. He refused. I told him that he had just a few minutes to reconsider before I started shooting. That proved a persuasive argument; in less than the allotted time the Russians were turned over to us safe and sound.

We took them back to their kolkhoz. That, for us, was the end of the episode. It was not, however, for the Russians. The expressions of gratitude, especially from their families, proved rather embarrassing, for they insisted on doing something for us. Finally, just to get rid of them, one of us suggested that it would be a nice change of diet if we could get a few crayfish, which we knew abounded in the canals nearby.

We did not realize what we were letting ourselves in for. The Russians, with typically Slavic expansiveness, were not satisfied with catching just a few of the crustaceans. They went fishing throughout the entire night—crayfish are best caught at night—with all the relatives they could muster. The results were stunning. Crayfish we had asked for, and crayfish we got—piles and piles, mountains of them. We ate crayfish morning, noon, and night, until we felt that we never wanted to see another crayfish as long as we lived. It was an unexpected end to what had begun as a matter of life and death.

It is perhaps well to state at this point that, although no non-commissioned officers or enlisted men were actively involved in our plot against Hitler, some, as in the instance described above, were witnesses of, or even parties to, our fight against the SS. This was not as risky as it sounds, for whatever the German soldier's faults may be, informing is not one of them. In addition, the army disliked the SS intensely.

As time went on, the non-commissioned officers of the Army Group Center headquarters, who formed the so-called *Unterstab* (Lower Staff) could not fail to notice certain of our activities. They all kept their mouths shut, even after the abortive coup of 1944. At that time, the ranking non-commissioned officer called the others together, told them that they knew the arrested officers were fine, decent men, and that the answer to any questions should be they had never seen or heard anything. Interrogating Gestapo officials were up against a blank wall when one non-commissioned officer after the other insisted that they had never noticed anything untoward. The silence of those soldiers meant the difference between life and death to some of the officers involved.

Aside from my military duties, purely political tasks took up much of my time during the years from 1941 to 1943. By frequent air trips from Russia to Berlin I kept up the contact between the resistance circles at the front and those in the Home Army. I briefed Oster on the psychological situation at the front, and on the conclusions we drew from our observations. Oster, in turn, kept me informed about the goings on at home, as well as about the political situation in Europe and the world. In this way, we both managed to keep a finger on each other's political pulse.

At irregular intervals, I also had conversations with Kurt Herbert Damgren, a Swedish diplomat living in Berlin at the time. His impressions were of great importance to us. Just to make sure that I was getting as complete a briefing as possible, I paid frequent visits to Baron Ernst von Weizsaecker, then State Secretary of the Foreign Office, and received from him the true facts about foreign affairs in exchange for a frank description of the current military situation. Through Weizsaecker, I found out that Ribbentrop, in his reports to the German missions abroad, was describing the military situation in irresponsibly rosy terms. The world situation was also quite different from the picture painted by Ribbentrop in his official reports to the army.

Another one of my contacts with a diplomat which dated from the early 'forties was that with former Ambassador Ulrich von Hassell. Hassell had been dismissed from the Foreign Service in 1937 after a clash with Ribbentrop. During the war, he kept in touch with many generals belonging to the resistance, among them Olbricht, Thomas, Stuelpnagel, and Witzleben. Hassell's hopes centered on action by the army against Hitler, after which he saw the possibility of truce, and later, peace negotiations.

While bitter battles raged in Russia, all was quiet in the West, where Field Marshal von Witzleben was Com-

ERWIN VON WITZLEBEN

1 8 8 1 — 1 9 4 4

The epitome of Prussian officers' traditions of honor and justice, Field Marshal Witzleben also was a kindly man who was horrified by the cruelty and baseness of the Nazi regime. Among the top military leadership, he was one of the earliest advocates of a coup d'état. Witzleben was hanged in August, 1944.

mander-in-Chief. I heard from Oster that Witzleben was planning a coup against Hitler from France. As the plan took on concrete form, the most important consideration became the way in which the army in the East, engaged in fighting the Russians, would react to a coup. I attended several discussions on that matter, but unfortunately we could not report much that was encouraging about the attitude of Bock, our Commander-in-Chief. All Tresckow could say was that he hoped to be able, once Witzleben had acted, to induce Bock to go along.

Witzleben sent one of his staff officers, Alexander von Voss, to General Halder in the Army Headquarters. Halder, in answer to a question about the situation in the East, pointed to a map of Russia and countered with the question: "Do you really think that with our limited forces we will ever be able to subjugate this continent?" When Voss came closer and closer to the key question of support for the planned coup, Halder, without letting himself be drawn into an actual discussion of the matter, indicated that he would be agreeable to anything Witzleben was planning to do. As for himself, however, he could offer no help because he was quite isolated and knew no one, at least not in an important position, within his sphere of influence who would voluntarily support a coup.

Before attempting to carry out his planned insurrection, Witzleben decided to go to the hospital for an operation. While still in the hospital, he was relieved of his command by Hitler's order, and was forced into retirement.

Another hope had gone up in smoke! General Thomas had supported Witzleben's plans for the coup d'état, as he had so many others. In the fall of 1941, he had visited two Army Groups at the Eastern front and had explained to the two chiefs of staff, generals von Sodenstern and von Greifenberg, that an early end to the war was an absolute necessity. Both generals were not without sympathy for Thomas' line of reasoning, but they had no influence on their respective commanders-in-chief.

Thomas then tried one more avenue of attack. Together with Goerdeler, he worked out a memorandum on the German economic situation in which the early end of the war was declared essential. This memorandum was signed by leading men of industry, commerce, and finance, and was then sent to Halder. Typical of what we had to contend with was the refusal, at the very last moment, by the so-called "great men" of industry to sign the memorandum because they considered it too dangerous.

When, in the winter of 1941, the command of the Army Group Center was transfered from Bock to Kluge, a turning point arrived in Tresckow's political activities. Kluge was in many ways sympathetic to our viewpoints. Up to that time he had been merely a non-Nazi, like Bock. Although he did not have the operational talents of the latter, and was not without vanity, he at least had a certain capacity for logical reasoning.

The fact that he had not been able to win over Bock failed to discourage Tresckow. Now his main task was to draw Kluge into our camp. In the years that followed Tresckow fought a persistent battle to achieve his aim of winning Kluge's cooperation for our plans, and only those who followed closely the intense and skillful way in which Tresckow conducted this campaign can appreciate the difficulties and obstacles he had to overcome. Each time Tresckow believed that he had finally gotten Kluge where he wanted him, he had to realize the very next day the

145

Commander-in-Chief had again started to waver. But Tresckow was untiring in his efforts, and in the long run Kluge succumbed to his influence—but to *his* influence alone. In jest, I used to call Tresckow the watchmaker who wound Kluge every morning and made him run all day. Only Tresckow was capable of winding the watch when it had stopped—and unfortunately it stopped quite often. Nobody can say today what would have happened if Tresckow had been at Kluge's side during the decisive hours on July 20, 1944. Very probably Tresckow could have forced Kluge onto the right road and kept him there.

By sheer accident, we got hold of a very delicate instrument through which we could—and did—apply pressure on Kluge. Even Hitler had not changed the traditionally low pay of German officers. However, in order to bind the officer corps more closely to him, Hitler made a practice of paying officers, from the army commander upward, sums of money from his own funds. These sums were not recorded in the army budget, and were tax free. Although this method of payment was an insult according to the honor code of the German officer, many succumbed because of the fear of losing their positions and the lure of the money. In this way Hitler held his higher officers on very effective golden leashes. However, not all the top generals accepted those payments. Witzleben, for example, refused them.

One day Kluge received a letter from which fluttered a check for 250,000 marks. On the check, in Hitler's handwriting, were the words: "For your birthday, my dear Field Marshal. 125,000 you may use to build on your estate—Reichminister Speer has orders." Kluge accepted the check, and also took advantage of the permission to make improvements on his estate, permission which other-wise was almost impossible to get during the war. We knew about this incident, and did not hesitate to tell Kluge that he could justify acceptance of that check before the judgment of history only if he could claim that he had done so to prevent his being dismissed from his post—a post which was essential to keep in order that he could do everything in his power to promote the planned coup d'état.

In the years 1942 and 1943, during which Kluge was Commander-in-Chief of the Army Group Center, I continued to work at political tasks. Through Oster, I became acquainted with his closest collaborators, Reichs Supreme Court Justice Hans von Dohnanyi, Baron Guttenberg, and Justus Delbrueck. Since 1933 I had known Guttenberg to be a resolute fighter against Hitler, and was happy to find him again in such an important position. He was in the same office with Delbrueck, the son of the great German historian. Delbrueck was rather slow in tackling problems and expressing his thoughts, but this slowness also had its advantages: His conclusions were usually correct. His cooperation with Guttenberg was smooth and bore good fruit.

Dohnanyi towered above both Delbrueck and Gutten-berg as far as political activity was concerned. A brilliant man, he exercised great influence over Canaris and Oster. His incisive intellect and indisputable logic made it possible for him to follow through to the last detail of all plans and ideas. Personal contact with him was at times made somewhat difficult by a certain coldness of attitude. In addition, his past career as public prosecutor had invested him with a manner which was not always condu-

147

cive to improving relations between him and his partners. However, his passionate anti-Nazi feelings made it possible for him to induce his superiors as well as his subordinates to work for the resistance. His influence on Oster and Canaris was so great that many things for which they accepted responsibility really originated with Dohnanyi.

During the same period, I made the acquaintance of Goerdeler and, through him, General Beck. Both these men, who represented the nerve center of the opposition, were to make an indelible impression upon me.

CHAPTER TEN

The Leaders

of the Resistance

As the organization of the German resistance crystallized, two men emerged as the leaders. One was the former chief of the German General Staff, General Ludwig Beck, and the other the one-time Lord Mayor of Leipzig, Carl Goerdeler. In characterizing the respective roles of these two men within the framework of the opposition, one could very well call Beck the head and Goerdeler the heart of the organization. Ever since July, 1942, I had been in almost constant communication with both of them and received lasting impressions which the passage of time has not been able to dull.

Beck, son of an industrial engineer from the Rhineland, was a man of wide-ranging cultural interests, a somewhat introverted intellectual whose main characteristic was that he thoroughly studied any matter before attempting to pass judgment on it. The fact that he was a General Staff officer was not immediately apparent; he gave the impression rather of being a profound philosopher. Every word he uttered, every gesture he made, bore proof of his inner balance and serenity. He also had the gift of great precision and clarity of expression. In addition, he radiated personal integrity and uprightness and commanded the attention of all who met him. Any show of disrespect was out of the question in his presence.

However varied and diverse were the backgrounds of the individual members of the resistance, Beck's position as the head of our organization was acknowledged by all and was never in doubt. Whenever controversies or arguments arose—and there were many, both personal and otherwise—Beck was called upon to judge each question. He handled this in a way which made his decisions acceptable even to those who lost out, for being a true gentleman, he coupled kindness with unquestioned authority.

On the other hand, the general staff officer was at all times very much alive in Beck. In that respect, he was a tragic figure. Fate had not only denied him the chance of exercising his own operational talents, but had also condemned him to watch helplessly from the sidelines while everything he had taught the German army was wasted in an insane war started against all reason by a military amateur suffering from delusions of invincibility. When, in the summer of 1942, I visited Beck and mentioned, in the course of conversation, that in Tresckow's opinion the war was lost because of the situation in Russia, his reaction was typical. "Whom are you telling this?" he said. "This war was lost before the first shot was fired." He then recounted the military diversions which had been made by Hitler. These included the occupation of Norway, the campaign in the Balkans, the war in North Africa —all of which, according to Beck, had to lead eventually to a German defeat. It was truly an experience to listen to the man while he slowly, weighing every word, unfolded the future of the war, so that his listener could see it all in his mind. When I look back today, I can say only that every one of his prophesies came true. He not only predicted the catastrophe in Russia, but also prophesied the course of the German defeat in the Western campaign of 1944–1945. The Allies, he said, would first land in Sicily, then in Italy, and one day the British would appear in Greece. Finally, ignoring Spain, the Allies would launch a colossal invasion on the northwestern coast of France. This invasion, Beck maintained, would be successful because of the combined use of Allied navy, air force, and airborne units.

What made these predictions remarkable was the fact that they were made in 1942, fully two years before the Allied invasion actually took place. Listening to Beck expound his theories, one received the impression that he was in the presence of a great military leader. A conversation with Beck was especially rewarding because one felt free to voice differing opinions. Such differences often appeared in the course of an exchange, and Beck would then give his entire attention to arguments which were contrary to his opinions. Quite frequently he picked these arguments apart, and in the end persuaded his opponent to his own point of view. And sometimes—and herein lay his greatness—he declared himself convinced by the other's arguments.

The outstanding qualities of Ludwig Beck's personality are so evident that few, if any, historians of the Hitler era dare deny his nobility of character, his personal and professional integrity, honor, and highmindedness. All the same, there is much misunderstanding of his true motives

151

LUDWIG BECK

1 8 8 0 — 1 9 4 4

A cultured but resolute introvert, Colonel-General Beck, the one-time German Chief of Staff became the military leader of the resistance because of his principles of justice and fairness, and his deeply-felt sense of historical responsibility. He committed suicide on the evening of July 20, 1944.

and convictions. William Shirer, for instance, while admitting his many superior qualities, insists that Beck was for years "pro-Nazi." Wheeler-Bennett calls him a "military opportunist." Much is made of the fact, by both Shirer and Wheeler-Bennett, that Beck appeared as a witness for the defense in the 1930 trial of three lieutenants from the regiment of which he was the commander. The three, Ludin, Scheringer, and Wendt, were accused of spreading Nazi propaganda in the Reichswehr, the German Army of that time. They were indicted on charges of high treason before the Supreme Court at Leipzig. Wheeler-Bennett sees Beck's testimony for his three subaltern officers as a sign of "cynical casuistry" (p. 217, *The Nemesis of Power*) implying that he was infected by Nazi doctrines. There is no basis for such a charge. Beck's testimony was no more and no less than the concern of a senior officer for his subordinates. It is difficult to imagine any army in which a commanding officer would not have enough feeling of responsibility to appear as a character witness for his young officers in a similar situation.

The trial aroused great public interest in Germany because Hitler also appeared as a witness. The three young men were defended by two lawyers, Hans Funk and Dr. Alfons Sack. Hans Funk later became a high Nazi official, and Governor General of Poland during the war. He was hanged, after having been found guilty of war crime charges by the International Military Tribunal at Nuremberg in 1946. Alfons Sack, a minor Nazi fellow-traveller, died in an air raid in Berlin in 1945. This is worth mentioning because both Wheeler-Bennett and Shirer confuse Dr. Alfons Sack with Dr. Carl Sack. Shirer, for instance, states that the three officers were defended by "two rising

Nazi lawyers, Hans Funk and Dr. Carl Sack." The latter was never a Nazi lawyer, took no part in the trial, and had nothing in common with Alfons Sack except his last name and the fact that he was a jurist. Carl Sack, who became the Judge-Advocate General of the German Armed Forces, was a resolute opponent of Hitler, an active member of the German resistance, and was hanged by the SS in the aftermath of the abortive plot against Hitler in 1944.

As far as Beck's early attitude toward the Hitler regime is concerned, it is true that he, although from the start opposed to the manners and methods of the Nazis, believed during the first few years after 1933 that Hitler's Chancellorship would work out well for Germany. His main reason for this opinion was that he considered German military equality necessary for a healthy development of domestic politics as well as for better relationships with other European nations. It must be stated at this point that Beck was strongly opposed to aggressive war—not for reasons of "military opportunism," but because of deep-seated convictions. The German army which he envisioned was to be an instrument of defense—but so strong and capable an instrument that any attack on Germany would involve great risks, and therefore make a European war less, not more, likely.

Beck's chief error was that, in the beginning, he saw Hitler more as the victim, rather than the instigator, of the excesses and illegal acts committed by the Party organization. Up until 1938, he believed that it would be possible to reform the regime by getting rid of the Party rule and the "Cheka" methods of the Gestapo and reinstituting law and justice in the country while retaining Hitler as chief of state.

155

In 1938, Beck's conversion into an active opponent of Hitler began when it became apparent to him that Hitler was by no means the victim but rather the main perpetrator of Party tyranny, and besides was planning a war of aggression against Germany's neighbors. First, as we have already seen, Beck tried to use his military knowledge to avert a war and at the same time convince his fellow generals that Hitler must be checked. In a number of detailed memoranda during the early months of 1938, he repeatedly warned against any aggressive war action. The fact that he used exclusively military arguments, all ending with the statement that Germany would ultimately lose a war of aggression, has led some non-German historians to charge that Beck was not concerned about the immorality of such a war but only about its chances of success or failure. This charge, however, is not valid. As a professional soldier, Beck could hardly be expected to use philosophical, scientific, economic, or other non-military arguments in his efforts to convince the other military leaders. His memoranda of that time clearly show that military arguments were the means by which he tried to avert a war which he considered wrong from a moral, political, and military point of view. In a memorandum prepared for the Commander-in-Chief of the Army of July 16, 1938, he warned:

"Ultimate decisions concerning the survival of the Nation are involved. History will burden these leaders with a blood guilt if they do not act as their professional and political conscience dictates. Their obedience as soldiers has its limits at the point where their knowledge, their conscience, and their responsibility forbids execution of an order.

"If their advice and warnings are not heeded in such a situation, they then have not only the right, but indeed the duty to the people and to history, to quit their positions. If all of them act in unision, execution of a war action becomes impossible. They then have saved their country from the worst possible fate—complete ruin.

"It shows lack of greatness and comprehension of his task, if a soldier in high position during times like these sees his duties only in the limited scope of his military tasks, without realizing his ultimate responsibility before the entire people. Unusual times demand unusual actions."

This memorandum shows that Beck was hoping for a démarche by all the top generals which would force Hitler to cancel his plan of aggression. From Beck's notes of July 29 of the same year, we may see that even at that time he was convinced that internal trouble with the Nazi Party would result if the Army moved to block Hitler.

"In regard to the memorandum of July 16 we have to expect internal unrest in any case. It therefore will be necessary to prepare the army not just for a possible war, but also for internal conflict which, however, could be limited to Berlin. Give orders. Bring together Witzleben with Helldorf." (Count Helldorf, Chief of Police in Berlin, had initially been a Nazi. Their excesses, however, had turned him into an active opponent.)

Beck's attempts to get his colleagues to join him in a concerted action against Hitler's war plans failed. Brauchitsch especially lacked the resolve for such a step. And so Beck resigned from his position as Chief of Staff. The seeds for his future role of leader of the resistance had been sown.

Important for any appraisal of Beck's character are his opinions about war in general, and "total" war in particular which he put down in writing after his retirement. Rejecting the theory that any future war must by necessity turn into a total war, he concluded that it would have to be the task of international politicians to restore war to its appropriate position as the ultimate instrument of politics to be used only after all others had failed. While Beck considered the hope of eternal peace unrealistic and rather naïve, he condemned the concept of total war, which, in Kant's words, "would create more bad men than it would eliminate," as disastrous to the future of mankind. Beck believed that the danger of total war could be averted only by the evolvement of what he called "a new ethical idealism."

Beck's unusual qualities, which set him apart from so many of his fellow generals with the same experience, have not been fully appreciated by historians. On both the German and Allied sides there is a tendency to judge military leaders in terms of their years of service and the positions they occupy because of such seniority. But it does not always follow that because someone has experience, he utilizes the knowledge acquired through it. This was never better expressed than by Frederick the Great, who once was asked why an officer who had been in the army for a long time was not being promoted. Frederick answered the question by telling the story of the pack donkey whom Prince Eugene, the famed Austrian military leader, took along on all his campaigns. The donkey witnessed some very important historical battles. "And when the war was over," concluded Frederick the Great, "the donkey was still an ass."

Beck weighed all the long-range effects of Hitler's policies, and judged military events within the framework of a larger concept. In so doing, he is worthy of a place among those military figures whose vision and wisdom allowed them to look beyond immediate and narrow military considerations.

Beck's ultimate sacrifice for his ideals of fairness, justice, and wisdom in national and international dealings was his life, which he gave in the fight against Hitler.

Goerdeler, the civilian head of the resistance, although similar in some ways to Beck, was quite different. When I said earlier that he was the heart of the opposition, I did not exaggerate. It is perhaps difficult for an outsider to realize the disheartening effects of the countless number of disappointments which we experienced during the war, and which at times left us feeling discouraged and depressed. Quite understandably, some of us gave up in despair or turned to other schemes.

Goerdeler, however, never wavered for one moment. He was the engine which drove the resistance movement forward through the depths of disappointment and over mountains of obstacles. He never despaired or doubted. His arguments had the forceful and convincing logic that comes from the heart. History one day will have to give him full and unstinting credit for having followed, without hesitation, doubt, or wavering, the dictates of his great heart. He was quick to grasp the whole of a situation and had a tremendous knowledge of international and inner-political conditions and of all facets of the German economy. In other words, his was a first-class and well-trained political mind. In addition, he shared Beck's virtue of being able to tolerate opposition. Goerdeler was capable of thoroughly discussing a matter and of changing his opinion if convinced of the validity of an opposing argu-

159

ment. For the sake of completeness, this sketch of Goerdeler's character must not overlook a trait which at times caused him to be overoptimistic: his fertile imagination. He occasionally considered matters finished when, in fact, they were only in the initial stages of development.

Before the First World War, Goerdeler had been an administration official. After the war, he again took up this work with vigor and industry in his special field of city and communal administration. He was a firm believer in maximum local self-government and a free, competitive economy. In 1930 he was elected Lord Mayor of Leipzig, a position he held until 1936 when he resigned in protest against the Nazis' removal of the Mendelssohn bust from its place in front of the Gewandhaus, Leipzig's famous concert hall.

Alarmed at the trend of Nazi policies, Goerdeler at first tried to convince members of the Hitler government of the folly and danger of their course. He believed so firmly that the human being is basically reasonable that it took him some time to realize that this was not true of the Nazi leaders. When he finally accepted this fact, he became one of the most resolute and active opponents of the Hitler regime.

His rejection of Nazism, once he had become aware of all its odious aspects, was complete, unconditional, and based primarily on moral and ethical grounds. After the Western Powers had handed Hitler his stunning victory at Munich in 1938, Goerdeler wrote a letter to friends in which he stated his opinion of the Nazi regime:

"I could, of course, say that this development (the Munich agreement) enlarges the power and *Lebensraum* of my country. Thus, as a German, I should be quite content. I know, however, that these dictators are nothing but criminals, and that their economic policy will lead to Bolshevism. Hitlerism is poison for the German soul. Hitler is determined to destroy Christianity. Not justice, reason and decency, but brute force will decide the future of the world."

The outbreak of the war, news of the atrocities commited in the occupied territories, and other Nazi outrages combined to increase Goerdeler's righteous indignation. In July 1940, at the height of Hitler's victories in the West, Goerdeler composed a memorandum which was originally meant for the officer corps of the German army. In this memorandum, he painted a desolate picture of a Europe conquered by Hitler:

"There can be no thought, by a system which in Germany lives on financial insanity, economic coercion, political terror, lawlessness and immorality, for a creative and constructive cooperation of free peoples under German leadership."

Goerdeler went on to state that a tyrant can institute only tyranny, that each new success makes him only more brutal and increases his lust for conquest. At the end of the memorandum, Goerdeler quoted the famous Prussian statesman Baron vom und zum Stein, who in 1808 urged King Frederick William III of Prussia to resist the victorious conqueror Napoleon Bonaparte:

"To have confidence in a man of whom it is in truth said that he has Hell in his heart and Chaos in his head is more than a fatal delusion. . . . If indeed we have to expect suffering and misfortune in any case, it is better to make a noble and honorable decision, which in case of failure offers at least some consolation."

161

DR. CARL GOERDELER

1884 — 1945

The civilian head of the resistance was a man of great administrative, political, and economic knowledge. Bolstered by unshakable principles of justice and decency, he devoted his untiring efforts to the fight against Hitler. Goerdeler was hanged in February, 1945.

The difficulties and dangers which beset our meetings with Goerdeler and Beck were legion. But these men never hesitated if they considered the meeting necessary. When I suggested in 1942 that it might be a good idea for Goerdeler to accompany me to Smolensk for talks with Kluge and Tresckow, he immediately agreed to make the trip. Although he could not come with me that time, he did come at the first opportunity. His friends in the OKW, the High Command of the Armed Forces, supplied him with the necessary papers. At the headquarters of the Army Group Center, Goerdeler met with Kluge and Tresckow. Their meeting was a great success. Tresckow from the beginning felt that here was a kindred spirit. The immediate bond of friendship and cooperation between these two men lasted until death separated them two years later.

One of Goerdeler's greatest gifts was his ability to talk to people from all walks of life and in each case find the right words to win them over to our cause. Kluge's case was a good example of Goerdeler's talent. Following up on what Tresckow had prepared, Goerdeler broke the ice with Kluge and convinced him of the necessity of moving against Hitler. Even though Kluge often wavered later on, in his heart he still considered himself our co-conspirator. Goerdeler knew how to appeal to Kluge's sense of honor. Each time Kluge wanted to bolt, one word from Goerdeler was enough to keep him in line.

What a battle Goerdeler fought for the cooperation of the generals! In the first six months of 1943, he wrote a lengthy memorandum and two letters, one to General Olbricht and one to Kluge. After many discussions and long deliberations, we decided not to send the letter to

Kluge because General Olbricht, who knew Kluge well, thought the letter would damage rather than help our chances with the Field Marshal.

At every occasion, Goerdeler reiterated his demands— at times tinged with bitterness—that the generals make up their minds and act. To stress the urgency, he pointed to the fact that Germany's situation was deteriorating from day to day.

As a last, desperate measure, Goerdler offered to talk to Hitler himself. However, he demanded immediate support from the generals. His friends had to use all their powers of persuasion to get Goerdeler to give up this idea.

The battle against the hesitation and vacillation of the generals had to be fought anew every day. They wanted either to get foreign-policy guarantees, or wait for the so-called "psychological moment." Their attitude was summed up best by one of our confederates, Captain Kaiser, who said, "One wants to act when he gets the order, and another wants to give the order when someone else has acted."

Because of the necessity of insuring smooth cooperation between the civilian and military resistance groups, we had to stay in constant contact with Goerdeler. In Berlin, his faithful friends, especially the staunch and upright Hermann Kaiser and Professor Jens Peter Jessen, often managed to arrange meetings. Also prominent among the people who deserve credit for helping us meet with Goerdeler was Colonel Berndt von Kleist, who scorned all personal danger and other difficulties in coming to our aid.

In order to gather without attracting undue attention, the "Wednesday Club" was called into life. We met under cover of night and darkness to keep our meetings secret

165

from the Gestapo. The "Wednesday Club" consisted of sixteen top scientists. Its leading members were the professors Sauerbruch, the famous surgeon, Spranger, Popitz, and Jessen. Beck was admitted to the club as a military scientist, and Ulrich von Hassell as a political scientist.

The acquaintance between Beck and Hassell dated from 1935. At that time, they were not yet determined to overthrow Hitler, for they thought that in the long run Hitler would not prevail against the forces of decency within the German people. By 1938, however, they realized that their earlier viewpoint could be upheld no longer.

Beck and Tresckow already knew each other from the years before the war, when Beck had been Chief of Staff and Tresckow one of his junior staff officers. At that time, they had met only through their military work; now the old bond was renewed on a different basis. And so, headed by Beck and Goerdeler, a group of people banded together, inspired by high ideals and a willingness to give all because all had to be won if all were not to be lost.

CHAPTER ELEVEN

The Shield

of the Resistance

In a totalitarian state no resistance movement can exist without the protection of persons in influential positions—persons who have access to the "lion's den" and who are, to all appearances, part and parcel of the ruling body. An underground movement cannot hope to suceed unless its members are capable of hiding their true feelings behind an impassive mask; the "shield" of the organization must consist of persons even more adept at playing a dual role, and playing it to the hilt. This takes iron nerve, stamina, presence of mind, and courage. It is not a game for the naïve and the timid. There is no room for mistakes.

Outstanding among those upon whom the resistance in Germany relied for protection were three men: Admiral Wilhelm Canaris, Chief of the Abwehr (Military Counter-Intelligence), SS Obergruppenfuehrer Arthur Nebe, officially one of Himmler's collaborators, and Dr. Carl Sack, the Judge Advocate General of the German Army.

The cooperation of Admiral Canaris was of paramount importance. The Abwehr, many of whose officers were anti-Nazi by inclination and tradition, was fertile soil for underground opposition activities. The very nature of the Counter-Intelligence organization, of necessity and legitimately cloaked in secrecy, permitted General Oster, Canaris' top assistant, to use the tremendous and widespread apparatus of the Abwehr to support, protect, and reinvigorate the resistance. In addition to giving Oster free rein to aid the resistance, Canaris did his best to thwart many of Hitler's plans and to save people who had fallen into the clutches of the Gestapo. Canaris' daring ventures included warning General Franco against entering the war on Germany's side. These warnings were doubly audacious because Canaris gave them during trips to Spain made ostensibly for the purpose of persuading Franco to do just the opposite. Franco, who had great respect for the German admiral, heeded his advice. On returning from each such visit to Spain, Canaris would blandly report to Hitler his inability to understand Franco's refusal to join the war, adding that he, Canaris, would have to try his luck again in the near future!

Franco undoubtedly owes the "little admiral" a special vote of thanks for his sound advice, and the Spanish government has acknowledged this by expressing its gratitude to the widow of Canaris. But the Allies also are indebted to the Abwehr chief, as anyone will readily admit when he considers what it would have meant to the Allies to have Gibraltar fall into Hitler's hands.

Whenever Oster and the other conspirators were at their wits' ends in their efforts to save some Nazi victim, they would turn to Canaris as a last resort. One of these cases, in spite of the deadly stakes involved, was not without its comic aspects. Dietrich Bonhoeffer, a young theologian and a member of our group, was informed one day that seven Jews he knew had been arrested by the Gestapo and were about to be shipped off to Auschwitz. He appealed to Oster for help, but in this case even Oster was at a complete loss, and could not think of any way to save the seven men. In desperation, he finally went to his superior and laid the facts before him. Grumbling that Oster always expected him to do the impossible, Canaris sent the younger man from the room. Then he called Himmler, and told the Gestapo chief that he must see him immediately on a matter much too sensitive to be discussed over the phone. Duly impressed, Himmler agreed to see Canaris at once. The SS leader was completely nonplused when the Abwehr chief, without preliminaries, began to complain about the Gestapo and charged that some of their officials were hampering the work of the Counter-Intelligence. "How do you expect me to carry on with the Abwehr, Reichsfuehrer, if your people arrest my agents? I know," Canaris added, cutting off Himmler's bewildered protests, "that it is not your fault, but it is causing me a lot of trouble." As a result of Canaris' complaint, Himmler called the Gestapo officials in question and ordered them to immediately release the seven Jews to the Abwehr.

A few hours after Oster had first informed his boss of the problem, Canaris called him in to tell him that "his" Jews were being delivered to the Abwehr headquarters. "And now," the chief added, "you'd better teach them a code or two, for I have claimed them as my agents."

This was easier said than done. Thoroughly confused and frightened, the Jewish ex-prisoners were in no condi-

WILHELM CANARIS

1 8 8 7 — 1 9 4 5

Head of the German Counter-Intelligence, Admiral Canaris abhorred National Socialism, and allowed his organization to be used for resistance purposes. A humane and kindly man, he repeatedly risked his life to save victims of the Gestapo. He was hanged by the SS in April, 1945.

tion to learn anything. Finally they were sent to Switzerland, and Canaris used Counter-Intelligence funds to reimburse them for part of their confiscated funds. The seven survived their saviors, Canaris, Oster, and Bonhoeffer, all of whom were hanged by the SS after the abortive coup of 1944.

Through the Counter-Intelligence, we received top secret information which enabled us to stay one jump ahead of the Gestapo. Invaluable aid and information were also given to us by the SS Obergruppenfuehrer Arthur Nebe. Nebe, one of the very few men within the SS to share our political and ethical viewpoints, had made the battle against Hitler his very special concern.

Because of the uniform he wore, Nebe was, and still is, a much-maligned and misunderstood figure. It is a cruel injustice to this brave man to refer to him as an "equivocal, shadowy figure" and a "renegade Gestapo official," as does Wheeler-Bennett in his book *The Nemesis of Power* (p. 389). Nebe was much more than that. His was one of the most nerve-racking assignments imaginable. He is dead, and cannot defend himself. Therefore it is up to those who know the facts to set the record straight. I feel especially compelled to do so because it was largely at my insistence that Nebe remained at his post during the latter years of the war. Sickened and weary of conditions he was all too often unable to change, he time and again was on the verge of giving up and retiring for reasons of "poor health." Each time I persuaded him that we desperately needed the pipe line to Gestapo inner circles which he alone could supply. In addition, I pointed out that he was capable of preventing many atrocities which surely would be committed if some other SS officer were to replace him.

My arguments prevailed, and I therefore must accept at least part of the responsibility for the fact that Nebe stayed to the bitter end.

To understand this man and the reasons why he ever became a member of the SS, one must know something of his background. Nebe had been a member of the German Criminal Police long before 1933, and his achievements in the field of crime prevention and detection were outstanding. After 1933 the Criminal Police were automatically taken over by the SS. Although never an enthusiastic Nazi, at first Nebe was not opposed to the regime, and the Nazis, needless to say, were happy to have such an outstanding specialist as one of their own. Very soon, however, Nebe began to change his mind about the Hitler regime—one could say a Saul was converted into a Paul. Long before the war even began, Nebe had entered the ranks of Hitler's opponents. He gave early evidence of his attitude when, in 1938, he joined forces with Dr. Sack and others bent upon uncovering Himmler's plot against General von Fritsch.

Oster, who had worked with Nebe for some time, informed us during the war of the latter's true feelings. And so, behind the mask of a high-ranking SS leader, we found a resolute and determined anti-Nazi. Despite Oster's assurances, however, Nebe's uniform was good reason for us to approach him with considerable caution. Tresckow assigned to me the task of testing Nebe, and making sure that Oster had not been deceived. The result of my investigations justified everything Oster had said about the SS Obergruppenfuehrer, and we soon established an excellent collaboration. Nebe was a past master in the art of hiding his true feelings. While sabotaging, to an almost incredible

173

degree, Hitler's orders for wholesale murder, he gave a most convincing performance as a dedicated SS officer. In the occupied Eastern territories, it therefore became possible, with Nebe's secret help, to save scores of people from certain death. This did not remain a secret to the population, especially in and around Borisov, where Army Group Center headquarters were located for quite some time. The people there knew very well how many lives we had managed to save and were ever eager to express their gratitude.

Nebe often contrived to thwart Himmler's orders for mass slaughter by falsely reporting that they had been carried out, and faking the numbers of those executed. It was a dangerous game that called for a good deal of nimble shifting and clever covering up, but Nebe handled it expertly.

Despite his caution and cleverness, Nebe could not help but be suspected by his own SS of being "soft." After a while, special SS commandos, *Sonderkommandos*, not subordinate to him were sent into the districts under his jurisdiction, where they did their bloody work without his knowledge.

One such case which I vividly remember involved an SS Sonderkommando consisting of Latvians. It must be explained that during the war the ranks of the SS were swelled by large numbers of non-German members, especially in the occupied Eastern territories. Large contingents of Ukranians, Latvians, Hungarians, and others of various nationalities were enlisted by the SS, which thereby was turned into anything but a "purely German" organization.

Information reached us at the Headquarters of the Army

174

Group Center that a special commando unit of Latvian SS had slaughtered five thousand Jews within a period of three days. An investigation revealed that the special unit had arrived in Borisov and had arranged an official "German Police Festival." After a noisy party, which ended at 4 o'clock in the morning, the commando unit surrounded that portion of the city inhabited by Jews. The Jews were roused out of bed and marched to a nearby forest. There the families were torn apart, and several groups were formed according to age and sex. One of these groups was ordered to dig a huge pit. When that had been done, the members of that group had to undress completely, regardless of age or sex. These Jews were ordered to lie down in the pit, whereupon the SS lined up at the edge of the excavation, and emptied their submachine guns into the poor tortured people crowded in the pit. Immediately afterwards, a second group of Jews were forced to cover the bodies with a layer of dirt, even though some in the pit were only wounded and still alive. Then the second and each subsequent group was slaughtered in the same way. Five thousand human beings in all were killed, layer by layer, in that one excavation.

News of this atrocity aroused such a storm of fury and indignation among the officers of the Army Group Center that many of them, with tears of rage in their eyes, demanded that Bock, Commander-in-Chief of the Army Group, intervene and put a stop to these outrages. It was the first time that we succeeded in getting Bock to take at least some action. It was ascertained that the Jews of Borisov had appealed for help to the German commandant of that city with the words: "We will not ask a German general for help in vain." After having been requested to

175

report on the incident, the commandant committed suicide. He considered it irreconcilable with his honor not to have been able to stop the slaughter.

Bock did not dare use force of arms against the guilty persons; instead, he wrote a memorandum to Hitler protesting the brutalities. Because of our protests, such atrocities as the one in Borisov were prevented from occurring at other locations within our district.

Although Nebe was often frustrated in his efforts to check, as much as was humanly possible, the reign of terror in the occupied Eastern regions, one does not dare think of what the toll in lives taken by the SS would have been without Nebe's intervention.

Nebe was also actively involved in our plans to overthrow Hitler. It was my task to keep in constant touch with him to receive the information he was able to get through his contacts with Himmler and other high Gestapo officials, such as Kaltenbrunner. Nebe's reports on what went on during the sessions of the Gestapo leadership gave us invaluable insights and allowed us to avoid certain pitfalls.

In my correspondence with Nebe, a code was used which had been carefully worked out, always with an eye on the possibility that these letters might one day fall into the wrong hands. The code was simple and effective: it employed those Nazi slogans that had become a part of the daily war propaganda. Each of these slogans had a special meaning when used by us. Our letters therefore had the outward appearance not only of innocence, but of remarkable loyalty to the Nazi cause. Any outsider chancing upon my correspondence with Nebe would have been convinced that we were both faithful and enthusiastic followers of Hitler. As an example, one of the favorite slogans of Nazi propaganda after the first setbacks in Russia was: "With complete confidence in the ultimate victory." Whenever I used this sentence at the end of one of my letters to Nebe, he knew that we were still working hard to perfect details for our plan to overthrow Hitler. Ironically, our using the slogan was not hypocrisy, for we meant it quite literally. The one slight difference, of course, was that we had in mind the ultimate victory of the resistance movement.

This trick of using the Nazis' own words for our purposes proved most helpful when I was arrested in the aftermath of the coup of July 20, 1944. The Gestapo had obtained some of my correspondence with Nebe, but they had to admit that there was absolutely nothing in the letters they could hold against me.

The third man in an influential position whose activities were geared to protecting and aiding members of the anti-Hitler conspiracy was the Judge-Advocate General of the German Army, Dr. Carl Sack. He very cleverly employed all juridical means within his power to help us, especially when members of our group within the Army ran into trouble and were arrested. Sack displayed great proficiency in dragging out and sidetracking proceedings against our confederates, and often succeeded in letting these proceedings peter out altogether. Sometimes Sack teamed up with prominent psychiatrists belonging to our group, who testified in court that the defendant in question was temporarily unbalanced and not responsible for his actions. In a few instances it was possible to have the accused man sent to a sanatarium instead of to the gallows or to prison.

177

Sack was instrumental in saving one of our friends, General Rudolf Schmidt, from a dire fate. Schmidt, one of the most talented of the German military leaders, possessed a sense of humor and an invincible optimism. He also had the distinction of having been one of the generals who told Hitler to his face that an aggressive war was not justified.

Schmidt was invaluable to us because he was always able to find a silver lining no matter how bleak the situation. Whenever we went through periods of depression, when everything looked hopeless and we were close to despair, we would go to see Schmidt. He would invariably cheer us up, infect us with his own attitude, and enable us to return to our task with renewed hope and vigor.

One day, however, Schmidt wrote a letter to his wife in which he ignored the cardinal rule of life in a totalitarian state: Always assume that you are being spied upon. The letter was opened and found to contain a scathing indictment of the Nazi leaders, whom Schmidt had lumped together under the term "criminals." Schmidt was immediately relieved of his command and would have faced capital charges if Sack had not intervened. By some deft manipulating, the Judge-Advocate General managed to sidetrack and minimize the issue, so that in the end all Schmidt lost was his rank and uniform.

Much later the Soviets captured Schmidt and accused him of war crimes. He spent ten years in Soviet prisons, including the infamous Lubjanka prison. But the evidence was so overwhelmingly in his favor that even the Soviets found no further reason to hold him, and eventually allowed him to return to Germany. Schmidt's long ordeal seriously impaired his health, and he died only a year after his return from Russia.

Without the protective shield furnished by such men as Canaris, Nebe, and Sack—and many others in less prominent positions—the German opposition would never have survived, or had a chance to develop right under the noses of the Gestapo. Proof of the effectiveness of our precautionary and protective measures was the fact that the Gestapo, as was revealed after the coup of 1944, never had the slightest idea of what had been going on for years before the final attempt on Hitler's life. No account of the German opposition against Hitler would be complete without acknowledgment of the invaluable services of those men who formed the shield of the resistance.

CHAPTER TWELVE

The Staff of the Resistance

Handling the work of a secret resistance organization within a totalitarian state calls for men who are exceptionally reliable, resolute, and discreet. Realizing that it could be only as strong as its weakest member, the German opposition exercised great care in selecting its confederates.

There has been much unfavorable comment on the small size of our group as compared to the German nation as a whole. Such criticism entirely misses an important point, which is that we were not at all eager to enlist the greatest possible number of people. On the contrary, it was to our own interest to limit the number of those involved in the actual plans of the plot. The smaller the circle of the initiated, the less the danger of discovery. From the men who were suited to our purposes by virtue of their character, we had to chose only those whose positions made it possible for them to help with, and contribute to, the work necessary for an eventual overthrow of the Hitler regime. These requirements eliminated all but a relatively small and select group of men.

As a member of the military group around Tresckow, naturally I knew best the people of that particular resistance circle, and the others with whom we had close contact. In this chapter, I should like to describe some of the men who formed the opposition staff under the leadership of Beck and Goerdeler.

Outstanding in this group was Henning von Tresckow, who played an important part in organizing much of the military resistance against Hitler. Although he was one of the best qualified German General Staff officers, Tresckow's mind was by no means exclusively military. In fact, after World War I, he had a successful career as a stockbroker. In 1924, he made a trip around the world and acquired considerable knowledge of the Americas as well as Europe. After his return, he joined the Reichswehr, the post-World War I standing army of Germany, and became a staff officer under Beck.

Tresckow possessed three qualities which are rarely found combined in one person. He was good, he was intelligent, and he was industrious. His noble character, keen mind, and capacity for hard work were admired by all who knew him—superiors, associates, and subordinates alike. One of his outstanding talents was his ability to inspire the people around him with his own highmindedness. He had become Hitler's implacable foe not so much through logic and reason, but rather because of his deep-seated aversion to anything base and mean. There was not an ounce of brutality in Tresckow's make-up. The only

181

HELMUTH STIEFF

1901 — 1944

Horrified and revolted by the atrocities committed by the SS, this gay and elegant young officer became an unconditional and dedicated enemy of Nazism and Hitler, and in 1943 actively joined the plot to remove him. Major-General Stieff was hanged in August, 1944.

time I ever heard him voice the necessity for ruthless action was when we were discussing the fate of the SS in case of a successful coup d'état.

Tresckow particularly disliked overemphasis on uniforms, drill, and all things military. He always encouraged his young officers to interest themselves in as wide a range of subjects as possible. Through his understanding of others, his innate kindness, and his integrity he managed to influence everyone who came in contact with him. By throwing himself heart and soul into the battle against Hitler, Tresckow won a place in the forefront of those who, regardless of the consequences to themselves and their families, dared to lift their hands against the German dictator.

One of the most important tasks of the opposition—the winning over of top military leaders to our side—was tackled by Tresckow with a zeal which was unflagging in spite of many disappointments. Here I must correct the misconception—commonly held outside of Germany—that the German officer's corps was a united, homogeneous body of men. It was no more united than, for instance, the German bishops or university professors. It is therefore a mistake to judge the corps as a monolith rather than the group of individuals it was, with wide variations in character, motivations, and outlook on life.

Because of the paramount importance of the OKW (the High Command of the Armed Forces) Tresckow arranged a visit to Berlin by General Helmuth Stieff, chief of the Organization Department within the Army High Command. Stieff was easily enlisted for the proposed coup d'état, for he was a long-standing and ardent foe of Hitler's. In 1939, when he saw and heard of the atrocities committed by the SS in Poland, he cried out in anguish: "I am ashamed to be a German! This minority has defiled the name of Germany with their murder, looting, and arson. They will be the doom of the entire German nation unless we manage to stop them soon." This conviction was the basis of Stieff's willingness to risk and, if necessary, sacrifice everything he had in order to remove Hitler.

Such books as Wheeler-Bennet's *The Nemesis of Power* and Shirer's *The Rise and Fall of the Third Reich* have distorted Stieff's personality, perhaps because of the nickname given to him by his comrades in the army. Vernacular and slang expressions in any language are easily misunderstood by foreigners. In Stieff's case, the nickname "Giftzwerg"—which translated literally means "Poison Dwarf"—led chroniclers such as Shirer and Wheeler-Bennett to believe that Stieff was a hunchback and a man with a venomous tongue. He was, in fact, nothing of the sort. He was a very short man, but his body was straight and well-proportioned. Far from being venomous, Stieff had a gay and sunny disposition, reserving his hatred exclusively for Hitler and the SS. I always found him pleasant and easy to get along with.

Besides Stieff, Tresckow also managed to win the cooperation of the Generals Erich Fellgiebel, Chief of Communications, Eduard Wagner, the Quartermaster-General, and Fritz Lindemann, Chief of Ordnance.

Two of the most important tasks on the day of the coup d'état were assigned to Fellgiebel. One was the demolition of the communication center in Hitler's Headquarters. In that way, all possibility of contact between Headquarters and the outside world by either telephone, radio, or telegraph was to be eliminated. This isolation of Hitler's

Headquarters unfortunately was not achieved on the fateful July 20, 1944.

Fellgiebel's second task was to keep open, on the day of the coup, all means of communication between the center of the resistance movement, the office of General Olbricht, and all other key offices. In this, he succeeded remarkably well—so well, indeed, that the Nazis nicknamed the abortive coup the "Switchboard Putsch."

Continuing his efforts to enlist military leaders from all branches of the Armed Forces, Tresckow also extended a few feelers to the Air Force and to the Foreign Armies section through its head, Colonel Baron Alexis Roenne. Roenne's aide, Count Friedhelm Matuschka, kept us informed about what was going on in the Western front.

Despite such successes, Tresckow was not satisfied. He was determined to win over at least two of the active Field Marshals at the front for the coup d'état, so as to assure effective collaboration between the Front and the Home armies. During Tresckow's absence in the summer of 1943. it had been impossible to keep Kluge firmly lined up on our side. Once again, as so often before, he started to waver; finally, however, he mustered the resolve to go to Berlin and talk with our confederates. Once Kluge was there, Tresckow quickly re-asserted his influence over him. A meeting of the two men with Beck, Goerdeler, and Olbricht resulted in agreement, so that cooperation between the armies at the Front and at home seemed assured.

In his untiring efforts to broaden the scope of the military resistance, Tresckow also tried to get the cooperation of Field Marshal Erich von Manstein. He had known Manstein earlier, believed him to be a talented officer, and thought that he might be of service in a good cause.

Tresckow's attempts to influence Manstein were supported by those of Colonel Schultze-Buettger, one of our group and Manstein's top staff officer, who did all he could to win over his superior to our cause.

Neither the efforts of Tresckow or Schultze-Buettger were crowned by success. Manstein, declining any political judgment, limited himself to weighing the German military chances against those of the other side. A meeting between him and Kluge, which Tresckow arranged, also was unsuccessful, for the two men did not get along well. The two Field Marshals agreed on only one matter—and that one purely military—that there should be a single Commander-in-Chief for the Eastern Front. Each of them probably considered himself the best candidate for that job.

Tresckow was not the man to give up easily. He told me that he once tried to persuade Manstein that his responsibilities were political as well as military. Although Tresckow's arguments affected Manstein so that he began to tremble, he still refused to support our efforts, claiming that according to his soldier's oath his primary responsibility as a top officer was to keep the Russians away from Germany's borders.

When I told General Beck of Tresckow's repeated attempts to win over Manstein for our cause, Beck said that he did not believe that Tresckow would be successful. The reasons for this he saw less in factual matters such as the military situation than in Manstein's character—or lack of character. Beck also told me that he thought future events would refute Manstein's arguments, for precisely by rejecting the rebellion against Hitler would Manstein contribute to the victory of the Russians. Beck mentioned a

187

letter he had written to Manstein, in which he had pointed out that further military operations had become senseless. Instead, he argued, the first consideration should be Germany's survival. Only with the help of an intact army would it be possible to protect the borders of the country and at the same time keep order internally. The mistake of 1918, Beck warned, should not be repeated. The army should be kept firmly in hand for the vitally important tasks inside Germany. Even this letter, however, did not draw any favorable response from Manstein.

Later, after Count Stauffenberg became an active member of the resistance, he also tried his luck with Manstein. The result of their meeting was as negative as had been all others; Manstein refused to become a party to the planned coup d'état. However, he told Stauffenberg that although he could and would not in any way take part in the efforts to overthrow Hitler, he would refrain from informing the Gestapo of the opposition's plans.

That Beck had been right in his estimate of Manstein's character was proved one day during a conference with Hitler, in the course of which the dictator complained about his generals and said that he expected them to desert him. Manstein took the opportunity to assure Hitler that he, for his part, would always remain loyal to the "Fuehrer."

However, two other generals declared themselves willing to join the plot. One was General Karl Heinrich von Stuelpnagel, Commander-in-Chief in France; the other was General Alexander von Falkenhausen, Commander-in-Chief in Belgium and Northern France. Both men were determined enemies of Hitler.

Similar to Tresckow in his relentless struggle to help

overthrow Hitler was Hans Oster, top officer in the Abwehr under Canaris. He, too, must be given a large share of the credit for organizing the resistance and for his attempts to check Hitler even before the war. Oster was one of the relatively few people who were unalterably opposed to the Nazis from the very beginning and who, at an early date, began to look around for likely allies and to collect material for his undercover war against Hitler. Oster never once wavered in his attitude, even after his arrest in the wake of the abortive July 20 plot. Typical of his personality are his last notes, jotted down in prison for his son:

"We shall remain to the last breath the decent fellows we learned to become at home and in the Army. Come what may! The only thing we fear is God's wrath, if we do not stay clean and decent and do our duty."

Oster was truly a man after God's own heart, of irreproachable character, great lucidity, and iron nerve in the face of danger. All his actions, including his warning to the Netherlands of Hitler's plan of attack in 1940, which has been the subject of much controversy, were dictated by the loftiest motives.

One of the outstanding members of the group around Tresckow was Colonel Berndt von Kleist. Although he had lost a leg in World War I, he rejoined the army in the Second World War. Kleist, the personification of dignity and integrity, was completely incapable of an ignoble act, and it was this, rather than political and military considerations, that turned him into one of Hitler's opponents. Kleist's untiring industry and diligence were invaluable to us, and he had great influence in our circle.

189

Berndt von Kleist also possessed a keen judgment of strategic military affairs, which enabled him to predict events which others often could not foresee. I once asked him for his appraisal of the German chances in the Russian campaign. "The German army," Kleist answered, "will fight against Russia like an elephant against an anthill. The elephant will kill thousands and thousands, probably even millions of ants, but in the end the ants will over-whelm him by sheer numbers, and devour him until nothing but the bare bones are left."

After Kleist, there was General Baron Rudolf von Gers-dorff, every inch the cavalry officer. He was endowed with a keen, lively mind, and quick perception. His elegant appearance and superb poise quickly won friends for him, and his talent to tell a story wittily and well was matched only by Schultze-Buettger. The latter, too, was a distinct personality, a solid and decent character who exercised great influence on his associates. Superior to most officers of his age in his operational talents, Schultze-Buettger had for years been the aide of General Beck while the latter was still the Chief of the German General Staff. No matter how exciting a situation might be, Schultze-Buettger would examine it calmly, strip away all extraneous detail, and go straight to the heart of the matter. In that way, he was able to correctly analyze even the most confusing events.

When Schultze-Buettger left us to become top staff officer to Field Marshal von Manstein, his successor was Alexander von Voss, son-in-law of General von Stuelpnagel. Voss was a very sensitive and high-minded person, who detested anything base or mean. During all the great political and military events, he was in a fever of apprehension until the outcome was known. The abortive coup of July

20 and its terrible aftermath caused him to take his own life.

Over the years, our circle changed and other members were added. One of these was Major Ulrich von Oertzen, whose capacity for hard, systematic work, talent for organization, and above-average intellect managed to bring order out of the greatest confusion.

At his side stood Captain Eggert, whose outstanding traits were his calm competence and logic. His political and religious convictions were unshakable.

Another one of our group, First Lieutenant Hans Albrecht von Boddien, added his great knowledge, understanding of human nature, and unerring instinct for matters that can be handled only by intuition to our pool of talent and ability.

Each of these members of the resistance had his own assignment, from trying to influence important persons whom we wanted to win over to our cause to any one of the myriad of technical details which our plan to overthrow Hitler and take over the government entailed.

At about the time that Schultze-Buettger was appointed first officer in the Army Group commanded by Field Marshal von Manstein, I became acquainted, through Hermann Kaiser, with General Friedrich Olbricht, the chief of the General Army Office of the Commander of the Home Army. Olbricht, a very religious man, was willing to use the great power of his position to depose Hitler. And so, towards the end of 1942, after many months of hard work, the opposition's plans for a coup d'état began to take definite shape. Finally, a meeting between Goerdeler, Olbricht, and Tresckow was arranged, as a result of which Olbricht promised to organize military resistance cells in

Berlin, Vienna, Munich, and Cologne, which would be instrumental in wresting power from the Nazis in those cities as soon as the blow against Hitler had been struck. The most important question was whether Hitler's assassination, which had to precede the coup d'état, could and should be handled by the field or home army. Ways and means of carrying out the assassination also were discussed at the time. It was clear that, after all the preparations in which so many members of the resistance had been involved, the moment for decisive action was now rapidly drawing near.

Other Opposition

Groups

Apart from the resistance group around Beck and Goerdeler, there were certain other opposition circles in Germany. One of these, the Kreisau circle with whom the Goerdeler group had many contacts, gained in influence as time went on.

The Kreisau circle got its name from the Silesian estate of the Berlin attorney Count Helmut von Moltke. His special interest was that field of international law which dealt with private rights. His mother was an Englishwoman who had been born in South Africa.

Moltke became the leader of a group of young people whose ideas were deeply anchored in the traditions of Christianity, and who believed that a Christian-Socialist ideology would become the leading political concept of the future.

One of Moltke's closest friends was Count Peter Yorck von Wartenburg, a gentleman farmer and administrative official. Since 1940, the two men had gathered around themselves a number of young people, with the idea of making preparations for the eventual military collapse of the Third Reich. Their work was aimed at supplying the spiritual and political equipment for those men who would one day have to take over the leadership of Germany, and they saw the Christian message as the foundation of a natural order. Their religious convictions prevented most of the Kreisau circle from active participation in the plans for Hitler's violent removal and the subsequent coup d'état. They saw their task not as ridding the world of Hitler and the Nazis, but rather as work that had to be done after the event.

Prominent in the Kreisau circle were men like Eugen Gerstenmaier, Erwin Reichwein, Theodor Steltzer, Adam von Trott zu Solz, and Fritz Count von der Schulenburg—theologians, teachers, jurists, diplomats, and administrators.

Moltke's wife played an important part in making possible meetings of the Kreisau circle and was in every way one of her husband's closest collaborators. Later on, when Moltke was in the hands of the Gestapo in the Tegel prison of Berlin awaiting his execution, his wife managed to hide in the home of the prison chaplain, Harald Poelchau, who was also a member of the resistance. With the help of Poelchau, who acted as a courier, she exchanged letters with her husband up to the very day of his death.

Quite apart from both the Goerdeler-Beck and Kreisau circles, other groups, mostly communistic, worked toward the downfall of the Third Reich. To illustrate the fundamental difference between these latter groups and those associated with Goerdeler, Beck, and Moltke, it will suffice to describe the history of one of them, a Communist group listed in the files of the Gestapo under the name "Red Chapel." The name has caused some confusion among non-Germans. In various books, such as Shirer's *The Rise and Fall of the Third Reich,* "Rote Kapelle" has been translated as "Red Orchestra." Although "Kapelle" can indeed mean orchestra—or rather "band"—it also means "chapel," and was used in the latter sense as the nickname of the Communist opposition group. The name actually stems from another Gestapo file, this one on Catholic dealings with the Vatican, which went under the code name of "Black Chapel." When the Gestapo later on came across evidence of a Communist conspiracy, they promptly named it "Red Chapel."

The "Red Chapel" was an organization that operated not only in Germany but also in France, Belgium, and the Netherlands. The central leadership of the group was situated in France and was directed from Moscow by radio and by couriers. In Germany, there were two subdivisions, the bigger and more important one in Berlin and the other in Hamburg. The organization was made up of people with very heterogeneous backgrounds who were, for the most part, members of the middle-class intelligentsia; the rest were organized members of the KPD, Germany's Communist Party. These two groups within the "Red Chapel" deeply distrusted each other, their only common bond being their political convictions. The Berlin division had members in many top government departments, such as the Reichs Aviation Ministry, the Army High Command (OKH), the Foreign Office, and the Reichs Economy Ministry.

The ultimate goal of the "Red Chapel" was the overthrow of the Hitler regime and its replacement by a German state patterned on Soviet Russia. This was to be achieved through the military defeat of Germany. The "Red Chapel" group never planned to assassinate Hitler or to destroy the Nazi regime by means of a coup. Rather, the activities of the "Red Chapel" consisted primarily of espionage for the Soviet Union. Leadership of the organization in Germany was in the hands of First Lieutenant Schulze-Boysen, of the Reichs Aviation Ministry, and Arvid Harnack, an administration official in the Ministry of Economy. Men such as Air Force Colonel Gehrts, the author Adam Kuckhoff, and the university professor Dr. Krauss also belonged to the group.

At the time of Hitler's rise to power, both Schulze-Boysen and Harnack were ideological adversaries of National Socialism. At the beginning of the war against Soviet Russia they joined the ranks of Nazism's active enemies. They were convinced not only that Germany *would* lose the war, but that she *should* lose it. This conviction was set forth in a number of pamphlets issued by the group.

Their entry into the ranks of Hitler's active foes was a direct result of their friendship with Soviet Russian officials. In Berlin, Harnack continued to keep up the acquaintances he had first made in the Soviet Union, especially with "Erdmann," the Soviet Russian Trade Attaché, with whom he had a close and friendly relationship. Through Harnack, Schulze-Boysen, Kuckhoff, and others were drawn into the circle around "Erdmann."

While "Erdmann" managed to win over Schulze-Boysen and Harnack on the basis of friendship, he put Kuckhoff under obligation by giving him money. By the time "Erdmann" left Germany—a few days before the start of the hostilities with Russia—he had won the cooperation of Schulze-Boysen, Harnack, and several others for the Soviet Secret Service. Also the methods of the proposed collaboration during the war with Russia had been determined. "Erdmann" left several radio transmitters for the use of the group as well as the code and code key and 10,000 Marks. The functions which were to be performed by each member had been decided upon while "Erdmann" was still in Berlin. Schulze-Boysen accepted the responsibility for gathering information, Harnack was assigned the job of transferring the messages into code, and a third collaborator was picked for the handling of the transmitter.

Soon after the German offensive against Russia started, the Schulze-Boysen group established radio contact with Moscow, and was able to supply the Soviet Information Service with secret material of all kinds until the fall of 1942. The number of collaborators steadily increased, new technicians were enlisted, faulty transmitters were repaired, and new assignments were accepted. All information was transmitted at night on wave lengths that had been designated by "Erdmann," some directly to Moscow, some to Brussels. The location of the transmitters was constantly changed to avoid detection; members of the group made their homes available for that purpose. Even the transmitter of Goering's Reichs Aviation Ministry was used to send to Russia coded information which concerned German military and economic affairs, information to which the conspirators had access through their connections with the various ministries. Repeatedly, exact data on German airplane production, specifying each type of plane, was sent to Russia. Plans for German offensive actions in the East, as well as plans for the use of local units and airborne actions behind enemy lines, were obtained and passed on to Russia. Other information dealt with German industrial plants and their products.

From time to time, Russian functionaries appeared in Berlin to pick up supplementary information and to deliver new instructions. In 1941, Russian parachute agents were also employed. For the most part these were German emigrés or former prisoners-of-war who had been trained in the Soviet Union for Secret Service work. These agents, equipped with all the necessary technical apparatus, including the most up-to-date miniature transmitters, were dropped by Russian planes in the vicinity of Berlin with addresses of members of the Schulze-Boysen group, in whose homes they found hiding-places. They were employed mainly to handle the actual transmission of information.

In time, the Gestapo managed to capture one of these agents. By forcing him to establish and maintain radio contact with the Russian Secret Service, they were able to gather information for months about the arrival of new agents, whom they captured the moment they set foot on German soil.

In this connection, an interesting sidelight was supplied by an old Communist family in Berlin. For years the home of this family had served as a meeting place for Soviet agents. The furniture in the apartment was fitted with many secret drawers, in order to keep incriminating papers and other material from being discovered in case of a search. A workshop for forged passports was also part of the setup. One day, for undetermined reasons, this family fell upon two newly-arrived parachute agents, robbed them of all their possessions, and then drove them from the house, thereby practically condemning them to death.

Hand in hand with the espionage activity of the Schulze-Boysen group went acts of high treason, but many more people were involved in this part of the operations. Organized in cells, quite a few of which had only loose connections with one another and which performed more or less independently, they employed the following methods:

1) Training of followers in small groups. This was done through a succession of discourse meetings, at which Schulze-Boysen frequently talked about the military and political situation, and each time pinpointed a subject which was then discussed in accordance with Communism's ideological concepts. Leaflets and other propaganda material were read and distributed.

2) Propaganda. Pamphlets were written in which Hitler's mistakes were listed, the power potential of the adversary expounded, and proof offered of the reasons why Germany had to lose the war. Schulze-Boysen was especially productive, and among many such leaflets wrote a study of Napoleon, whose Russian campaign was compared to Hitler's. In these leaflets, Schulze-Boysen openly asked for sabotage by Germans and urged German soldiers to throw away their weapons and desert to the other side. Harnack, on the other hand, wrote a rather scientific study on Hitler's monopolistic capitalism. The leaflets were hectographed and distributed from hand to hand.

When, in the summer of 1942, a propaganda exhibit with the title "The Soviet Paradise" was shown in Berlin,

Schulze-Boysen started a counter-action. He wrote a pamphlet called "The Nazi Paradise." This pamphlet, which was also printed on large posters, was distributed at night in the streets of Berlin by young members of the group. Schulze-Boysen went along in an Air Force uniform to provide protection for the others in case of trouble with the police.

The two leaders of the Berlin division of the "Red Chapel," Schulze-Boysen and Harnack, were completely different in character. Schulze-Boysen, a great-nephew of Grand Admiral von Tirpitz and son of a Navy officer, was intelligent and capable, but uncontrolled and devoid of scruples, a fanatic and a born revolutionary. He was by far the most active person in the "Red Chapel," and as its more or less acknowledged leader he organized the political as well as the espionage activities of the entire group.

Arvid Harnack, on the other hand, was a very different kind of man. He had spent a good deal of time abroad, had studied in the United States, and had married an American woman of Jewish descent, Mildred Fish. After 1939, he was a member of the German commission which conducted economic negotiations in the wake of the German-Soviet non-aggression pact. He was an expert on the economic situation in both the United States and the Soviet Union. By nature circumspect, reserved, and non-revolutionary, he did not have the strength to free himself from Schulze-Boysen's influence and from the fetters which his friendship with the Russians had imposed upon him. Although he coded information and met with Russian as well as with German emigré parachute agents, he was primarily active in the political sector of the "Red Chapel's" work.

The continuous radio transmissions of the Schulze-Boysen group finally gave away the existence of their secret station. Some of the messages were intercepted and decoded. In one of the messages from Brussels, the name Schulze-Boysen was mentioned instead of the usual code name. As a result, he was immediately arrested, as were most of his colleagues a short while later.

The trial of the "Red Chapel" group was conducted by the Supreme Military Court against the wishes of Hitler, who was suspicious of military justice. Terence Prittie, in his otherwise quite laudable account of various anti-Hitler opposition groups, *Germans Against Hitler*, states that the trial of the "Red Chapel" members was a farce. This is not accurate. The court observed to the full the legal rights of the defendants, but it was so obviously a case of espionage that the death sentence was passed in most cases. The court did spare the life of American-born Mildred Harnack; but this did not suit Hitler, who personally ordered her condemned to death.

It is clear that there could be no collaboration whatever between the "Red Chapel" and the resistance movement under Beck. The fundamental difference dividing the two most certainly cannot be found in the field of criminal law—in this case, the laws defining high treason and its penalties. Both groups were engaged in what technically was high treason. So long as states exist, they will always seek to protect themselves against anything which threatens their structure and status. Criminal law legislation, however, can never be more than a superficial barrier to the morally responsible person—a barrier that has to be reckoned with only to the extent of correctly evaluating the results of breaking these laws. By themselves, criminal law legislation exercises moral influence only when it coincides with the dictates of ethics and morality. Such coincidence was notably lacking in all the political laws of the Third Reich. Therefore, actions taken in accord with a higher duty were morally justified even if and when, from the point of view of the existing criminal law, they constituted high treason.

The decisive difference between the "Red Chapel" and the Beck-Goerdeler groups has to be sought on another level, and this difference becomes clear when we examine their respective principles. Rejection of Nazism was the one thing the groups held in common. Beyond that, the "Red Chapel" remained bogged down in controversy between two rival political ideologies—National Socialism and Communism. The resistance movement under Beck, on the other hand, reached over and above politics to religious and moral values. Political considerations and even the nation itself were secondary. No one will set himself lightly against his country, especially during a war, but when religion and ethics are in danger, the nation is less important than the moral structure which alone can supply a lasting and solid foundation for any state. This does not mean that we were not patriots. On the contrary, every line written by Goerdeler during that time shows the value the resistance movement set upon the nation. We considered the survival of Germany our very special task.

In comparing the aims of the "Red Chapel" and Beck-Goerdeler groups we find that they agreed only in their desire to overthrow the Hitler regime, not in answering the question of what was to happen afterwards. The "Red Chapel" wanted to turn Germany into a Communist state modelled on Soviet Russia; the goal of the resistance groups led by, or associated with, Beck and Goerdeler was to create a state along traditional European and German lines. We certainly did not want to remove Hitler only to have his regime replaced with another kind of totalitarianism in the form of a Soviet-controlled Communist state.

Even when considered from an anti-Nazi viewpoint, the espionage activities of the "Red Chapel" could not be condoned for two reasons. The first was that their espionage and sabotage were not aimed primarily at eliminating Hitler and his regime with one stroke, but rather at bringing about the fall of the Third Reich through military defeat and economic collapse. The victims of this activity would be the common German soldier and other helpless and innocent individuals who were not responsible for the policies and crimes of the regime. Our fight, on the other hand, was directed solely against the guilty ones.

The second reason for rejecting the methods of the "Red Chapel" was the group's total subservience to a foreign power. This does not mean that we shunned all contact with other countries. Germany, like any other state, is a part of the world and in its policies must consider the international situation. A diplomat is justified in negotiating with a foreign power as long as he does not harm the interests of his own country. Only on this basis can the secret negotiations by members of the German resistance before and during the war be appreciated. In the common European interest, it could even become necessary to discuss military matters, as when General Oster warned the Netherlands against an imminent attack by Hitler in 1940. Those who call his action treason will have to ask themselves whether this attack was really in the best interests of Germany, or whether it was not better for the country that a German should act as Oster did. Because his country had fallen under the tyrannical rule of an alien dictator, Oster found the courage for a truly great deed. For this, he suffered the penalty of being called a traitor—but he also proved that there did exist courageous internal opposition to Hitler and his amoral policies. At no time, however, was he or any other member of our resistance group a tool or agent of any foreign power.

In retrospect, it is clear that those who obeyed every order and every regulation of the Third Reich destroyed, by their compliance, more spiritual values than all the members of the resistance could manage to preserve by their combined efforts and "treasonable" activities. These activities were at all times in the long-range best interests of Germany, and had nothing in common with espionage and sabotage as practiced by the "Red Chapel."

CHAPTER FOURTEEN

Blueprint for a

New Germany

In all the long-range plans for the creation of a post-Hitler Germany all political groups had been included in the proposed distribution of government power. To that end, Goerdeler had conferred for years with the various groups, from far right to far left—with the exception of only the Communists—and had succeeded in achieving a considerable amount of unity, the kind of unity that had been so conspicuously absent in the years before 1933. Through his connections with leading Catholics, Goerdeler won the cooperation of those Catholic groups which, before Hitler's takeover, had made up the bulk of the old Center Party. On the Left, too, he found support, especially from two representatives of the German workers, Julius Leber and Wilhelm Leuschner, both extremely able men. Before the Nazis' rise to power, Leuschner had been Minister of the Interior in Hesse. Leber, who for years had been a prominent newspaper

JULIUS LEBER

1 8 9 1 — 1 9 4 5

A representative of German Labor, and a leading Social Democrat, Leber spent many years in Nazi prisons. After his release in 1937, he devoted his time to the fight against Hitler, and became one of the prominent figures of the civilian resistance. He was executed in January, 1945.

editor in Luebeck, was arrested in 1933, and spent the next four years in prison.

Both Leuschner and Leber fought hard against National Socialism. To camouflage their political activities, Leuschner had acquired a small manufacturing plant, while Leber had become a coal merchant. Both used their homes as centers for their political work. They and their political friends realized that there was no constitutional way to rid Germany of the Nazi rule; only in close cooperation with the army could these labor leaders hope for the overthrow of the Hitler regime.

In addition to the representatives of the Socialist labor unions, Goerdeler also counted among his collaborators the former leader of the Christian trade unions, Jacob Kaiser. Leuschner and Leber both were executed after the abortive coup of 1944; Kaiser was destined to survive.

It was not always easy to get the various factions of the opposition together under one roof. Nevertheless, although he did not remain unchallenged, Goerdeler managed to keep the reins of political power in his hands.

All the plans for rebuilding the German government and the cleanup of the entire administrative structure after Hitler's fall had been hammered out by Goerdeler and his assistants through years of work. Among the measures to be taken immediately after a successful coup was the reinstatement of those pre-Hitler statutes of the criminal law which guarantee freedom of the individual; that is, from the moment of a takeover by the resistance forces, arrests could be made only by legal court order or when the criminal had been apprehended while actually committing the crime. In the latter case, the defendant was to be brought before a judge within twenty-four hours, who would then decide whether or not he was to be kept under arrest. During the state of emergency the judge would be obliged to keep persons in custody if requested to do so, in the interests of internal security, by the Chancellor, the Minister of the Interior, the Minister of Justice, or the Commanding General.

So far as the economy was concerned, Goerdeler intended to leave the existing organizations intact, but make them self-administrating in order to encourage civic responsibility. He also planned to have both workers and employees take an active part in deciding important economic questions. Although he was, of course, an implacable enemy of all forms of economic collectivism, Goerdeler realized that the stark facts of existing realities in the Germany of that time would demand the continuation of a planned economy, at least for a while.

Goerdeler's plan for the churches included self-determination and self-administration as well as the separation of church and state. The Police would again become the responsibility of individual communities and districts; only the security police would be the concern of the Reichs Government.

As for the constitution of the new Reich, Goerdeler wanted to reorganize its entire structure from the bottom up. He was of the opinion that the jurisdiction of the individual communities should not be limited. His plan called for local elections within three months after demobilization. Goerdeler's aim was to revitalize the natural interest of every individual in his local community. All honorable citizens, both men and women, over twenty-four years of age were to have the right to vote. Any citizen in good standing who was at least twenty-eight years old would be eligible for elective office. Under Goerdeler's plan, the candidate with a plurality of votes within his district would win the election; an absolute majority was not necessary. Three quarters of the community representatives were to be chosen in this way, while the remaining quarter was to be selected by the Chambers of Commerce of each community, on the condition that in each case one delegate should be an employer and one a worker or employee.

As soon as the community had chosen its representatives, the latter were to elect a mayor and his deputies for a period of twelve years.

Goerdeler planned to reorganize all phases of the administration from the individual community upward, in a way which would have insured a maximum of self-government. The Reichs Government was to have no more than a supervisory role.

The Reichs Government itself was to consist of the following ministries:

1) Defense
2) Interior
3) Foreign
4) Justice
5) Economy
6) Finance
7) Education
8) Transport

The government was to be headed by a Reichs Chancellor. The Minister of Defense would have had jurisdiction over Army, Navy, and Air Force. Goerdeler did not plan to have a separate Ministry of Labor. He wanted to have all the members of the Reichs Government meet regularly under the chairmanship of the Reichs Chancellor. Popular representation, in the form of a Reichstag (Parliament) and a Reichsstaendehaus (Congress of representatives of the various professions), was to exercise a controlling influence over the government.

Correctly appraising the German national character, and in an attempt to avoid the dangers which had resulted from the constitution of the Weimar Republic, Goerdeler favored a monarch as head of the new German state. He preferred the inherited to the elective monarchy as a guarantee for the continuity of the state. The constitutional monarch was to be above party and politics, and, like the English king, he was to be the Supreme Commander of the Armed Forces and the personification of public power. Because he wanted to avoid disputes about personalities, Goerdeler planned to leave the actual choice of a king to a later date; first there was to be a Reichs Statthalter (Regent), as head of state. Beck was the natural choice for this position, for he had all the prerequisites: integrity, dignity, objectivity, and age. The last qualification was important in Germany as a sign of firmly-rooted authority.

Goerdeler himself was to be the new Reichs Chancellor. His long years of battle against Nazism, his comprehensive mind, and his talent for unifying opposing views made him the logical choice for the Chancellorship. Leuschner was selected for the position of Vice Chancellor, while the post of Minister of the Interior would have gone either to Leber or to Count Fritz von der Schulenburg. The other ministries were to be filled partly by men of the political Right, partly by those of the Left. A career diplomat, either Ulrich von Hassell or Count Werner von der Schul-

211

enburg, would have been chosen to head the Foreign Ministry.

Through our participation in the talks about the political aims of the resistance group, Tresckow and I also heard about other activities within this organization; those, for instance, of Joseph Mueller, a Munich lawyer, and his negotiations with the Vatican, and of Hans Bernd Gisevius and his work in Switzerland.

Toward the end of 1943 Goerdeler formulated the guiding principles and aims of the future Reichs Government, as he visualized it, in a declaration which represented the collaboration of a number of opposition members. The text of this declaration, which would have been released for publication shortly after a successful takeover by the resistance, ran as follows:

"The members of the new Reichs Government never wanted this war, nor did they ever deem it necessary. Instead, they looked upon this war as the greatest misfortune that could have befallen Europe and the world. They therefore consider it their most urgent and important task to end the war without delay by concluding a true and lasting peace. This peace should enable all nations, great and small, to govern themselves within their own borders in security and national independence, and to unite in healing the wounds of the war and rebuilding the stricken Continent.

"The Reichs Government is aware that immense obstacles have to be overcome on the road to this goal; obstacles which consist of broken treaties and acts of senseless violence. Prerequisite to any understanding among the peoples of the world is a return of trust and confidence. Only a world filled with mutual trust can establish a peace worthy of the stupendous sacrifices made by the peoples of this earth, one which can give men's lives a true and lasting foundation deserving of the name of peace, and can avoid, after the disaster of this war, the worse disaster of a thwarted peace.

"The Reichs Government is determined to contribute toward this return of confidence. While so engaged, it will not hesitate to take drastic measures against those who would destroy this foundation of national and international understanding.

"Trust is based upon respect for truth and reverence for the right. Hitler had only contempt for both truth and right. In place of truth he put propaganda; in place of right, violence. Propaganda and the Gestapo were his means of staying in power. For him, only one ultimate value existed: the state. Therefore he called it total and turned Germany into such a state, a state which took the place of all other values and determined the aim and purpose of every endeavor. The state was above and beyond right and morality. The individual and society alike were completely subordinate to the state. The old theory that the end justifies the means, a theory abhorred by all right-thinking men, was proclaimed in its new form: 'Right is what benefits the people.' The concept of individuality, peculiar both to Christianity and the Germanic people, was denied by him. Man was to be no more than a part, member, and functionary of the state; he was to be remodelled in the cast of a collective being, and to give up his right to face the state as an individual. This concept of the state fitted in with the one-party system, its central theme being the development of an authoritarian political purpose which prevailed by means of propaganda and violence.

"In place of this caricature of a true state community, the Reichs Government will establish a state in accordance with the Christian traditions of the Western World, and based upon the principles of civic duty, loyalty, service, and achievement for the common good as well as on respect for the individual and his natural rights as a human being.

"The Reichs Government solemnly rejects the idea of the

totalitarian state, which can never unite the forces of a nation, and which does not aim at forming a higher unity of action from the various national currents and diversities, but which intends a single concept to triumph ruthlessly over all other opinions, and aims at exterminating all minorities as well as those Germans who do not concur.

"The cure for this condition is to be found in the constitution which takes into account the organic structure of the nation, one which permits all political and social factions to live peacefully side by side. In addition, the constitution should help direct all the diverse forms of community life, typical of our times, into channels of peaceful activity, without allowing this activity to affect the power of the state to uphold law and order—a power indispensable to the welfare of the people. The Reichs Government begins by subordinating the power of the state to the laws of morality and justice. It respects the individual, the family, religious creeds, professional societies, local administrations and free trade unions. In return, it demands that all citizens feel obligated to contribute to the common welfare.

"The Reichs Government will, of course, give back to the German people the unadulterated means for informing themselves on the policies and actions of their government, as well as on the situation in the Reich, in Europe, and in the world, and to freely express their opinions on all these and other matters.

"The Reichs Government therefore declares war on all suppression and falsification of truth. The German people, freed from the fog of propaganda, must learn the truth and nothing but the truth. Without illusions, they must recognize their true condition so that they may go about building a future free from all wishful thinking. Those who believed that the easy victories of the first two years of war were a gift from a Divine Providence to the German people will have to learn to recognize that idea either as blasphemy or as a frivolous error for which the German people have had to pay with two and a half million dead, and six million homeless men, women, and children.

"The Reichs Government, in serving the truth, need fear nothing and nobody; therefore, as one of its first measures, it has cancelled all penalties for listening to foreign broadcasts. To all enemy propaganda which is not conducive to peace and international reconciliation, the Reichs Government will supply the necessary answers.

RIGHT AND JUSTICE

"During the past ten years, in accordance with the character of the totalitarian National Socialist state, justice and its administration have become a travesty. Unscrupulous violators of right and justice have abused their powers and degraded the courts by turning them into tools of state propaganda and henchmen of the executioners. The laws must be restored as the basis for all judicial decisions. Judges, freed from all political and police directives, will once more become servants of the community, in their capacity as servants of right and justice. Warrants of arrest will, from now on, be issued only for offenders against the laws of the newly-established German community.

MORALS AND SEX MORALITY

"National Socialism exemplified deification of every kind of brutality that could serve its purpose. This, in addition to the slackening of morality inevitable in times of war, has brought about a widespread moral decay, which the Reichs Government plans to check by all available means. We must put an end to the separation of families, frivolously contracted marriages, and state premiums for illegitimate children. Not be-

215

cause of prudish prejudices, but for the sake of the health and future of our nation, young men and women must be taught to realize that happy families, lasting marriages, and healthy children can exist only on the solid foundation of respect for eternally valid laws.

RELIGION AND CHURCH

"While allowing all religious freedom to the individual, the Reichs Government affirms its adherence to the Christian faith as one of the fundamental forces which have shaped the German nation and its history.

"The Reichs Government knows full well that political measures are incapable of restoring the disrupted religious traditions and customs. It does, however, immediately abolish all persecutions of Christian churches by the State, as well as all arrests, banishments, and prohibition of preaching directed against the clergy. All religious communities shall fulfill their sacred mission, free from government interference. The Reich will protect them and their ministers.

YOUTH AND EDUCATION

"All schools are to be freed immediately from the noxious role of having to falsify facts, to offend youth's instinct for the truth, and to teach young people phrases instead of knowledge, hypocrisy instead of moral courage, brutal coarseness instead of true achievement.

"The right to educate is vested primarily in the parents. The school should support them in this endeavor by encouraging children, through teachers who are qualified professionally and by character, to attain the maximum development of their individual mental and physical faculties.

"Gifted children from all strata of the people shall be admitted to any school for which they are qualified. The Reichs Government rejects the idea of any exclusively state-sponsored youth organization. It will, however, support any effort by religious communities, professional unions, and physical education clubs designed to encourage young people to develop a sense of civic duty and service to the community.

"Universities should receive stature and dignity from their task, which is to be truly free places of research, learning, and instruction. Academic self-government, which will determine the rights and duties of both teachers and students within the appropriate boundaries, must regulate the internal affairs of the universities and the student bodies.

ECONOMY AND SOCIAL POLICY

"As long as hostilities continue, the national economy must do everything in its power to supply the troops with all they need in the way of food, clothing, and arms. The Reichs Government is convinced that all economic planning in a Germany impoverished by war and the preparations for war, can, at the beginning, have only one aim: to feed and clothe the German people, to help them rebuild their shattered homes, and to replace their ruined household furnishings. Besides providing for the victims of this war—the widows, orphans, and disabled soldiers—this must be the foremost task of German social policy.

"The Reichs Government is determined to conduct the economic policy of an impoverished Germany in a way that results in a truly united national community, inspired by public spirit and neighborly love; and, no longer serving to camouflage the corruption of tyrants, to stand watch over the remaining resources of the German people.

"The degree of economic liberty to be restored after the war will be determined solely on the basis of how much it will contribute toward the common good. An economic bureaucracy which has become an end in itself, and which by endless red tape hampers the economy and increases the cost of labor, also reduces production and is therefore a serious mistake.

Wherever free competition serves to increase efficiency, permits a cheaper supply of necessities, and keeps the consumer from becoming the last, helpless link in a long chain of distribution, it should be encouraged.

"The export trade, reduced to barter in the present war economy, should be made, as soon as possible, to serve the vital requirements of the German people. It will have to supply them with all the food, clothing, raw materials, and other goods which the industry and labor of the German peasant and workman cannot produce at all, or which would be uneconomic to produce and which the German natural resources cannot supply.

"Relaxation of wage and price controls can begin only after our home needs have been assured. Economic power positions can no longer be unilaterally exploited. The development of wages should be determined, as far as possible, by independent wage agreements between employers and trade unions. Experienced government mediation is obligated, as in the past, to offer helpful assistance. The law which provides 'for the protection of national labor,' which was exploited for the sole purpose of reducing the German worker to a state of dependence, will be changed without delay. Those employers who have perverted their economic responsibility, and have sunk to a level where they were nothing more than automatic receiving stations for the orders of the political bosses, must be removed from all responsible positions in Germany's economic life.

"National Socialist mismanagement has shattered the German Social Insurance system—at one time the most progressive in the entire world—and left it in ruins. The remnants of the system are to be transferred to an autonomous administration by the workers and employees, for which it is intended, and is then to be combined into a uniform foundation for the entire structure of Social Insurance.

PUBLIC FINANCE

"The reckless accumulation of public debts during the past ten years has increased Germany's national debt from ten billion to three hundred billion Reichsmark. To this sum must be added the immense damages caused by the war. This almost intolerable burden, which far exceeds the total national assets, has been imposed upon us and upon future generations. The Reichs Government is determined to discharge these debts without having recourse to a new inflation. Instead, the government will institute a severe tax policy and other measures appropriate to the general impoverishment of the German people. In addition, there will be a balanced budget of income and expenditure, of which public accounts will be rendered, thus laying the foundation for a solid and lasting economic life.

THE END OF THE WAR

"The Reichs Government is well aware of the fact that its future task—that of giving new constitutional shape to the life of the German people, and of filling it with peaceful achievement—can be undertaken only after the end of the war, which it fervently desires. Ready as it is to make peace, the Reichs Government realizes that this does not depend entirely upon its own attitude. It will, however, seize upon every opportunity offered in declarations made about the future of the world by foreign statesmen and thus demonstrate its willingness to conclude a lasting peace, one which will open the way for all peoples to live together in freedom and mutual respect."

These proclamations, which represented the aims and attitudes of the resistance, were to be made public shortly after a successful coup d'état, giving the German people as well as the world a clear indication of the policies of the new regime.

219

CHAPTER FIFTEEN

To Kill—

Or Not to Kill?

From the very beginning, long before the war, one thing was quite clear to all the members of the German resistance: The only possible basis for the ultimate success of our coup d'état was Hitler's complete removal from power. No other alternative could be considered. While we were in complete agreement on the *fact* that he had to be removed, there was some difference of opinion among the various factions of the opposition as to the *means* by which this goal should be achieved. In the years before the war, plans for the overthrow of the Nazi regime had not included the assassination of Hitler; he was to have been forced to resign or taken prisoner. Quite a few of the conspirators—mostly among the civilian group—remained convinced even during the war that it would be advantageous for us to take Hitler alive. One of the arguments advanced in support of this theory was that the taking of Hitler's life would be considered a disgusting and revolting deed, even by many non-Nazi Germans. Others reasoned that killing Hitler might backfire and hurt us later by giving rise to the myth that "everything would have turned out all right if only Hitler had been alive." But the strongest argument for keeping Hitler alive was that the resistance movement would then be able to bring him to trial before the eyes of the world, and thus record for the annals of history the viciousness and absurdity of the man and his system.

This last argument was strongly supported by Goerdeler, the leader of the civilian group within the resistance. It was just as strongly opposed by most of its military members, even though they realized that a case could be made for Goerdeler's point of view. But the soldiers who were actually to undertake the difficult task of removing Hitler believed that it would be almost impossible to take him prisoner. Besides, the military leaders, well acquainted with the mood of the troops, could correctly gauge the reactions of the average German soldier. They knew exactly how much the oath of allegiance meant to him, especially now that the country was at war.

Another aspect of the problem which these leaders did not dare overlook was the fact that not only the greater part of seventy million Germans, but also much of Europe's non-German population remained under the spell of Adolf Hitler. This spell caused a kind of paralyzing hypnosis that penetrated into the very ranks of even those nations at war with the Third Reich. Europe during the war years could be compared to a school class of frightened youngsters faced by a malevolent teacher who carried a big stick. All the pupils apprehensively watched the teacher, each fearful that he would be picked out next for punishment.

Such considerations, which were based upon a sober evaluation of the known facts and eliminated all wishful

221

thinking, had convinced the leading military members of the resistance that the spell emanating from the person of Adolf Hitler could not be completely broken so long as he was alive. To remove this spell with one bold stroke, and at the same time to relieve the German army of its oath of allegiance to the "Fuehrer," seemed to the military group the most urgent task by far, and a necessary prerequisite for the success of any coup. This view, sponsored mainly by General Beck, was finally adopted after some debate in the fall of 1942. The die was cast, and the resistance movement, dropping all plans to take Hitler alive, decided on his assassination.

At this point it should be stated that killing for political reasons can be justified only under the most extreme circumstances. Barring such circumstances, assassination is unethical and must be condemned. The members of the German resistance, both civilian and military, were in complete agreement on this point. We were not revolutionary terrorists, to whom assassination seemed the logical method for gaining personal political power or other advantages. On the contrary, many of us hesitated on religious grounds to endorse Hitler's assassination, although we were dedicated to fighting the evil personified by him. When we finally agreed to go along with the decision to kill him, it was only after considerable inner struggle and because we had become convinced that there was no other way left. Every day and in ever-increasing numbers, innocent people were dying in concentration and slave labor camps, soldiers of all nations were being killed or maimed, and Germany was being pushed closer to total national disaster in a war unleashed by one man against all dictates of right and reason. His death—and his death only—would signal the end to this senseless slaughter. It was Hitler's life against the lives of hundreds of thousands of human beings. If ever in history an assassination was justifiable on moral and ethical grounds, this one was.

The code of ethics applicable to assassination applies equally to the much-debated question of military obedience. Although an army must give unquestioning obedience to its leaders under normal circumstances, there are situations when disobedience becomes the duty of the soldier. Very few people outside Germany—and by no means all Germans—realize that in the pre-Nazi Prussian army this principle of disobedience under certain circumstances was an established and legal custom. In fact, the Prussian Code of Military Law contained a clause which stipulated that orders of criminal content were not to be obeyed, and that the soldier who did obey such orders was liable to punishment. The so-called "blind obedience" of the German army was a purely Hitlerian creation, and there cannot be the slightest doubt that it is invalid from both the ethical and military point of view. In extreme cases, a man has to reserve for himself the ultimate decision on what constitutes his duty. Obeying orders cannot be used as an excuse for committing or condoning a crime. This was the guiding principle of the military members of the resistance. Although technically engaged in high treason, and, with the decision to kill Hitler, in preparations for political murder, they felt that they were actually doing their duty according to the highest standards of ethics, morality, and patriotism.

Here, of course, we come to the very core of the controversy that has been raging ever since the plot of July 20, 1944: Should the personal oath of allegiance to Adolf Hitler have been obeyed unconditionally by the German officer? The difference of opinion on this point is responsible for the seeming paradox that, while the German resistance during the war was largely supported by the army, the army contributed most to the failure of the strike against Hitler. The split on the matter of the oath of allegiance ran deep. On one side were those officers who considered an oath an oath, and who felt themselves bound to it. Also there were those who used the oath as a convenient excuse to avoid involvement in dangerous activities. On the other side were those officers who considered it their higher duty to fight Hitler in spite of their oath. In this connection, it is interesting to note what a non-German and non-military authority has to say about conventional versus "higher" duty. The Swiss historian Ernst Gagliardi touches on this question in his discussion of the background of Bismarck's dismissal by William II, the last German Emperor. In the first volume of Gagliardi's history of these events, he sides with William II and against Bismarck on domestic and especially social matters, in which he considered Bismarck behind the times. In the second volume, however, which deals with foreign policy, he is on Bismarck's side, stating that in certain instances it is a man's highest virtue, not to simply obey the head of state and government, but to do his best for his country, even if this includes moving *against* the chief of state.

The significance of this remark was not lost upon Hitler. He had allowed the first volume to appear in Germany, but when the second volume was published, he immediately had all the copies confiscated and destroyed.

We may say that those officers who made up their minds to act against Hitler were operating on that level of "highest virtue" ascribed by Gagliardi to Bismarck in his quarrel with Emperor William II, while the officers who felt themselves bound by their oath to remain loyal to Hitler must be relegated to a much lower level of "manly virtue."

It was, of course, quite clear to everyone involved in the conspiracy that killing Hitler would be only the spark needed to set off the coup d'état itself. The second step would have to be the seizure, by military force, of all the vital positions and buildings in and around Berlin. In order to contact representatives of world powers, carefully picked men were to be assigned to key government and administrative posts immediately after Berlin had been seized by the military. After all, the purpose of our coup was not just to eliminate Hitler and overthrow the National Socialist system, but to create a new government capable of filling the resulting vacuum and thus preventing chaos. The first step—Hitler's death—had little meaning unless we could follow it immediately with the second step.

Under the circumstances existing in the winter of 1942–1943, preparations for the spark that was to set off the chain of events planned by the resistance had to be handled by the field army. The threads of the entire plot were gathered in the hands of General Oster, who placed all matters of importance before General Beck, the chief of our group. It was Oster's task to prepare, with the help of General Olbricht, head of a key department in the army reserves, all the steps necessary for the capture of Berlin.

Olbricht and Oster, incidentally, had drawn up, in great detail, the first serious plans for taking over power in Germany during the war. What they needed now was a man in the field army capable of initiating the first step—

the assassination of Hitler—which would be the signal to go ahead with their plans to seize Berlin. The man they sought was finally found in General von Tresckow.

As soon as Tresckow joined the plot, the work of the others took on shape and form. Instead of more or less theoretical tea-time discussions, a concrete project with all the earmarks of the real thing was drawn up. It was part of my duties, as a member of the military group within the resistance, to see that the communication between Oster and Tresckow—who, by the way, never once met face to face—was established and continued without interruption. Only those who lived in Germany under the Nazi rule will be able to appreciate the constant and extensive precautions which had to be taken by us to prevent discovery of our activities by the Gestapo. For this reason, we avoided all meetings and discussions which were not absolutely necessary and took great care to draw as little attention as possible to those involved in the plot. Even among the closest allies, only those names essential to the understanding of developments were mentioned, thus reducing the danger of accidentally arousing the suspicion of the ever-present Gestapo spies. It hardly has to be stressed that our precautions, necessary though they were, slowed down and hampered the pace of our preparations.

For those who have never had to live under such pressures, it will be quite impossible to imagine the persistent, nagging anxiety that was our constant companion by day and helped to rob us of our sleep at night. The ever-present fear of spies and the possibility of being under surveillance by the Gestapo were a paralyzing burden which every member of the resistance had to bear day after day, month after month, without a moment's relaxation or relief.

Shaking off this weight anew each morning was in itself an effort that sapped much of our energy and stamina.

During the last conference between Olbricht and Tresckow in the winter of 1942, during which the date for Hitler's assassination was discussed, Olbricht asked for another eight weeks' time to complete a more detailed draft of his and Oster's plans for the seizure not only of Berlin, but also of Cologne, Munich, and Vienna. After the eight weeks had passed, I represented Tresckow in another conference with Olbricht at which he spoke the long-awaited, fateful words: "We are ready. The spark can now be set off."

To make sure that every detail was fully understood, and that the various phases of the coup would be executed as smoothly as possible, one more conference between our group at the Eastern front and our allies in Berlin was necessary. This meeting did not take place in Berlin, as had all the others, but in Smolensk, at the headquarters of the Army Group Center. As a cover for our conference, Admiral Canaris, the chief of the German Military Intelligence, organized a service flight from Berlin to Russia. He brought along a large number of officers of his entourage, and to make the whole thing even less conspicuous, he arranged a general meeting of Intelligence officers. The really important meeting, however, took place far removed from the bustle of activity, in a small and modest room ordinarily used by one of the minor officers in Headquarters. Here, late at night, Tresckow, Supreme Court Justice von Dohnanyi—one of Oster's collaborators —and I met. Tresckow told Dohnanyi of our plan to take decisive action as soon as possible, and was himself informed of all the details of the preparations in Berlin. We

227

then conferred on ways and means of communicating with each other, and set up a code intelligible only to those intimately involved in the plot. Then we parted.

Late that night we joined the other Intelligence officers for a round of drinks. During that party, Canaris mentioned that he was going to fly to Hitler's Headquarters the following day to take up a matter with Himmler. I knew that, as so often before, this conference with the SS chief had to do with people who had fallen into some Gestapo trap, and whom Canaris wanted to save under the pretext that they could be useful for counter-intelligence work. Only his intimates knew how many people Canaris had snatched from the clutches of the Gestapo with his clever, persuasive reasoning.

His officers naturally could not know this, for they were unaware of the dangerous activities in which their chief was engaged. When they heard that Canaris was planning to meet with Himmler, they heatedly declared that they would no longer be able to shake hands with Canaris, for anyone who had exchanged a handshake with a "swine" like Himmler could never again give his hand to others without befouling them. Canaris grinned as he listened to these outbursts, for although he was in no position to explain the situation or divulge his real reason for meeting with Himmler, he secretly was pleased with the honorable and straightforward attitude of his collaborators. Naturally, he did not change his mind about talking to Himmler.

As for Tresckow and me, the meeting earlier that night had settled the last few questions, and everything was now ready for us to go ahead with our plans for Hitler's assassination.

CHAPTER SIXTEEN

The First

Assassination Attempt

In the meantime, Tresckow had been busy with preparations in anticipation of a final agreement concerning details for the coup d'état. Redoubling his efforts to win over to our side his superior, Chief Commander of the Army Group Center, Field Marshal von Kluge, Tresckow tried to get the latter to accept and actively support the idea of eliminating Hitler. Tresckow was convinced that the unqualified support for the coup of such an important military leader would lend enough prestige to our undertaking to exert pressure on other field and reserve commanders who were still wavering. He also wanted to persuade Kluge to begin without delay the long-overdue regrouping of the eastern front demanded by the General Staff in a more easily defensible position further west. Once such a movement was started, the other Army Groups of the eastern front would have been forced to follow suit.

Besides working on Kluge, Tresckow was plotting to arrange a situation favorable to an attempt on Hitler's life. A pretext had to be found which would lure the "Fuehrer" away from his headquarters in East Prussia and persuade him to visit the staff headquarters of the Army Group Center, which was located in a forest near Smolensk. To increase our chances of success, Tresckow wanted to get Hitler in surroundings with which the latter was unfamiliar while we had the advantage of knowing every detail.

It was no easy task to try and arrange Hitler's visit without arousing suspicion, but Tresckow was aided by his longstanding acquaintance with General Schmundt, Hitler's Chief Adjutant. Schmundt, a thoroughly devoted follower of the "Fuehrer," was not intelligent enough to perceive that Tresckow's suggestion that Hitler visit Kluge's headquarters was nothing but a pretext. Much less did he dream that Tresckow was using him to arrange for a deed which, if successful, would alter the course of history.

Finally, everything was arranged. Hitler advised Kluge to expect him in Smolensk during the early part of March, but as was his habit in such cases, he announced his visit several times, only to cancel it each time at the last minute. Finally he arrived by plane in Smolensk around noon on March 13, 1943.

If Kluge at that moment had been ready and willing to act according to his inner convictions, there cannot be any doubt whatsoever that the tyrant would have been eliminated on that day in March. With Kluge behind us, Hitler's assassination would not have presented too much difficulty. The Army Group Center had a cavalry regiment under the command of Colonel Baron von Boeselager, who belonged to our group and had offered to take on the task of killing Hitler. The entire corps of officers of the regiment had been carefully selected for our purpose. Boeselager, who combined military foresight with personal courage bordering on recklessness, was ready to act.

Such action, however, could not have been undertaken without Kluge's knowledge and consent, and Kluge, although he recognized the right course, did not have the strength of character to follow through. At the last minute, he hesitated. Again and again he brought up various arguments, claiming that neither the world, nor the German people, nor the German soldier would understand such an act at this time. He insisted that it would be much better to wait until the military situation had developed to a point that would force Hitler's elimination.

Kluge's attitude was a blow, for it made it impossible to use the military apparatus of the Army Group Center for the assassination, as we had originally planned. Tresckow decided to wait no longer, but to take matters into his own hands and, by using an alternate plan for killing Hitler which we had worked out some weeks before, force matters to a head. We felt that once Kluge was faced with a fait accompli, he would hesitate no longer, but follow the dictates of reason and conscience and join us.

To make this easier for him as well as the rest of the military command, we conceived a plan that differed somewhat from the original one. Dropping the idea of shooting Hitler, we planned instead to eliminate him by smuggling a time bomb aboard his plane. In this way, the stigma of an assassination would be avoided, and Hitler's death could be attributed—officially, at least—to an accidental plane crash.

Although Tresckow was especially ill-fitted for the odious and repugnant role of a sneak assassin, he accepted the responsibility of doing the "dirty job" of getting Hitler out of the way. No one except his most intimate friends knew what this decision had cost him. Once he had made up his mind, however, he hesitated no longer, but began to look around for the necessary materials. Several months before Hitler's visit to the Army Group Center's headquarters, Tresckow had managed to get explosives through Colonel Baron von Gersdorff, a staff officer of the Army group, who could obtain such material without arousing suspicion. Gersdorff, although solidly anti-Nazi, was not yet involved in the plot to kill Hitler. Here, however, was a person of such complete integrity that we did not hesitate to approach him.

Trying to find the right kind of explosive was quite a problem. We soon realized that the types used by the German army were not at all suited to our purpose, for the fuse that ignited them made a slight hissing noise which might have been noticed by some alert bystander.

We finally decided on British explosives of the plastic type and British fuses. British planes had been dropping large amounts of such material over Germany and German-held territory, in an effort to equip Allied agents for acts of sabotage. Naturally, a good deal of this material fell into the hands of our own military.

The British explosive had two great advantages. It was extremely powerful, but not bulky. A package no bigger than a thick book was capable of tearing apart everything within the space of a fair-sized room. We had our choice of three different types of trigger mechanism, each very clever in its construction. One set off the explosion after a few minutes, the second after about half an hour, and the third after two hours. We therefore could select the one which best suited our timing. Most important, however, was that triggering the bomb did not cause the slightest noise. Simply by pressing down on the head of the fuse, a small bottle containing a corrosive chemical was broken. This chemical ate through the wire holding down the firing pin, which, on being released, struck the detonator and set off the explosion.

Before doing anything else, Tresckow and I had to make enough tests with these bombs so that we would be familiar with every detail—familiar enough so that we could almost handle them in our sleep. Most of our tests were successful, and proved the explosive to be amazingly powerful. Our main difficulty, for we possessed no technical knowledge in this field, was to find out exactly what had gone wrong in the few tests that had not worked out as expected. In all these cases, the moment of explosion had been much—and to us unaccountably—delayed, thus throwing off our timing. Noticing that this had happened only with the bombs we had tested outdoors, we engaged in conversations with members of the Pioneer squad, casually bringing up the question of British explosives. We soon found out that the Russian winter had been responsible for the unsatisfactory results of some of our outdoor tests, because extreme cold tended to slow down the action of the chemical.

After we had concluded our experiments we went ahead with preparations for the assassination. Tresckow thought of a way to camouflage the bomb. Taking two packets of explosive—just to make doubly sure—we fashioned them into a parcel which looked like two bottles of Cointreau—the only brandy that comes in square bottles. The wrap-

233

ping was arranged in such a way that the fuse could be triggered from the outside without disturbing the package. On the morning of March 13, I took the bomb to my quarters and locked it away. Kluge and Tresckow drove to the airport to meet Hitler, who, as usual, arrived with an incredibly large entourage including both his personal cook and his private physician.

The official conference with Hitler took place in Kluge's quarters, with Tresckow and the other commanders of the Army Group Center present. It would have been easy to smuggle the bomb into that room, but had we done so, we would have killed not only Hitler, but all the other army leaders, including Kluge, whom we needed for the success of the coup.

After the official meeting, lunch was served in the officers' mess. Once again the fact that the bomb would have killed everybody in the room forbade an attempt at that time.

Hitler was served a special meal, every part of which had been prepared by his personal cook. It was tasted before his eyes by his physician, Professor Morell. The entire procedure was reminiscent of an Oriental despot of a bygone age. Watching Hitler eat was a most revolting spectacle. His left hand was placed firmly on his thigh; with his right hand he shoveled his food, which consisted of various vegetables, into his mouth. He did this without lifting his right arm, which he kept flat on the table throughout the entire meal; instead, he brought his mouth down to the food. He also drank a number of non-alcoholic beverages which had been lined up beside his plate. On his orders, no smoking was allowed after the meal.

During the luncheon, Tresckow approached Colonel

Heinz Brandt, a member of Hitler's entourage, and asked him casually whether he would be good enough to take along a small parcel containing two bottles of brandy for General Helmuth Stieff of the High Command at Headquarters. Brandt readily agreed.

Now everything was arranged. Earlier that morning, I had telephoned Captain Gehre, the liaison officer whom Oster had designated in Berlin, and had given him the code word which meant that Operation Flash—Hitler's assassination—was about to be set off. We had agreed on this way of communicating, and I knew that Gehre would immediately inform Dohnanyi, who in turn was to advise General Oster of the developments. These two were then to get everything ready for the second, vital step of seizing the German capital.

After lunch Hitler started back to the airport, accompanied by both Kluge and Tresckow, while I fetched the bomb from my quarters and drove to the airport. Upon my arrival there, I waited until Hitler had dismissed the officers of the Army Group Center and was about to board his plane. Looking at Tresckow, I read in his eyes the order to go ahead. With the help of a key, I pressed down hard on the fuse, thus triggering the bomb, and handed the parcel to Colonel Brandt who boarded the plane shortly after Hitler. A few minutes later both Hitler's plane and that carrying the other members of his party, escorted by a number of fighter planes, started back to East Prussia. Fate now had to take its course.

Tresckow and I returned to our quarters, from where I again called Gehre in Berlin, and gave him the second code word, indication that Operation Flash was actually under way.

We knew that Hitler's plane was equipped with special devices designed to increase its safety. Not only was it divided into several separate cabins, but Hitler's own cabin was heavily armor plated, and his seat was outfitted with a parachute. In spite of all this, Tresckow and I, judging from our experiments, were convinced that the amount of explosive in the bomb would be sufficient to tear the entire plane apart, or at the very least to make a fatal crash inevitable.

With mounting tension we waited for news of the "accident," which we expected shortly before the plane was to pass over Minsk. We assumed that one of the escort fighters would report the crash by radio. But nothing happened.

After waiting more than two hours, we received the shattering news that Hitler's plane had landed without incident at the airstrip at Rastenburg, in East Prussia, and that Hitler himself had safely reached Headquarters.

We could not imagine what had gone wrong. I called Gehre in Berlin immediately, and gave him the code word for failure of the assassination. Afterwards, Tresckow and I, stunned and shaken by the blow, conferred on what our next move should be. We were in a state of indescribable agitation; the failure of our attempt was bad enough, but the thought of what discovery of the bomb would mean to us and our fellow conspirators, friends, and families, was infinitely worse.

Finally, after considerable deliberation, Tresckow decided to telephone Brandt, and asked casually in the course of the conversation whether the Cointreau had been given to General Stieff. When Brandt replied that he had not yet had the chance to do so, Tresckow told him that the wrong parcel had been sent by mistake, and asked him to hold it until the following day, when it could be exchanged for the one Stieff was supposed to get. Brandt's pleasant answer made it clear that at least the bomb had not been discovered. We realized that it had to be retrieved at all costs, but as Stieff at that time was not yet a member of the conspiracy, we had to keep him out of it, and could only pray that the bomb would not go off belatedly and before we could get hold of it.

On some military pretext, I flew to Headquarters the following day in one of the regular courier planes, and immediately went to see Brandt. As I exchanged parcels with him—the one I had brought along actually *did* contain two bottles of brandy—I felt my blood running cold, for Hitler's aide, serenely unaware of what he was holding, handed me the bomb with a grin, juggling it back and forth in a way which made me fear a belated explosion. Forcing myself to display an outward calm which I most certainly did not feel, I took the bomb and immediately made my way to the nearby railroad junction at Korschen, where a special train of the High Command was scheduled to leave for Berlin that night.

As soon as I arrived in Korschen I boarded the train and went to the sleeping compartment that had been reserved for me. Locking the door behind me, I began gingerly to open the deadly package with a razor blade. After gently removing the wrapping, I could see that the condition of the explosive was unchanged. Carefully dismantling the bomb, I took out the fuse and examined it. The reason for the failure immediately became clear. Everything but one small part had worked as expected. The bottle with the corrosive fluid had been broken, the chemical had eaten through the wire, the firing pin had been released and had struck forward—but the detonator had not ignited! One of the few duds that had slipped past a British inspection was responsible for the fact that Hitler did not die on March 13, 1943.

Mingled disappointment and relief flooded through me as I looked down at the dismantled bomb. Disappointment, because our long and carefully laid plans had ended in failure through no fault of ours; and relief, because we had at least been able to prevent discovery of the plot, with all the terrible consequences such a discovery would have brought in its train.

After a night on the train, I arrived in Berlin on March 15, and immediately went to see Oster, Dohnanyi, and Gehre, to whom I gave a detailed account of the failure of our attempt. I had saved the detonator, and showed the others by what a freak of fate our plans had been frustrated. Oster remained calm, wasting no breath on recriminations or regrets.

A few days later we were given what looked like another good chance for an attempt on Hitler's life, this time during the annual ceremony for soldiers killed in battle, which was to be combined with an exhibition of captured Russian weapons in the Zeughaus in Berlin. By sheer coincidence, Baron von Gersdorff was detailed for duty at that ceremony. Tresckow took this as a sign that fate was playing into our hands. He confided in Gersdorff, and won not only his complete cooperation, but his promise to make an attempt on Hitler's life—at the cost of sacrificing his own. Tresckow told me of this offer in a code which no outsider could have understood. This information reached me late at night. Early the next morning I went to Gersdorff at the Hotel Eden and gave him the bomb. It was most difficult to find a suitable fuse on such short notice, but Gersdorff finally figured out a way to trigger the bomb and went off to the ceremony with the explosive in his coat pocket. However, he never got a chance to use it, for Hitler appeared only briefly and left after a few minutes. Gersdorff needed at least a quarter of an hour for the fuse to work in the cold hall of the Zeughaus.

How different would have been the course of the war and the fate of the world if we had succeeded in our attempt to kill Hitler that March of 1943! It would have meant an early end of the war, and an immediate end to the concentration camps and the terror in the occupied countries. We would have been spared the horrors of another two years of Nazi rule.

Bitter as the disappointment was for all of us, there was a bright side: Olbricht had found that his preparations in Berlin had not been adequate. Now we had another chance to correct and improve the plans. Shortly afterwards, I returned to Smolensk and to Tresckow, and found him not disheartened by failure, but instead all the more determined to go forward on the road he had chosen, fully convinced that difficulties existed only to be overcome.

CHAPTER SEVENTEEN

Preparation of the

Coup d'État

The failure of our attempt of March 13, 1943 was for us not just a great disappointment, but also a lesson. We were willing to learn from the events, and to redouble our efforts so that we could get set for a new blow against Hitler. In the course of our discussions following the abortive attempt, we came to the conclusion that, even if we had succeeded in killing Hitler, the subsequent coup d'état would not have gone smoothly. The main obstacle was a lack of coordination between the activities of the resistance groups within the army at the front and our confederates in the Home Army. To eliminate this weakness, Tresckow claimed that he urgently needed rest after the strain and stress of the Russian campaign. He received a sick leave of several months duration. Ten weeks of that leave were spent at his sister's home in Neubabelsberg, between Berlin and Potsdam. During that time Tresckow devoted all his energies to problems of the resistance.

Four different problems were foremost among those that had to be tackled by the opposition, and all had to be handled with circumspection and energy. These four tasks were:

1) Preparations for the coup which would give us control of Berlin. These preparations had to be drawn up according to general staff methods, just like any other major military action;

2) Formulating the political aims and objectives of the coup d'état;

3) Renewal of our efforts to influence those Field Marshals and Generals who appeared to be not too far removed from our way of thinking;

4) Preparations for a new assassination attempt against Hitler.

Preliminary work on those four problems was completed during the summer months of 1943. The coup of July, 1944, was based on the preparations that had been made a year before. Needless to say, a great many meetings and discussions were needed to get everything settled, and now more than ever it was necessary to exercise the utmost caution and discretion. However, we managed to succeed in keeping our clandestine activity secret during those months.

Shortly before we began this work in the summer of 1943, we received a severe blow. Several of our associates were arrested, among them Supreme Court Justice von Dohnanyi and Pastor Bonhoeffer. They remained silent in prison and gave nothing away, so that the Gestapo did not get on our trail. But in these two our group had lost men

241

who were hard to replace. Dietrich Bonhoeffer, for instance, had connections in Britain which were very valuable to us, connections that dated from the years 1933-1935. During that time Bonhoeffer had been pastor of the German Protestant congregations in Britain, and had become friendly with the Lord Bishop of Chichester, George Bell. During a meeting with Bell in Stockholm, in 1942, Bonhoeffer told Bell about our plans for a coup d'état. The Lord Bishop subsequently tried to interest the British Foreign Office in the plans but received a negative answer from Anthony Eden.

Dohnanyi and Josef Mueller, an Abwehr man, were accused of having contacted the enemy through the Vatican in order to explore the possibilities for a peace. Because of this accusation, Dohnanyi's office was searched. During the search, someone noticed that Dohnanyi tried to push a folder in Oster's direction. The folder was confiscated and was found to contain Bonhoeffer's name; as a result Bonhoeffer was drawn into the proceedings.

The Bonhoeffer-Dohnanyi investigation was conducted with considerable tenacity. Canaris tried in every way to torpedo the chief investigator, for Judge-Advocate General Sack had indicated that the man could be transferred only if he were discredited in some way, and Canaris found the way. The chief investigator had once said that the members of the Division "Brandenburg" were quitters. This division was under the general command of Canaris, who repeated the derogatory remark to the commander of the division, and suggested that the commander teach the investigator a lesson. The commander, enraged, did just that: He went to see the chief investigator and punched him in the nose. As a result the latter was transferred, and the entire matter subsided, to be dug out again only after the events of July 20, 1944.

Although the Bonhoeffer-Dohnanyi investigation did not get far at that time, it had undermined the position of General Oster. Canaris could no longer hold him. He was transferred to the so-called "leadership reserve" and removed from active service. This meant that we had lost our "general manager" and now had to look for a suitable successor to Oster. The man we found was Colonel Count Claus Schenk von Stauffenberg, whose military position at the time was Chief of Staff of the Allgemeine Heeresamt, the General Army Office, headed by General Olbricht. From a purely military point of view, Stauffenberg's was a much more important position than Oster's. While Oster had the advantage of many years of political experience and the authority that comes with age, he had become somewhat removed from the mainstream of purely military events. Stauffenberg, on the other hand, was a born general staff officer with outstanding talents in the tactical and operative field.

Born in 1907, Stauffenberg had joined the "Bamberger Reiter," a famous cavalry regiment. The Stauffenbergs were an old Swabian family, deeply rooted in Catholicism. Count Claus von Stauffenberg's career in the army had been exemplary. Transferred early to the General Staff, he had excelled in all matters of organization. For this reason he worked mainly within the organization department of the OKH, the Army High Command, during the early years of the war. Later Stauffenberg was transferred to the Afrika Corps in North Africa, where he lost an eye, his right hand, and two fingers of his left hand. Because of these injuries, he was transferred back to the General

Staff. His experience and great ability got him a position in the General Army Office, where he had access to inside information on all the military and political operations of the German army. He also was able to exercise a considerable influence on the formation of the Army Reserve.

Tresckow and Stauffenberg first became acquainted in the summer of 1941. At that time, Stauffenberg belonged to the Organization Department of the OKH, and visited the headquarters of the Army Group Center in Borrisov. We had the impression then that he was a gifted General Staff officer. He indicated to us that he was not a Nazi, and indeed saw a danger in Hitler and Nazism. But we did not realize at the time that Stauffenberg was a man whose name would rank high among those who fought against Hitler. We therefore were much impressed when Olbricht, whom we asked in the summer of 1943 to suggest a likely candidate to succeed Oster, named Stauffenberg and arranged to have us meet with him.

Stauffenberg was a far cry from the average German career officer: To appreciate this, one must understand that military one-sidedness was, in a way, the strong point of the German officer. Immersed in the military matters which were his work and his life, the German officer was probably, on a purely professional basis, superior to many of his foreign colleagues. This strength, however, was also his weakness, for it rendered him incapable of judging anything but military matters. Tresckow, of course, was in a class by himself, not only because he had had a successful civilian career, but also because of his broad outlook and his knowledge of foreign countries.

These were advantages Stauffenberg did not have. But he had something else that set him apart from his fellow officers. From an early age, he had been interested in matters of the mind and spirit, in poetry and literature, an inclination which brought him into contact with the poet Stefan George, who soon realized the young officer's spiritual qualities and drew him closer into his circle. Stauffenberg was strongly influenced by Stefan George's writings. One of his pleasures was to recite George's famous poem "The Antichrist," the last three verses of which seemed to him especially descriptive of Hitler and his rule:

The Lord of all Vermin enlarges his realm;
No treasure he lacks; no luck ever fails.
And down with the rest of the rebels!

You cheer and delight in the devilish hoax,
You squander the rest of the earlier strength
And feel not the need till the end comes.

Then you hang out your tongues o'er the emptying trough,
Stray like cattle confused through the burning corral . . .
*And fearfully then sounds the trumpet.**

Thus Stauffenberg's objection to Hitler was fundamentally a spiritual one and in no way based on a fear of impending German military defeat or any other materialistic considerations. Moral conviction and the acknowledgment of Christian truths turned Stauffenberg into an uncompromising fighter against the German dictator.

A few meetings with Stauffenberg were sufficient to let us realize that we had found in him a worthy successor to Oster. His calm courage, his circumspection, clarity of mind, tenacity and persistence, as well as his professional

---

* This poem was translated by Hilda Simon especially for this edition.

CLAUS SCHENK
COUNT VON STAUFFENBERG

1 9 0 7 — 1 9 4 4

The brilliant, dashing, handsome young staff officer became the resistance movement's "general manager" in 1943. Convinced that Hitler was "evil incarnate" and had to be removed, he decided to undertake the assassination himself after other attempts had failed. He was executed by a firing squad on the evening of July 20, 1944.

knowledge and ability made him a natural "general manager" of the resistance.

While detailed plans for the coup d'état were being drawn up during 1943, one thing was clear to all of us: To get firm control of Berlin, the political, military, and economic nerve center of Germany, the most careful and elaborate military preparations were necessary. This became Stauffenberg's main task. Tresckow supplied him with a top-notch aide: Major Ulrich von Oertzen, a staff officer of the Army Group Center. Oertzen was talented and experienced in the field of military organization. Stauffenberg and Oertzen, under the general direction of Tresckow, were the men who, in long days and nights of intensive work, formulated the orders which, on the day of the coup d'état, were to make possible a take-over of Berlin by the forces of the resistance.

In view of the flood of vilification directed against the men of the resistance by the Nazis after the abortive coup of July 20, 1944, it is interesting to look at the appraisals made by the General Staff during the war of men such as Stauffenberg, Tresckow, and Oertzen *before* it was known that they were members of the opposition. Stauffenberg, for instance, was considered a "born leader, capable of handling any situation; courageous; sense of humor; far above average." There were similar favorable opinions of Oertzen and Tresckow. These, then, were the men who were later described as cowardly, traitorous wretches—when it became apparent which side they had chosen.

One of the first problems was to find out the exact number of army units stationed in and around Berlin and then to determine the comparative strength of the SS forces with which they would have to deal. This was made more difficult by the constant fluctuation in the numerical strength of the Army Reserve which, at irregular intervals, had to send replacements to the front or form whole new divisions.

Those army units stationed in the capital itself, as well as the military training schools in the vicinity of Berlin, had been earmarked for the take-over in Berlin. Only relatively weak forces were stationed in the city. They consisted of the Guard Battalion (Wachbataillon), the Army Fire Brigade Training School, the Army Ordnance School, and the territorial battalions 311 and 320. The strongest of these units was the Guard Battalion, whose name was misleading, for it had, in terms of arms and men, practically the strength of a regiment.

Outside the city limits we could count upon some units that were in training, as well as the complements in the Infantry Training School of Doeberitz, the Cavalry Training School at Krampnitz, the Tank Training School at Wuensdorf, and the Artillery Training School at Jueterbog. The question of how well these troops were armed, especially for street fighting, had to be carefully studied.

One of the most important problems was a correct appraisal of the officer corps for the delegation of command posts. We had to take into account the attitude of local commanders and influence them without making them confidants. We also had to reckon with the fact that the German officer could not do anything he wanted to with his troops. National Socialism had so thoroughly permeated all facets of German life, including the army, that some way had to be found to convincingly explain our acts to the troops.

A great difficulty, and one about which we could do

very little, was the activity of the Personnel Office, which, because it could transfer important people from one position to another without warning, could easily destroy our best-laid plans. That was shown on July 20, 1944, when the command of the Guard Battalion was found to be in the hands of a man who, in that fateful hour, chose to side with Hitler.

Finally, it was no simple matter to get precise information about the numerical strength of the SS units stationed in and around Berlin, as well as the kind and amount of arms and ammunition they had at their disposal. The government district was important, as was the radio station, the press quarter, the electricity, gas, and water works, and the railroad junctions; superiority in arms and men could easily become the deciding factor in the coup. Our disadvantage was increased by the short distance between the above-named vital areas and the SS barracks. On the other hand the army units we wanted to employ had to cover a long distance before they could reach the key districts. Even with the best organization there was no way of avoiding the fact that the first twenty-four hours would remain a period of risk. After that time, strong army units could be brought into Berlin, so that the original numerical superiority of the SS could be quickly overcome and reversed.

The important thing, then, was to weather that first twenty-four-hour "danger period" and to concentrate on occupying the government district and the radio station. Later, the SS could be destroyed, and resistance forces could proceed to take over all of Berlin.

Last among our considerations were the considerable complements of Blue Police in Berlin. This question did not pose too grave a problem, however, as the President of Police in Berlin, Count Wolf Heinrich von Helldorf, had turned from an early Nazi into an anti-Nazi. We could even expect that at least a part of the Blue Police would fight on our side, especially because Helldorf was supported by SS Obergruppenfuehrer Nebe, who had returned to his post as head of the Criminal Police in Berlin.

In the fall of 1943 all the necessary preparations had been completed, and we were looking forward impatiently to the moment we could translate our plans into action.

CHAPTER EIGHTEEN

Plans for the

"Day After"

In looking beyond the coup d'état itself, it was clear to all of us within the resistance that swift and decisive action against the top Nazi leaders and the SS would have to be taken immediately following the overthrow of the Hitler regime. It was imperative that we render powerless, within the shortest possible time, those representing the might of the Nazi Party, thereby eliminating with one stroke any danger of the Nazi forces regrouping and endangering the interim government which was to take over after Hitler's death. Our plans were complicated by the facts that Germany was at war and that Soviet troops were close to the Eastern borders. We knew, from our clandestine contacts with non-German countries, that we could expect little change in attitude by those at war with Germany, even in the event of an overthrow of the Nazi regime and the creation of an anti-Hitler government. We should in fact have to fend off the external adversary with one hand while trying to eliminate the internal enemy with the other—hardly an easy or enviable task.

As I mentioned before, our most immediate worry centered on the crucial twenty-four hours after Hitler's assassination. The preparations worked out by Stauffenberg and Oertzen went under the guise of measures to be taken in the event of internal unrest. The commander of the Home Army was to give the code word *Walkuere* (Valkyrie) to all military district commanders, which was the signal for them to alert certain army units and to have them occupy all public buildings. At the same time, these military commanders would take over all executive power from the civilian authorities.

Of prime importance to us was the reaction of Military District III, which included Berlin and the province of Brandenburg, for its commander was a Nazi. But we did succeed in coming to an understanding with his chief of staff, General Rost. The commandant of Berlin, General Paul von Hase, had for some time been firmly on our side.

Completing the plans for "Valkyrie" down to the last detail called for a tremendous amount of work. Tresckow, Stauffenberg, and Oertzen translated all these measures into precise military orders, which were taken down by two female members of our conspiracy, Margarete von Oven, who had for many years been secretary to the late General von Hammerstein, and Erika von Tresckow, General von Tresckow's wife.

The Valkyrie orders were signed with the name of General Fromm, Commander-in-Chief of the Home Army. Although Fromm did not belong to our circle, we had to use his name to avoid arousing suspicion among the troops.

The orders began with the statement that the SS had attempted a putsch, which it had been necessary to suppress. The Reserve Army units were ordered to disarm the SS in the barracks of Lichterfelde, a suburb of Berlin. We hoped in this way to eliminate the advantage of the

SS over the regular army troops, which were not stationed in Berlin itself, and thus alter the time element by several hours in our favor.

The second order, which was to complete the coup and in which we could more or less show our true colors, was signed by Field Marshal von Witzleben, who was to be Commander-in-Chief of the Armed Forces. It was a great moment for us when Tresckow submitted this order to Witzleben, who, after listening to Tresckow's brief explanation of the details, signed the order without a moment's hesitation. Incidentally, this was done in the summer of 1943, a full year before the coup actually took place.

The order signed by Witzleben was to be the instrument through which we hoped to eliminate the SS as a potential threat to our coup in the first crucial hours after Hitler's assassination. Therefore, it had to sound plausible to the army troops whom we planned to use against the Blackshirts. The order read as follows:

1. The Fuehrer Adolf Hitler is dead. An unscrupulous clique of Party leaders, who have no feeling for the fighting front, have tried to exploit the situation and to stab the struggling army in the back. In this hour of supreme danger the government of the Reich, in an effort to uphold law and order, has proclaimed a state of military emergency. At the same time, the Supreme Command of the Armed Forces has been entrusted to me.

Accordingly, I issue the following orders:

1) I herewith transfer the Executive Power, with the right of delegation, to the territorial commanders—the commanders of the Army Reserve in the Home territory, and the Chief Commanders in the occupied territories.

2) The following persons and authorities are subordinated to the holders of the Executive Power:

   a) all government boards and commissions in the respective districts; all units of the armed Forces including the Waffen-SS, the Reichs Labor Service, and the Organization Todt;

   b) all public authorities of the Reich, and the entire police force—regular, security, and administrative police;

   c) all officials of the various branches of the NSDAP and its associated organizations;

   d) the traffic and transportation systems and the public utilities.

3) The entire Waffen-SS is to be immediately incorporated into the army.

4) The holders of the Executive Power are responsible for maintaining law and order and public security. Any resistance to the military executive power is to be relentlessly suppressed.

5) In this hour of supreme peril to our country, unity within the Armed Forces and the maintenance of discipline are of paramount importance. I therefore expressly proclaim it the duty of all commanders of the Army, the Navy, and the Air Force to support with all possible means the holders of the executive power in the fulfillment of their difficult task, and to ensure compliance with their orders by all subordinate authorities. The German soldier is faced with an historic task and it will depend on his energy and attitude whether Germany is to be saved.

THE COMMANDER-IN-CHIEF
von Witzleben, FIELD MARSHAL.

This order would have made all holders of power in the Reich subordinate to the armed forces. In a subsequent order, we planned to make use of this fact. The text of this one read as follows:

By virtue of the authority delegated to me by the Commander-in-Chief of the Army, Navy, and Air Force, I invest the Commanding General of each Military District with executive power. The following measures are to be taken immediately:

a) Occupation of all communications systems; radio amplifiers, and main transmitting stations; of all gas works, power stations, and waterworks.

b) The following are to be relieved of office, and to be placed in top security confinement: all Gauleiters, Reichs-Governors, Cabinet members, Provincial Presidents, Police Presidents, all high-ranking SS and Police Chiefs, all chief officials of the Gestapo, the SS Administration Centers, and the Propaganda Bureaus, as well as the District Leaders. Exceptions only by my express command.

c) The concentration camps are to be seized without delay, all guards disarmed and confined to their barracks. The political prisoners are to be informed that, pending their liberation, they are to abstain from all demonstrations and independent action.

d) If compliance with the orders by leaders of the Waffen-SS appears doubtful, or if they seem to be unqualified, they are to be taken into protective custody and replaced by officers of the army.

e) To deal with all political questions arising in connection with the State of Emergency, I shall attach a political delegate to each Military District.

f) In all its dealings the holders of the Executive Power must tolerate no arbitrary or revengeful acts. The population must be made aware of the gulf between the new regime and the ruthless methods of the former rulers.

> (signed) *Fromm*, COLONEL GENERAL,
> *Count Stauffenberg.*

All these orders were placed in safekeeping with General Olbricht.

During the summer months of 1943, Tresckow had not confined his work to the staff plans for the proposed takeover of Berlin. He was also in constant communication with Beck and Goerdeler on the political aims of the coup, which were becoming more and more urgent. The resistance had been founded, and for many years nourished and kept alive, by civilians. The cooperation of the military had occurred at a later stage. It was almost inevitable that, during the war, the influence of the military would increase, but this did not mean that the military group had taken over the movement, or intended to do so. The civilians, conscious of their priority, did not want to surrender control, and the military members, because of their experience, did not wish to have a military regime. Men like Beck, Witzleben, Tresckow, and Stauffenberg were absolutely convinced that, while the Army was the only instrument for wresting power from the Nazis, it would be a mistake to let it attain political power of its own, and this was therefore never part of our plan.

We all realized, of course, that an armed conflict with the SS could not be avoided, and that only the Army was then in a position to cope with it. For this reason, the execution of this stage of the coup would have to remain

257

exclusively in the hands of the military. But even after this struggle had been won, a period of unrest and instability throughout Germany could be expected. Here again, the Army was the logical instrument to cope with such an emergency. We planned, therefore, to set up a military dictatorship for a short period immediately following Hitler's removal. All the leading men of the resistance, both of the military and civilian groups, agreed to limit military rule to the shortest possible time—no longer than three months at the outside—after which the Army would recede into the background, and civilian authorities would take over control of the state.

One question has often been asked: If the coup d'état had been successful, how would the resistance have handled the problem of dealing with the SS, Gestapo, and the prominent Nazi leaders guilty of the crimes committed against the victims of the Third Reich? The way this question is asked, especially by non-Germans, often implies a doubt that a German regime—even an anti-Nazi German regime—would have moved energetically against the malefactors of the Third Reich. Even today, when so many facts about the German opposition's persistent struggle against Hitler have come to light, many people seem to doubt that we could have been trusted to punish the perpetrators of Nazi crimes as sternly as they were punished after the war by the victorious Allies.

In view of this stubborn belief, it is necessary to explain that not only had we made plans for dealing with the Nazi leaders, but that, quite contrary to a widely-held but erroneous idea, we would have been much more efficient than the Allies. There were two reasons why we would have done a better job in eliminating those who had been responsible for instilling the poison of National Socialism in the German people, and for committing the crimes in the occupied countries and concentration camps. First, we knew exactly who the guilty ones were: we did not have to search them out, we would have made no mistakes, and they could not hide from us. Secondly, our action would have been swift: there would have been no trials against Nazi officials years after their crimes had been committed, trials such as we are still witnessing today, twenty years after the war, when the passage of time has dulled the meaning and confused the issues.

Our plans for dealing with the top Party officials, SS, and Gestapo leaders had been worked out by leading jurists in the resistance, primarily by Dr. Carl Sack, Judge-Advocate General of the Army, a distinguished member of our group. The jurists whose task it was to hammer out the legal details of our planned action against leading Nazis were especially anxious to avoid the stigma of introducing retroactive laws, that most odious of all the many unlawful measures of the Nazi regime. The resistance therefore looked for an *existing* law under which the Nazi leaders could be prosecuted, and found one: the law making it a capital offense to "impair the defensive capacity of the German people."

In accordance with this plan, all the top leaders of the Nazi Party from the Kreisleiter (District Leader) upward, as well as all Gestapo and SS chiefs, would have been indicted on charges of impairing the defensive capacity of the German people. The trials would have taken place before special military courts; the death sentence would have been passed and executed within twenty-four hours after the defendants had been found guilty. The Nazi

259

officials could not have complained of being judged un-fairly by laws that had not previously existed—a charge which could legally be leveled at the Nuremberg trials. We, on the other hand, could have made out a convincing case showing how the Nazi leadership, by its insane pol-icies and criminal acts, had roused the world to take up arms against Germany, and thus had not only impaired, but had virtually destroyed the "defensive capacity" of the German nation and come dangerously close to de-stroying Germany herself.

Using these tactics, it would have taken us only a short time to get rid of the entire Nazi hierarchy, on clear and defensible grounds, both legally and morally. There would have been no question of illegal "retroactive" laws which later could be used to reproach the new regime. The Gestapo and SS individuals directly involved in crimes against the lives of concentration camp inmates and other victims of Nazi terror were to be indicted on charges of murder, rather than high-sounding charges of "crimes against humanity." Murder is sufficiently serious.

By necessity these measures against the Nazi leadership would have had to be both harsh and swift. We had no intention of risking all, only to leave intact part of the cancer that had all but destroyed Germany and brought so much pain and suffering to people throughout Europe. Any chance of Nazism rallying and perhaps winning an-other day had to be eliminated.

Our way of dealing with the top leaders of the Third Reich would therefore have differed markedly from the way the victorious Allies handled the problem after the war. It was my opinion then, as it is today, that the trials at the International Tribunal would one day be considered a great political mistake, at least by the Western Powers. I also think that this view has gained considerable acceptance in the past years among jurists and historians of both the United States and Great Britain. It certainly is getting increasingly difficult to come by the records of the Nuremberg trials.

My conviction in this case stems not from any hindsight. On the contrary, I was given the opportunity to express my opinion even before the trials began through my acquaintance with the late Major General William J. ("Wild Bill") Donovan, formerly Director of the Office of Strategic Services (OSS). During the war, one of the many tasks of Donovan's office was to keep up clandestine contact with the German resistance. After the war, I became acquainted with him and we met a number of times.

At Nuremberg, Donovan was appointed a deputy prosecutor under the Chief Prosecutor, Supreme Court Justice Robert A. Jackson. As the preparations for the trials progressed, Donovan began to have doubts about them. Knowing that I was a jurist, and familiar with my role within the anti-Hitler resistance, he wanted to get my professional opinion and asked me to come to Nuremberg to look at the draft of the indictment against the accused Nazi leaders. I accepted that invitation, and spent some time carefully studying the lengthy draft Donovan gave me. After going over the document word by word, I set down my professional opinion rejecting the entire indictment on four counts:

1) It used retroactive laws—precisely the kind of method we had come to consider one of Hitler's most repugnant and unlawful acts. No law against so-called "crimes

against humanity" had been in existence at the time the defendants had committed the offenses they stood accused of at Nuremberg.*

2) The indictment was based upon Anglo-Saxon trial law, with which the defendants were completely unfamiliar, and which had no validity in German legal custom.

3) The accusations dealt exclusively with offenses against *Allied* citizens. Justice, however, demands that no such discrimination be made—all human beings, no matter of what nationality, who had been victims of the Nazis should have been included.

4) Contrary to every basic juristic rule, the accusers in this case were also the judges. An old proverb says: "Only God can help him whose accuser is also his judge."

After reading my memorandum on the draft Donovan was more than ever convinced that he had been right in questioning the wisdom of the trials. He began to search for ways of shortening and limiting the proceedings as much as possible. He finally hit upon the idea of having Goering assume all responsibility for what had happened in the Third Reich, so that Goering alone would be indicted, as the representative of Hitler. In this way, the trial would have been over in the shortest possible time, with the conviction, sentencing, and execution of Goering by the Allies. The rest of the defendants could then have been turned over to a duly appointed German court, consisting of German jurists with anti-Nazi records. If all trials of Nazi crimes had been handled in this way, many high SS officials would have been prevented from turning "state's evidence," a legal practice unknown and unac-

---

* The same argument, I found out later, was advanced by the late Senator Robert Taft as one reason for his rejecting the Nuremburg trials.

ceptable to German law, which resulted in long delays and in some cases failure to bring to justice a number of the main perpetrators of Nazi crimes.

When Donovan asked me what I thought about the chances of persuading Goering to assume all responsibility for the policies of the Third Reich and plead guilty, I advised him to wear full uniform with all the medals he had ever received for that visit to Goering in prison. I also urged him to appeal to whatever was left of Goering's sense of officer's honor, making it plain at the same time that his life was forfeit in any case.

I was not mistaken in my appraisal of Goering. After returning from his visit in Goering's cell, Donovan informed me that the latter was willing to cooperate. The Allies, however, most certainly were not, as Donovan soon found out when he submitted his plan to Chief Prosecutor Jackson. The idea of seeing their carefully prepared, mammoth trial going down the drain did not at all appeal to the Allied officials, who were looking forward to months in the spotlight while the case against the accused Nazis was being presented to the world.

When I next saw Donovan, he was shaking with anger and frustration after what had evidently been a stormy session with Chief Prosecutor Jackson. He told me that he was resigning from his post as deputy prosecutor because he did not wish to be in any way connected with the coming trials; he had become thoroughly convinced that they were legally and politically unsound. He also suggested that it would be wise for me to get out of Nuremberg at once—advice I lost no time in following.

Years later in New York, Donovan told me that he was more than ever convinced that history would justify his

263

decision to walk out on the Nuremberg trials.

In retrospect, and with the objectivity gained by the passage of time, there can be no doubt that, if the coup d'état against Hitler succeeded, it would have been followed by swift, clear-cut action on the part of the new regime against those responsible for the crimes and misdeeds committed during the Nazi rule. Moreover, ludicrous situations such as that resulting from the Katyn case could never have happened.

In the forest of Katyn, my friends and I personally inspected the mass grave of thousands of Polish officers who had been shot in the back of the neck. There was never the slightest doubt that these officers belonged to cavalry regiments which had been employed not against Germans but against Soviet troops. Many of these officers still had notes in their pockets which made it plain that they had been captured by the Soviet Army and that they believed they were about to be released and sent to their homes.

I believe the Katyn case, where the murderers were also serving as prosecutors and as would-be judges, is unique in legal history. The International Tribunal passed over this particular accusation, and with good reason. The mere fact, however, that the prosecution was allowed before the world to blame the Germans for this atrocity will always remain a shameful blot on the record of international law.

Even from the distance of two decades, I still believe that the German resistance had basically sound, just, and feasible plans for preparing a strong foundation on which a post-Hitler Germany could have been built. What the future would have brought must, of course, remain forever in the realm of speculation.

CHAPTER NINETEEN

New Frustrations

In the course of 1943, the necessary over-all preparations for a coup d'état had been completed. These included agreement on political aims and general staff plans for a takeover of Berlin by resistance forces. In addition, Field Marshal von Kluge, an active commander of an Army Group, had been won over to our cause. In the West, inclusion in our plans of Generals von Stuelpnagel and von Falkenhausen gave us an additional margin of safety. Now everything depended upon the initial spark which was to signal the overthrow of the Nazi regime.

Judging from our experiences, this spark could be supplied only by another—this time successful—attempt on Hitler's life. For such an undertaking two things were needed: an assassin and a bomb. The necessary explosives were furnished by Colonel Baron Wessel von Freytagh-Loringhoven, who was in the Abwehr under Admiral Canaris. Although there was some difficulty in obtaining the British explosives we wanted, he managed to get them for us.

This first lot of explosives caused a mishap which could have meant trouble for us. It had to be shipped to East Prussia, where Hitler's Headquarters were located. General Stieff agreed to arrange its transport and delegated the job to two of his aides, Major Kuhn and First Lieutenant von Hagen, who took the explosives to East Prussia and hid them under a wooden tower within the area of the Army High Command Headquarters.

For some unexplained reason, the explosives blew up. This unfortunate incident naturally attracted the attention of various security officials, and an investigation followed. However, Colonel Werner Schrader, who headed the investigation, was our confederate and managed very cleverly to let the entire thing peter out.

In an attempt to replace the explosives, Stieff sent Hagen to the Army Group Center. There, Oertzen directed him to the staff of a Pioneer unit, where he received some German explosives, which he took back to the OKH. As before, however, this type of explosive proved unsuitable for us because there was no way of setting it off without causing a slight hissing noise, which we could not risk. Once more we had to turn for help to Freytagh-Loringhoven, who managed to get us more of the British explosive. This second lot, by the way, was used some months later for the assassination attempt of July 20, 1944.

For the assassination itself, we first had to get our man into Headquarters. The choice was automatically limited to a relatively small group of people, for the great majority of the conspirators did not have access to Headquarters and could have been introduced there only with considerable difficulty by using some pretext.

To explore the possibilities of an attempt on Hitler's life

in his Headquarters, I flew there twice during the summer of 1943 and discussed all pertinent matters with Colonel Dietrich von Bose, who knew every detail of the location.

Through Bose, I obtained an exact schedule of Hitler's daily routine. At ten o'clock in the morning, he was awakened by his valet; his breakfast was sent up to his room by dumbwaiter and excerpts from foreign newspapers, selected by Ribbentrop, were submitted to him. Because Hitler knew no foreign language, these excerpts had to be translated into German. Any reading matter submitted to him had to be either written or printed large enough for him to read without glasses, or typed on a special typewriter with unusually large characters, for Hitler was short-sighted. Nobody was to deduce from the way he held a document that he had trouble with his eyes. Only while looking at a map did he use glasses or a magnifying glass, but it was strictly forbidden to photograph him with his glasses on, for Hitler maintained that a bespectacled dictator would lose authority.

At eleven o'clock, Hitler received his Chief Adjutant, who reported mainly on matters of personnel. At noon, the conference on the military situation began, during which the Chiefs of Staffs of the Armed Forces had to report on the situation at the various fronts. Other officers were called in whenever necessary, but Hitler personally decided all military questions.

At two o'clock in the afternoon lunch was served. This meal usually dragged on until four because of the monologues with which Hitler entertained the company. Then followed Hitler's afternoon nap, from which he rose only at six or seven o'clock to give official audiences. Supper began at eight and lasted until ten, when Hitler gathered

267

around him a group of people whom he himself selected and engaged in conversations—or rather monologues, for he did most of the talking. During these after-dinner sessions he expounded his ideas of the "blessings" he had in mind for the peoples of the world. His two female secretaries attended these nighttime meetings; other women close to him stayed at his mountain retreat, Obersalzberg, in Berchtesgaden, and were not present at Headquarters.

At four o'clock in the morning, Hitler finally went to bed. It was strictly forbidden to disturb him during his periods of rest, and his daily schedule was altered only for the most urgent reasons.

Opportunities for an attempt on Hitler's life were therefore sharply limited. Only someone who could manage to get himself invited to one of the nighttime gatherings or who had access to the military conferences in the morning had any chance at all. Furthermore, to try to shoot Hitler with a pistol was an almost hopeless undertaking, since several SS men were always in the room with him or in the immediate vicinity. Anyone who has ever handled guns will appreciate the difficulty of killing a man in such circumstances with only one shot. If the shooting is done in anger or some other strong emotion, there are more chances for its success than when it is a coldly premeditated deed. Even a hunter is gripped with feverish anticipation when the long-awaited object of his hunt finally appears within his sights. How much greater then is the turmoil in one's heart and mind when, after overcoming a multitude of obstacles, and with the knowledge that the odds are unfavorable, one pulls out a gun at the risk of one's life, fully aware that success or failure of the deed will decide the fate of millions!

A check on who would be willing to attempt an assassination in this way showed that even men whose courage was beyond doubt and who had proven it innumerable times in combat frankly admitted that they did not feel equal to the job. Young Colonel Baron Georg von Boeselager, one of our confederates who had received the Knight's Cross with Oak Cluster and Swords because of his exceptional courage in combat, rejected the idea of killing Hitler this way. Instead, he offered to storm Hitler's headquarters with his regiment, whose members were unconditionally loyal to him. But Boeselager's regiment was stationed in Russia, and all attempts to have it transferred to East Prussia met with failure.

And so we were forced to return to the idea of killing Hitler with a bomb. One of our confederates, First Lieutenant Werner von Haeften, considered attempting the assassination, but because of his Christian beliefs felt that he could not assume the responsibility for killing other people around Hitler, always a likely possibility in a bombing attempt. A young captain, Axel von dem Busche, overcame such scruples after an inner struggle; just as he had, he was gravely wounded at the front, removing him from the list of candidates.

Finally, General Stieff and his two aides, Major Kuhn and First Lieutenant von Hagen, offered to undertake the assassination. But after trying to solve the problem of getting the bomb into the room where Hitler's conferences took place, Stieff concluded it to be too difficult. He then came up with another plan, involving a new type of uniform which was being considered. The plan was to have the uniform demonstrated by an officer who was willing to sacrifice his life. During Hitler's inspection, the officer was to set off the bomb hidden under the uniform, throw his arms around Hitler, and blow up both himself and the dictator.

The demonstration of the uniform was scheduled several times in the fall of 1943, but each time Hitler cancelled the visit, almost as if he had some premonition of what was awaiting him. Another demonstration was scheduled for a day in November; this time Hitler's visit seemed assured. The day before, an Allied air raid caused so much destruction that the demonstration had to be called off.

Finally, Tresckow declared himself willing to make another attempt. That, of course, would have necessitated his meeting Hitler under circumstances that would not arouse suspicion. Tresckow tried two different ways of bringing about such a meeting. First, he tried to persuade General Schmundt, Hitler's Chief Adjutant, to establish a new office which would evaluate the psychological and political data collected from combat units and bring this material directly to the attention of Hitler himself. Although Schmundt found the plan interesting, he did not act upon it, either because he had become suspicious or because he thought it impractical.

Then another plan seemed to offer itself. General Heusinger, at that time Chief of the Operation Department of the OKH, was planning to take a leave of absence. The question of a deputy and possible successor for him arose. Many attempts were made to secure this position for Tresckow. Finally, Tresckow himself approached Heusinger in the winter of 1943, when we were quartered in a small village in the Pripet Marshes. He wrote to Heusinger, who was a non-Nazi, begging Heusinger to appoint him his deputy for the duration of his leave. At the same time, Tresckow also wrote a letter to Stieff, to whom he explained the mechanics of the bomb. This was a necessary precaution because both bomb and fuse were in Stieff's safekeeping at the time.

I flew to Minsk with these two letters, where I caught the connecting plane to Headquarters. I went to Heusinger first and gave him Tresckow's letter, which he read in my presence. Without any change in expression, he said: "An answer will not be necessary." I had the impression that Heusinger had seen through Tresckow's plan, and wanted to express his refusal by not answering at all.

From Heusinger I went to see General Stieff, who received me with his usual nonchalance and gaiety. He opened the letter, read it quickly, chuckled approvingly, and then tore it into small pieces. He tried to throw the pieces into the wastepaper basket, I stayed his hand and asked him to let me get rid of them. He immediately agreed, and thanked me for my good advice.

It should be noted that nobody in the winter of 1943 considered Stauffenberg for the task of killing Hitler. We felt him to be irreplaceable in Berlin on the day of decision. Furthermore the fact that he had only one eye, one arm, and only three fingers left on his other hand would have made us feel that he was not cut out for the role of Hitler's assassin.

Finally we thought of still another possibility. A new attempt was to be made to persuade Hitler to visit the headquarters of the Army Group Center. During that visit several officers, including myself, were to try and kill Hitler with our pistols in what could be described as a "collective assassination." Even though we did not think that all the shots would find their target, half of them, we were sure, would be enough to finish him off. The collective action was designed to help ease the burden felt by any person with a conscience who is considering such a deed. Preparations for this attempt were made several times, first at Smolensk, then at Orsha, and later on at Minsk. However, nothing and no one could persuade Hitler to repeat his earlier visit to the Army Group Center.

While these plans were under consideration, Field Marshal von Kluge had a serious automobile accident on the road from Orsha to Minsk, and was incapacitated for several months. This removed an important link in our chain of cooperation between the field and home armies.

Kluge's successor as Commander-in-Chief of the Army Group Center was Field Marshal Busch, who had made a name for himself as a brave soldier in World War I. However, he had neither the ability to command an Army Group nor any political judgment. Busch is best characterized by a story he told us about his actions as a member of the "People's Court." Because he had no knowledge whatever of the law and juridical matters, he said, he had decided to sentence all the defendants to death. This he did, even in those cases where the learned judges had been of a different opinion. After Busch told this story, we talked about an outrageous order from Hitler, according to which all enemy parachutists were to be shot regardless of whether they wore civilian clothes or uniform. Busch defended that order, even though he did not dispute the fact that it was a breach of international law.

As though we did not have enough troubles, General Beck became ill and had to undergo a serious operation. At about that time, I was in Berlin to discuss the situation with Stauffenberg and Olbricht. During the meeting, Olbricht told us that he had more bad news for us, worse news, in fact, than at any time during the war. "A short time ago," Olbricht continued, "Admiral Carnaris came to see me and told me of a conversation with Himmler. Himmler said quite bluntly that he knew very well that influential circles within the Army were hatching plans for a rebellion. He said, however, that he would not let it get that far, but would put a stop to it in time. He had waited only to find out who was behind it. Now he knew, and would deal with people such as Beck and Goerdeler."

Olbricht was very much depressed by Canaris' story. He believed that Himmler was poised to strike. There was nothing for us to do, however, but to keep our nerve and hope for the best, knowing that, as in all things in life, luck would have to play an important part in our undertaking. Much later, it became clear that the Gestapo, although it had vague suspicions, never had any real knowledge of our conspiracy.

In the meantime, the military fortunes of the Third Reich had sunk to a new low, so low that Beck believed we would not be able to avoid that most unfortunate of all Allied demands, the unconditional surrender. The situation on the Eastern Front was becoming daily more untenable, and for this Hitler himself was largely responsible. After dismissing Brauchitsch in December, 1942, he had assumed military command and, to keep tight control, had issued two orders whose effect proved disastrous.

The first of these orders cancelled a system originally devised by Frederick the Great. Under this system, a superior officer indicates in his military orders only the goal of a particular operation; the means by which this goal is to be achieved are left for the local commander to decide.

Hitler eliminated this element of freedom, and directed that all military orders should designate the tactical means as well as the goal. Hitler also ruled that, on the entire Eastern Front, no officer was to give an order to retreat unless Hitler had personally endorsed it.

These two orders restricted the freedom of action by military leaders to such an extent that all military tactics came to an end and encirclement by the enemy, it seemed, had come to be considered the apex of military wisdom by Hitler. He stubbornly refused to consider the repeated proposals by his Field Marshals that the overextended Eastern Front should be brought back and an "East Wall" built farther to the west. Hitler's orders to hold existing positions at all costs prepared the way for the great successes of the Russian army.

In view of the German military situation, Germany's allies began to waver. Around the turn of 1943-44, I heard from Stauffenberg and Olbricht that Hitler had made special plans for Hungary. He was going to confront Hungary with certain demands, and if these demands were rejected all Hungarian units in Russia were to be disarmed; German troops would then occupy Hungary and proclaim a new regime. We considered informing the Hungarians of Hitler's plans, but we could not find a suitable partner for so delicate a discussion.

The Hungarian project was a prime example of Nazi propaganda at work. Long in advance of troubles with the Hungarian government, newspaper articles had been prepared, decrying the purported "betrayal" by the Horthy regime and calling for liberation—by German troops—of the "true" Hungary. Photographs showing the boundless

274

enthusiasm of the Hungarian population over the entry of German troops were all ready for use.

The Allied invasion—openly announced by Churchill—could be expected at any time after the beginning of 1944. We realized that our plans for a coup would have to materialize before the invasion, were they to have any immediate political import. However, one mishap after the other beset our efforts, making us so desperate for a chance to kill Hitler that we were ready to grasp at a straw. Thus, when one of our confederates, Colonel von Breitenbuch, declared himself willing to try to shoot Hitler, even those of us who saw scant chance for success in such an attempt encouraged him to go ahead. His plan involved getting Field Marshal Busch to take him along on a proposed visit to Hitler. Breitenbuch's plan succeeded up to a point: Busch took him along to Hitler's mountain residence in Berchtesgaden, and Breitenbuch even managed to get into the room where the conference took place. Once there, however, he could not even put his hand in his pocket to pull out his gun. Several tall SS men, who were always around when Hitler received anybody, watched all the people in the room, ready to throw themselves upon anyone who made the slightest suspicious movement.

And so it was disappointment all the way. All our plans to assassinate Hitler had been frustrated, and time was fast running out. To make things worse, Admiral Canaris was forced to retire in February, 1944. This was especially unfortunate because Canaris had access to much information which was valuable to us. Not the least of it was what he knew about the tapping of telephone lines by the Gestapo.

Spring 1944 thus saw us desperate for action and ready to take almost any chance for the long-overdue coup d'état.

CHAPTER TWENTY

July 20, 1944

On June 6, 1944, the Allied invasion in France began. A few days later, General Kurt Zeitzler, Chief of the German General Staff, summoned all the army commanders from the Eastern Front to Headquarters. On that occasion, Tresckow took me along to East Prussia, where we visited our friend and confederate, Count Heinrich von Lehndorff, on his estate at Steinort. Steinort was one of the oldest and most beautiful of East Prussian castles, and for many centuries had been owned by the Lehndorff family. Now, however, Hitler's Foreign Minister Joachim von Ribbentrop had more or less taken over, and had transformed part of the castle into his headquarters, so that he could always be near Hitler.

Because Ribbentrop felt the castle was not grand enough for him, he had it partially rebuilt, installing, among other things, a cinema on the first floor, where he watched a movie every night. He called Steinort his "field headquarters," but his way of life remained strictly on a peacetime level. Rare flowers and gourmet foods, so choice that even Germans with the most discriminating taste had not seen them in years, were flown in from Copenhagen and elsewhere, despite the fuel shortage.

Count Lehndorff had just returned from Berlin and a meeting with Stauffenberg, with instructions to ask Tresckow whether now, after the invasion, there was any point in continuing with our plans for a coup d'état, since a practical political effect no longer seemed likely. Tresckow's answer was explicit and to the point:

"The assassination must be attempted at all costs. Even if it should not succeed, an attempt to seize power in Berlin must be undertaken. What matters now is no longer the practical purpose of the coup, but to prove to the world and for the records of history that the men of the resistance movement dared to take the decisive step. Compared to this objective, nothing else is of consequence."

Tresckow asked Lehndorff to deliver this answer to Stauffenberg, adding that Stauffenberg should go to France and see General Speidel, Chief of Staff to Field Marshal Rommel, and suggest to Speidel that a gap be opened in the Western Front so that the Allied troops could break through. Otherwise, Tresckow warned, the Russians would soon break through in the East and overrun Germany.

Our visit to East Prussia was important for another reason besides seeing Lehndorff: It gave us a chance to learn the official opinion of the situation created by the Allied invasion. General Heusinger, Chief of the Operations Department, submitted a report on the military situation to the assembled Army Chiefs of the Eastern Front. He expounded the view of the OKW, which centered on the statements that the Supreme Command considered it possible to keep the British and American invasion forces confined to the peninsula of Cotentin and that there was no reason to fear a breakthrough into the plain beyond. This appraisal of the situation in the West was based upon the erroneous assumption that the Allied invasion had succeeded purely by accident. That assumption was made, in turn, as a result of the delayed reaction by the Supreme Command to the invasion. Tresckow, who had heard the details of that incident from General Schmundt, told me all about it.

It seems that the Germans were caught by surprise when the Allied invasion began on June 6; it had not been expected at that particular time. Rommel was in Germany, and had to be summoned back to France in a hurry. In the meantime, the news of the invasion was relayed to the OKW through the usual channels, but the officer in charge did not dare, in view of the early hour, to waken Colonel General Jodl, the Chief of Staff of the OKW. As a result, Jodl heard of the invasion only after some delay, and he, in turn, waited to inform Keitel. Both Keitel and Jodl felt themselves bound by the order never to disturb Hitler's sleep. Consequently, it was not until the military conference at noon that Hitler was informed of the invasion.

The fear of disturbing Hitler's rest was to have grave consequences. Stationed directly behind the Atlantic Wall was a Tank Corps whose special task was to attack a landing enemy. Hitler had reserved for himself personally the right to employ this Tank Corps; not even Rommel or Rundstedt could command the Corps. When Hitler finally gave the order to attack, it was already two o'clock in the afternoon, and priceless time has been lost. In the meantime, part of the Corps had been crippled by an American air attack. There could be no doubt that Hitler's uninterrupted sleep had *aided* the invasion, but the conclusion drawn by the Supreme Command was that it had *succeeded* only because of that accident. This was a mistake that led the German Command to underestimate the Allied action.

As the mouthpiece of official OKW opinion, Heusinger gave a rather foggy picture of the situation in the East. He said it was difficult to get a clear indication of Russian plans due to poor German reconnaissance both on the ground and in the air. The possibility of a Russian attack could not be excluded, although it seemed more likely that the Russians would not launch any big offensive.

Tresckow did not agree with this conclusion. He believed that the Russians were keeping their main armies far enough in the rear to avoid being reached by German air reconnaissance. But his opinion was rejected, nor was he heeded when he warned that the Russians would attack the bulging "belly" of the Army Group Center front at several points, would break through the thin line of German defenses, and, by pushing their armies into the gaps, would open the entire front. Tresckow's prophesies became grim reality when, on June 22, the Russians started their offensive. It took them only three weeks to destroy twenty-seven German divisions, making Germany's position in the East untenable.

In view of the situation, Tresckow could not bear to watch any longer without taking action. At the end of June, he sent Colonel Baron von Boeselager to Kluge, who had become Commander-in-Chief in the West. Boeselager's instructions were to explain to Kluge the situation in the East, to beseech the Field Marshal to open up the front in the West, and, above all, to urge him to fight Hitler instead of the Americans and British. Otherwise, Tresckow warned, all Germany would be lost. Tresckow's message also contained an urgent appeal to Kluge to arrange for Tresckow's transfer to the West as the Field Marshal's aide.

In the second week of July, Boeselager returned with Kluge's answer. Kluge stated that there was no need to do any "opening up" of the front in the West, for it was only a question of time before the Allied troops would break through. There was not a chance, Kluge said, of preventing this breakthrough. He also declared that, even though he was Commander-in-Chief in the West, he did not feel at all sure of his staff and was indeed so hemmed in that he could not undertake anything in line with our wishes. Neither, he added, would he be able—at least for the time being—to arrange for Tresckow's transfer.

In the meantime, on July 1, Lehndorff visited us in the East. He brought the bad news that our confederates Halem and Mumm had been condemned to death by the "People's Court." Lehndorf told us that the Judge-Advocate General, Dr. Carl Sack, was making every effort he could to persuade the Chief Prosecutor of the "People's Court" to postpone execution of the sentence. However, the failure of the July 20 coup was to spell doom for all our rescue plans.

Lehndorff at the same time brought us a message from Stauffenberg, informing us that he, too, agreed that we had to act at all costs. Stauffenberg's reasons for his decision were the same as ours. From now on, he said, we were to expect the assassination at any time. He himself would carry it out because he was the only person in our group who had access to Hitler. Stauffenberg also told us that he wanted Oertzen to come to Berlin immediately, for many things had changed since the summer of 1943 and he needed Oertzen for his plans in Berlin.

Stauffenberg suggested that Tresckow remain at his post for the time being. He would be summoned to Berlin by a teletype message from Field Marshal von Witzleben as soon as the latter had officially taken over the Supreme Command after Hitler's death. I, on the other hand, was to stand ready for a trip to Berlin immediately after the assassination, when I would receive a telephone call from Colonel Mertz von Quirnheim, Stauffenberg's successor in the General Army Office.

Because of his outstanding talents for organization, Stauffenberg had been appointed Chief of Staff to General Fromm, Commander of the Home Army. When Fromm told Stauffenberg that he had been selected for this important post, the latter demurred, saying that he no longer believed that the war could be won and that he believed Hitler alone was responsible for the impending German defeat. Fromm listened without argument, and finally told Stauffenberg that his own appraisal of the situation was not so radically different. Stauffenberg had the courage to present the same argument during a conversation with the Army Chief of Staff, General Zeitzler. He, too, quietly heard Stauffenberg out, and then told him that he appreciated subordinates with the moral courage to express their opinions frankly. Zeitzler, who had succeeded Halder in the summer of 1942 as Chief of Staff, had originally been one of Hitler's partisans. Later his daily controversies with the dictator had caused him to change his views considerably.

Shortly before July 20, Colonel von Voss called and told me that Oertzen wanted us to know that "it"—the assassination—had been scheduled twice already, but both times something had gone wrong. Now, however, "it" would be tried a third time, with every hope of success. Even before we received that message, Tresckow informed our confederate Schultze-Buettger of the imminence of the assassination, so that he would not be caught by surprise on the day of the coup d'état.

Meanwhile, in Berlin, the Socialists within the resistance group had decided to establish contact with Communist circles, in spite of the grave misgivings of all the other members. The first meeting took place on June 22 in the eastern part of Berlin, with a second meeting scheduled for July 4. Before that date, however, all those who had participated in the first gathering, including Julius Leber, were arrested. It was discovered later that one of the Communist participants had been a Gestapo spy.

These arrests acted as an added incentive to Stauffenberg, who admired Leber greatly, to act as quickly as possible. His new position gave Stauffenberg access to the war council conferences held at Hitler's headquarters. Thus Stauffenberg had taken on two separate—and basically incompatible—tasks: first, the assassination; second, the direction of the military coup in Berlin. It became clear only later that this double responsibility was the error which contributed most to the failure of the coup d'état.

Hitler spent almost the entire half of July in his residence on the Obersalzberg, near Berchtesgaden. Because of the approaching Russian armies, the officials of the OKW moved his headquarters from East Prussia to Zossen, near Berlin. This move had already begun when Hitler ordered an important military conference at the Obersalzberg for the beginning of July. Carrying the bomb, Stauffenberg flew to Berchtesgaden in a special plane, but when he arrived at the conference he found that Himmler was not present. Because he wanted to eliminate Himmler along with Hitler, Stauffenberg did not attempt the assassination that day.

Hitler was furious at the removal of his headquarters from East Prussia and ordered its immediate restoration to the old location. Therefore, the next military council took place in East Prussia, on July 15. Stauffenberg had access to that conference, and was getting ready to activate the mechanism of the time bomb when Hitler left the room and did not return. One more attempt had been foiled.

The next meeting in which Stauffenberg was to take part was scheduled for July 20. Again, he made his preparations. In the meantime, General Beck had intervened and ordered the assassination attempt at the next opportunity, regardless of whether or not other important Nazi leaders besides Hitler were present. The urgency of this decision was underscored by the alarming news from the Western front, relayed to us by Colonel Caesar von Hofacker on July 16.

Hitler's headquarters in East Prussia was surrounded by three security zones. Because a separate pass was needed for each zone, it was extremely difficult to get past the checkpoints.

When Stauffenberg arrived at Headquarters shortly before noon on July 20, he found to his surprise that the conference was not being held in the customary concrete bunker but in the so-called tea house, which was constructed partly of wood, and whose floors and ceiling were not reinforced with concrete.

In the conference room stood a long table, seating ten people on each side. Hitler was present, as were most of the others who usually took part in these councils, with the exception of Himmler and Goering. During the report on the military situation in the East, Stauffenberg managed to excuse himself, ostensibly to answer an important telephone call. A few minutes earlier, he had started the fuse mechanism of the bomb. Before leaving the room, he leaned the briefcase containing the bomb against the table leg near Hitler's seat. He went outside and waited. Minutes later, the explosion came, just as Hitler was bending over the table to look at a map.

Because the tea house was partly wood rather than stone, the air pressure caused by the explosion found an outlet through the nearest wall, which collapsed. Most of the people in the room were hurled through this opening and escaped with their lives. Four people were killed: Hitler's stenographer, a man named Berger; Hitler's Chief Adjutant, General Schmundt; Colonel Brandt, first staff officer of the Operations Department of the OKH; and General Korten, Chief of the General Staff of the Air Force.

Hitler was thrown clear of the room, and received only a few minor burns and bruises. But the scene of the explosion was a terrible sight: It appeared as though all the occupants of the room were lying dead or dying in pools of blood.

Stauffenberg had waited nearby until the usual quiet of the Headquarters area was shattered by the deafening roar of the explosion. He saw the members of the conference, Hitler among them, being hurled out of the room, their clothes torn and bloody. Convinced that the bomb had done its deadly work, Stauffenberg started back to Berlin at once, only to find that the alarm had already been given. The security zones around Headquarters were being sealed off, but aided equally by sheer luck, his presence of mind, and clever bluff, Stauffenberg managed to get out. He drove to the air strip, flew to Berlin, and took over the direction of the coup in the capital.

General Beck arrived at the War Ministry. He telephoned the Commanders-in-Chief of all the Army Groups, and demanded their unconditional subordination to his command. He ordered the Army Group North to evacuate the Baltic territories and to withdraw to East Prussia. He also tried to persuade Kluge to act and to make preparations for the evacuation of France and Belgium.

In the meantime, things were happening in the office of General Fromm, Commander-in-Chief of the Home Army. Details of the conversations and events that took place in those fateful hours were told to me weeks later by Fromm himself, when we both were inmates of the Gestapo prison. At that time, I also got a chance to read Fromm's indictment, which contained all the statements made in the course of those conversations.

In the early afternoon of that ill-starred July 20, General Olbricht came into Fromm's office and informed him that he had to tell him something "under four eyes." Fromm thereupon interrupted the military report to which he was listening and, as soon as they were alone, Olbricht announced that Hitler had been assassinated.

"Who told you that?" Fromm demanded. Olbricht re-

285

plied that the message had come from General Fellgiebel, who had personally transmitted the news from his office at Headquarters to that of the Communications General of the Home Army Command.

"Under the circumstances," Olbricht continued, "I propose that the code word for internal unrest be issued to all Deputy Commanders, thereby taking over the executive power." Fromm, however, insisted that he could take so far-reaching a measure only if he were completely convinced that Hitler was indeed dead. Olbricht, who was quite sure that Hitler was dead, picked up Fromm's telephone, and requested a priority call to Field Marshal Keitel. When the connection had been established, Fromm asked Keitel:

"What has happened at Headquarters? Wild rumors are afloat in Berlin."

"What is supposed to be the matter?" Keitel retorted, "Everything is all right here."

"I just had a report that the Fuehrer had been the victim of an assassination," said Fromm.

"That's nonsense," Keitel replied, "It is true that an attempt was made, but fortunately it has failed. The Fuehrer is alive and only slightly injured. Where, by the way, is your Chief of Staff, Colonel Stauffenberg?"

"Colonel Stauffenberg has not yet returned to my office," said Fromm.

This conversation between Fromm and Keitel was heard by Olbricht. On the strength of what Keitel had told him, Fromm decided that the code word for internal unrest should not yet be issued.

A short time afterwards, Olbricht again appeared in

Fromm's office, accompanied by Stauffenberg. Olbricht informed Fromm that Stauffenberg had confirmed Hitler's death.

"But that is impossible!" Fromm protested. "Keitel just assured me of the opposite."

"Field Marshal Keitel is lying as usual," said Stauffenberg. "I myself saw Hitler's body being carried away."

At this point, Olbricht said to Fromm: "In view of the situation, we have issued the code word for internal unrest to the District Commanders." Upon hearing this, Fromm sprang to his feet, banged his fist on the desk, and shouted: "This is open insubordination! what do you mean by 'we'? Who issued the order?"

"My Chief of Staff, Colonel Mertz von Quirnheim," replied Olbricht.

Fromm demanded that Olbricht fetch the Colonel at once. When Mertz appeared, he admitted that he had issued the code word for internal unrest to the military district commanders without waiting for Fromm's authorization. Still standing behind his desk, Fromm told Mertz: "You are under arrest. We shall have to see about further developments."

At this moment, Stauffenberg rose and said icily: "General, I myself set off the bomb during the conference with Hitler. There was an explosion as though a 15-centimeter shell had hit the room. No one who was in that room can still be alive."

"Count Stauffenberg," said Fromm, "the assassination has failed. You will have to shoot yourself at once."

"No, sir, that I shall not do," replied Stauffenberg.

Olbricht again intervened in the conversation. Turning

287

to Fromm, he said: "General, the moment for action has come. If we do not strike now, our country will be ruined forever by Hitler."

"And you, Olbricht," said Fromm, "are you too involved in this coup d'état?"

"Certainly," replied Olbricht, "even though I am not one of those who will actually assume power in Germany."

Upon hearing this, Fromm declared: "All three of you are herewith under arrest."

"You cannot arrest us," Olbricht retorted. "You are deluding yourself about who actually has the power. It is we who are arresting you."

A scuffle between Olbricht and Fromm followed, in which both Stauffenberg and Mertz von Quirnheim intervened. Fromm was overpowered. An officer, pistol in hand, appeared in the room, and Fromm was forced to stay in his office. At the same time he was informed that his telephone was being cut off. Fromm submitted to this confinement until evening. However, two Generals managed to get in touch with him during the afternoon. They told him that rumors of the assassination's failure had spread like wildfire, that the officers' corps and the officials of the Home Army were unwilling to take part in the coup d'état, and that an attempt was being made to get troops to Berlin and arrest the insurgents.

Shortly after his arrest, Fromm was also visited in his office by General Hoepner, the man who had been expelled from the Armed Forces in 1941. Hoepner told Fromm that he regretted Fromm's personal discomfort, but that nothing would happen to him. He informed him that the command of the Home Army had been transferred from Fromm to himself, while Field Marshal von Witzleben had taken over the Supreme Command, and that General Beck, designated by the resistance as head of the new German state, also was present in the War Ministry. So far as they were concerned, Hoepner declared, Hitler was dead, in spite of Keitel's statements to the contrary.

In the meantime, the first measures had been started in Vienna, Prague, Paris, and Kassel. Units of the army stationed in the vicinity of Berlin were marching on the capital. The Commanding General of Berlin and the province of Brandenburg, known to be a Hitler partisan, was summoned to the War Ministry and arrested on his arrival. His successor was General Freiherr von Thuengen, one of our collaborators.

On the orders of General von Hase, the Commandant of Berlin, the initial steps were taken for seizure of the capital's vital districts. He issued orders to surround the government quarter. The commander of the Guard Battalion received the order and proceeded to execute it. The troops who were to arrest Goebbels and occupy the radio station were assembled in the Zeughaus (Armory) Unter den Linden, but at that moment a fateful incident occurred. Major Remer, commander of the Guard Battalion, was urged by the Nazi propaganda officer attached to the unit to call Goebbels and find out what had happened before taking further action. Remer called Goebbels, who demanded that the commander come and see him at once. In Remer's presence, Goebbels telephoned Hitler in East Prussia, who told the young Commander that the orders he had received were part of a revolt. Hitler's voice had the expected effect on Remer, and the Guard Battalion was turned against us.

Even this misfortune would not have caused the coup

d'état to fail, for the Military Training Schools were still marching on Berlin. However, rumors that the assassination had failed spread all over the War Ministry, causing great confusion. Many officers began to waver, others deserted our cause, and still others, who until then had remained quietly in the background, gathered for a counterblow. Shots were exchanged, SS units and detachments of the Guard Battalion arrived and freed Fromm, who earlier in the evening had requested—and received—permission to leave his office and go to his quarters in the Ministry.

While all this was happening, the Gestapo had remained in their headquarters without lifting a hand. When they heard details from East Prussia, they sent SS Oberfuehrer Pifrader to the War Ministry, where he was promptly arrested. Only after his liberation did Pifrader get a chance to call Gestapo headquarters. Until then, the Gestapo officials had thought only about arrangements for the defense of their headquarters. There was much confusion, and even the top leaders could not make up their minds about what they should or should not do, so completely had they been caught by surprise. This alone clearly proved that the Gestapo, although they vaguely suspected something, had no definite knowledge of the coup d'état. Apart from a few unimportant facts, all the plans formed by us over the years in connection with Hitler's overthrow never became known to the Gestapo until after the coup of July 20. The Gestapo leaders themselves were forced to admit that this was true.

After his liberation, General Fromm set up a court martial consisting of three generals who passed the death sentence on the insurgents. With this sentence, Fromm went to his office, where Beck, Olbricht, Hoepner, Mertz von Quirnheim, Haeften, and several others were assembled. Fromm declared them all under arrest, and read the sentence to them.

Hoepner asked Fromm to postpone his execution, for he thought he would be able to justify his actions. Fromm agreed, and had Hoepner taken to prison. Olbricht asked only for permission to write a few lines to his wife. Fromm granted this request also.

When Fromm ordered the condemned officers to surrender their weapons, Beck replied: "Surely you will not ask me, your former chief, to do that. I myself will accept the consequences of this sorry situation." Fromm indicated his acquiescence. Beck then sat down in an armchair, drew his pistol, and tried to shoot himself through the head, but the bullet only grazed his skull. Beck made another attempt, while Stauffenberg supported the general in his chair. The second shot inflicted a fatal wound, but did not kill Beck instantly.

Fromm then ordered Olbricht, Stauffenberg, Mertz and Haeften executed by a firing squad in the courtyard of the War Ministry. In the moment before the shots were fired, Stauffenberg shouted:

"Long live our sacred Germany!"

Later Fromm asked about Beck. When he was told that Beck was still alive Fromm gave orders to end his suffering. The failure of the coup d'état was complete and absolute; the death of the first five of our confederates was only the opening round of the orgy of death and terror that was to come.

General Fromm did not save his life by turning against

the insurgents on July 20. In February, 1945, he was sentenced to death for cowardice by the "People's Court." The sentence affected him the more profoundly because he had not expected it. He was shot on March 19, 1945, by prison officials in the Brandenburg penitentiary. He died with the words "Heil Hitler!" on his lips.

CHAPTER TWENTY-ONE

The Price

of Failure

In the weeks after July 20, a great wave of arrests swept over Germany. Among those arrested were not only persons who had been closely connected with the conspiracy, but also many who were only indirectly involved. The Gestapo raged unchecked. Hundreds of people, many of them members of the Armed Forces, were executed during the months following the abortive coup d'état. I shall not attempt to give a complete account of those events. Instead, I shall concentrate mainly upon the incidents with which I was most intimately connected.

Early in the morning of July 20, I had visited the headquarters of the Army Group Center for a conference with our confederates. I had just returned to my quarters when a call from Colonel Mertz von Quirnheim was received at the Army Group Center indicating that the assassination had succeeded and that I should get ready to leave for

Berlin without delay. Soon after came the first official news bulletin over the radio, announcing that an assassination had been attempted but had failed, and that Hitler had suffered only minor injuries.

At first, Tresckow and I thought that the official bulletin was a lie. Our first doubts came when an order arrived through the usual military channels, directing us not to accept any orders from Berlin, because certain circles in the capital were trying to fish in troubled waters in the wake of the assassination attempt. One thing was clear: the great strike had been attempted, but I knew it had failed when I heard Hitler's speech over the radio at midnight.

I immediately rushed to Tresckow, who had already gone to bed, and told him what I had heard. He listened, and then said, "I am now going to shoot myself, for they are bound to find out about me during the investigation, and then they will try to extract the names of others from me. To prevent this, I shall take my own life."

I tried to dissuade him, advising him to wait and watch the developments. We argued all through the night, but I could not persuade Tresckow to change his mind. He remained firm in his decision to take his own life at the front the following day. He begged me, however, to try to stay alive as long as it seemed at all possible.

On the morning of July 21, Tresckow and I parted. He was quite calm and collected. "Now they will all fall upon us," he said, "and cover us with abuse. But I am convinced, now as much as ever, that we have done the right thing. I believe Hitler to be the archenemy, not only of Germany, but indeed of the entire world. In a few hours' time, I shall stand before God and answer for both my actions and the things I neglected to do. I think I can with a clear conscience stand by all I have done in the battle against Hitler. Just as God once promised Abraham that He would spare Sodom if only ten just men could be found in the city, I also have reason to hope that, for our sake, he will not destroy Germany. No one among us can complain about his death, for whoever joined our ranks put on the poisoned shirt of Nessus. A man's moral worth is established only at the point where he is prepared to give his life for his convictions."

Tresckow drove to the 28th Rifle Division, whose first staff officer was Major Kuhn. Informing the latter of everything he knew, Tresckow then drove into no man's land. There, using two pistols, he pretended an exchange of shots, and then set off a rifle grenade which blew off his head. At first it was generally assumed that Tresckow had been killed in action. I was assigned the task of taking the body to Germany, where it was buried near his parents' grave at his home in Brandenburg.

In the days and weeks that followed, the death toll of the abortive plot rose rapidly. Some of the people involved committed suicide, but the majority were hauled before the "People's Court." Only the first few of these trials were publicized. All the others, in accordance with the official statement that only a "very small clique of ambitious officers" had been involved in the revolt, were never brought to the attention of the public.

On August 7, 1944, the first of the publicized trials was held. The defendants were Field Marshal von Witzleben, General von Hase, General Stieff, General Fellgiebel, Count Fritz von der Schulenburg, Count Yorck von Wartenburg, and General Hoepner.

PETER COUNT YORCK VON WARTENBURG

1904 — 1944

Descendant of a general who won fame in the fight against
Napoleon, Yorck, a prominent member of the "Kreisau Circle," fought Hitler and Nazism because of his unshakable
devotion to Christian moral principles. He was hanged in
August, 1944.

Wheeler-Bennett, in his book *The Nemesis of Power*, has described what he calls the "pitiable performance" of these men before the "People's Court." He charges that they "did not present even that degree of courageous riposte which was permitted to them." This charge is unjust, and, as we shall see, untrue. It is, however, a good illustration of the tremendous part success plays in the lives of men. Nothing, indeed, "succeeds like success." The successful man is forgiven even the most questionable action and behavior while the man who fails is subject to contempt and merciless criticism. The men of July 20 were failures, and were widely judged and condemned on that basis alone.

The fact remains that these defendants, who had been treated mercilessly and subjected to every kind of abuse, who, on Hitler's express orders, received not even a minimum of fair treatment, whose every word was cut off by a torrent of invective from the president of the court, Ronald Freisler, still maintained an amazing amount of dignity. They also, even more amazingly, managed to get in more retorts to Freisler's invective than would have seemed possible under the circumstances. "You can have us hanged," Witzleben said to Freisler after sentence had been pronounced, "but within three months' time the people will drag you alive through the filth of the gutter." And General Fellgiebel's reply to the sentence was: "You had better hang us in a hurry, otherwise you will hang before we do!" In subsequent trials, there were many other cases of spirited answers to Freisler's taunts and abuses. When he sneeringly told Joseph Wirmer, a Catholic lawyer who had been very active in the resistance: "Well, now you will soon be in Hell," Wirner fired back: "With pleasure, Mr. President, just so long as you soon follow me there."

The ever-widening scope of the Gestapo investigations also proved fatal to our friends who had been arrested prior to July 20 and whose cases had come to a virtual standstill before that date. Now the Gestapo took a new interest in these cases, among them those of Dohnanyi and Bonhoeffer. Nikolaus von Halem and Mumm von Schwarzenstein also were victims of the abortive coup's bloody aftermath. Halem was executed on October 20, 1944, and Mumm on April 20, 1945.

The attitude with which these men faced death is best illustrated by two letters written by Nikolaus von Halem. Two days before the trial, Halem wrote to his mother:

"My dearest, my poor dear, that you have to go through this anguish! Autumn is coming, I hope it will not break your heart. I am writing this two days before the trial, ready for whatever may happen, and with great serenity of mind. How comforting is the thought that my sufferings will soon be ended. But the fact that yours begin only now and will continue troubles me greatly. Believe me, so far as death is concerned, I have all the advantage the Stoics claim in their philosophy, although I sympathize with the form rather than the content of their teaching. Whether we know it or not, we are all imbued with the spiritual essence of twenty Christian centuries. Now a period seems to be approaching in which even the apparently un-Christian philosophies of such European thinkers as Kant, Schopenhauer, and Nietzsche reveal this common background. Understandably we all fear death—chiefly because it usually overtakes us so unexpectedly. The reason why the death of a man of eighty is only mildly saddening is because the time of death seems to harmonize with the universal order; in other words, it can almost be predicted. The Catholic Church rightly

299

attaches great importance to preparing the dying, since the outward ceremonies induce the mind to face the imminent end gravely, and so to concentrate upon this mood. He who is prepared need not fear death.

I feel almost shy about touching on the mystery of Grace, to which the high and holy mystery of Death is in a way the threshold. One step, and we are through. I know that the conventional words of comfort, especially those of the Church, will not find the way to the depths of your heart, and I should not be your son if I, too, had not had to travel my own road. However, even though the primitive way of expressing your grief, by crying, wailing, and tearing your clothes, is barred to you as a member of our civilization, please try again and again to penetrate with all the keenness of your mind into the true meaning of life. Cleopatra says to Antony:

> "Oh infinite virtue! com'st thou smiling from
> "The world's great snare uncaught?"

Only a woman could see it that way. You, however, are one of the few of your sex who are capable of achieving the fortitude of inner freedom and detachment from the world, and thus also from the death of your son, so that you, too, can smile as freely as I shall smile on my last way.

Read—and think of me while reading—the second volume of *The World as Will and Concept*. The second, remember, at least to begin with, even though this is contrary to your habit. Read at random, and do not let yourself be influenced by Schopenhauer's repeated grim demand that one read every word he has written. You will see that it will lead you forward, possibly to the Monadism of Leibniz, which Schopenhauer despises, but which I love: if I can, I shall help you.

Greetings to all my sisters and to my brother. With each one of them I share strong mutual bonds. I am going to write another letter to Marie, whom more than any of the others I recommend to your care. She, I am afraid, has lost her home in more than the usual sense. The sweet thought of her and our happy years together causes me bitter pain. My little Fritz! And little Wilhelm, how fortunate that he cannot know what is happening. Hold on to them, support them, teach and console them! I beg you with all my heart, do not consider it too much trouble!

As a result of time and circumstances, I have no house to put in order, and so I am leaving all practical matters aside. Marie will prove her strength in managing things, and our friends will help her with it.

When the troubled waves of this storm have one day grown calm again, and you can place some memorial for me—perhaps on father's grave—please add the Bible verse which even as a child moved me as though coming from the very depths of the universe: "Fear not, for I have redeemed thee. I have called thee by thy name, thou art mine." It is found in Isaiah, but I do not recall where.

I believe that the war will end this year or at the beginning of next. Ah, if only, like Moses gazing out over the Promised Land, I could see a bright future for you, even from afar!

And now, farewell, my dearest, my heart's beloved! After so many words, the essential still remains unsaid. But that is indeed beyond words. Let it rest in silence in our hearts, where we both can be infinitely sure of keeping it forever.

Once more, farewell! Do not think that you have lost me. My thanks, a thousand times my thanks, my deepest love and tenderness I gather together in one last kiss."

Your son,

A few minutes before his execution, he wrote these few words with shackled hands, on a slip of paper:

Dear Mother!
Now I have overcome even that last slight unrest that makes the treetop tremble before the tree falls! And thus I have

attained the goal of mankind, for we can and ought to endure knowingly what the plant undergoes unknowingly.

Farewell, they have come to fetch me. A thousand kisses.

Your son,

The price in blood that had to be paid for the failure of the coup of July 20 assumed staggering proportions before the fall of the Third Reich finally put an end to Hitler's life. The number of those arrested was in itself a striking refutation of the claim—too often echoed by other nations—that the German opposition to Hitler had been restricted to a "very small clique." Our group was not large compared to the 70,000,000 Germans, but then the number of men who will risk their lives for an undertaking such as ours will never, in any nation, be more than a tiny percentage of the population. In Germany, the aftermath of the abortive plot wiped out all but a handful of those who had fought so long and so hard to rid their country and the world of Hitler.

CHAPTER TWENTY-TWO

Gestapo Prison

Danger sharpens our mental faculties and develops the instinct for imminent perils in a way that people living in normal, civilized conditions can hardly imagine. A kind of sixth sense warns of impending danger while at the same time allowing us to weigh and analyze all chances of escape.

Ever since the failure of the plot of July 20, I had thought it highly probable that I would be involved in the investigations; after the publication of the first long list of people who had been arrested in connection with the plot, the probability became a certainty. I want it understood that, in describing my arrest, trial, and, finally, my liberation, I do so not because I consider my fate to be of any special interest, but merely because my experiences and ordeals were typical of what happened to most of my friends and all the others in the German resistance who shared our convictions.

In accordance with my agreement with Tresckow, I waited with suppressed anxiety for what the days after July 20 would have in store for me. I was not overly surprised when, on August 17, a staff officer roused me from sleep and placed me under arrest. My first impulse was to grab the pistol beside my bed and put an end to my life; yet at the same time some instinct warned me against this step and prompted me to wait and abide. This instinctive feeling that in the end I was destined to escape the Gestapo was not always equally strong during the long months of my imprisonment. It was often quite powerful, and, although it weakened many times, it never completely forsook me and helped support me through all the trials and tribulations that lay ahead.

This intuition was also the main reason why I refrained from any attempt to escape, although two chances for flight offered themselves during the first two days after my arrest. The first opportunity came immediately after I had been taken into custody at Mackow in Poland, near the German-Russian front line. I was taken under military guard to a house in a village only a few miles away. The sentry at the front door could not have prevented my escaping through the unguarded back door and into the nearby woods.

On the following day, still under guard, I was taken by car to Ortelsburg in East Prussia, and from there by train to Berlin. We arrived in the German capital late at night, and found the station jammed with people, for in those days the trains were badly overcrowded, a condition which later was to become worse as the masses of refugees began to arrive from the East.

My guard consisted of one lieutenant and two sergeants,

none of whom knew their way around Berlin, so that I had to direct them from the platform across the station to the guard house. That was my second chance for escape. The two sergeants were carrying my luggage, and the officer was busy telephoning for a car from the guard house; it would not have been difficult at all for me at that moment to disappear into the crowd. I resisted the temptation mainly because of the instinct I mentioned earlier. Of course, I also was acutely aware of the difficulties such an escape would have entailed in regard to shelter and food.

And so, during the night of August 18, I was brought to Berlin's notorious Gestapo prison in the Prinz Albrechtstrasse. From that moment, there was a marked change in my treatment. My military guard had been correct and polite, but the minute the Gestapo took over, correctness was replaced with rudeness.

At the prison, I was kept in solitary confinement. The washroom, however, was designed to be used by several people at once, and so, in the days that followed, I had an opportunity to get to know my fellow prisoners. Among them I discovered many well-known faces: Admiral Canaris, General Oster, Ambassador Count von der Schulenburg, Ambassador von Hassell, Count Lehndorff, the former Minister of Finance, Popitz, Pastor Bonhoeffer, Lord Mayor Goerdeler, the lawyers Mueller and Langbehn, General von Falkenhausen, and many, many more.

In the past, while we had been busy with preparations for the coup d'état, it had often been extremely difficult to get in touch with our co-conspirators; now we were all gathered together, like the characters in the last act of a cheap comic opera. Of course we were not permitted to talk to each other, but even a glance or a hastily spoken word, at a moment when the guards' attention was diverted, was often enough for an understanding.

The Gestapo had established a special guard for us prisoners connected with the plot of July 20. This guard was made up of police officials, who for the most part were in civilian clothes and who had come from those Gestapo quarters that had been bombed. Many of these officials were not unfriendly, but this was often nothing but a false front, a means of extricating information from the prisoners. A few of these guards, however, were genuinely sympathetic. These latter had been police officials prior to 1933, and had later been retained by the Gestapo. Whenever they felt themselves unobserved and alone with one of the prisoners, they did not conceal their aversion to Hitler and National Socialism. Many among us owed a number of small comforts to these officials—and even, occasionally, a valuable hint. The trusties detailed for menial jobs, most of whom leaned toward Communist views, tried with much zeal to make life bearable for us.

After two days in prison I was handcuffed and taken for my first questioning. The interrogation was conducted by Habecker, a Commissioner of the Gestapo. He began by informing me that I was charged with having taken part in the preparations for the plot of July 20, and that this accusation had been corroborated by a number of witnesses. He told me that it therefore would be useless to deny the charge, and much better for me if I confessed at once. I would have been willing to do this only if I could be absolutely convinced that the Gestapo possessed real evidence of my complicity, but from the beginning I had the impression, which was confirmed during the course of the interrogation, that they in fact knew nothing about me. Although they had a strong suspicion, or rather the right instinct concerning me, they had no concrete proof.

I therefore decided to deny everything. The fact that I was confronted with criminals masquerading in the guise of lawful authority made me feel morally justified not to tell the truth. The Gestapo countered my denials with the accusation that I had visited Count Lehndorff on a trip to East Prussia with Tresckow. They insisted that during that visit we had engaged in conversations amounting to high treason, conversations that had concerned the immediate preparations for the plot of July 20.

By pure coincidence, I had had a chance earlier that same day to exchange a few words with Count Lehndorff in the prison washroom. Therefore I knew that, although he had admitted the *fact* of our meeting—which could not be denied because others knew about it—he had withheld the *nature* of our talks from the Gestapo. Accordingly, I flatly denied the accusation. I was then shown a protocol—supposedly signed by Lehndorff—which the Gestapo advanced as proof that I was lying. Due to my longstanding knowledge of Gestapo methods I immediately guessed that both the protocol and the signature were forgeries. I therefore stuck to my denials, and demanded to be personally confronted with Lehndorff. This request was, naturally, refused.

My cell opened on the same corridor as Lehndorff's, and so I had the opportunity to observe that he was kept under unusually heavy guard. There was a special reason for that. Lehndorff was high on the list of those whom the Gestapo wanted, for he was the one who, on July 19, had undertaken the task of visiting Koenigsberg and getting in touch with the Commanding General of that region. His idea was to try to win him over to our side as soon as the first word of a successful coup came from Berlin. It was of course obvious that the cooperation of the military in East Prussia would have had far-reaching effects, for here, in a comparatively small area, were concentrated the headquarters of Hitler, Himmler, Goering, and Ribbentrop. In addition, a considerable part of the High Command was stationed there.

Lehndorff's trip to Koenigsberg and Steinort had of course not gone unnoticed, and he was aware that he could expect his immediate arrest. Almost immediately after the abortive plot, an attempt was made to take Lehndorff prisoner on his estate in Steinort. A large number of Gestapo officials had surrounded his castle, but Lehndorff had succeeded in getting out and safely reaching the forests belonging to his estate. Eventually, however, he had been forced to leave his hiding place, and in the end openly approached the Gestapo agents who were searching for him. The Gestapo, much relieved that he had surrendered, took him first to Koenigsberg and from there to Berlin, where Lehndorff made a second attempt at escape. When the car that was to take him to the Gestapo prison stopped in front of the Reichs Security Office, Lehndorff took advantage of an unguarded moment, leaped out of the car, and disappeared into the darkness. From Berlin he made his way on foot to Mecklenburg, where he intended to hide on the country estate of his married sister. He managed to cover the long distance in four days, and to him, having always felt at home in the outdoors, being out in the open day and night was a pleasure rather than an ordeal. But dogs had been put on his trail, and in the end he was apprehended just before he reached his destination. The Gestapo brought him back to Berlin.

At the beginning of the interrogation, Lehndorff denied all charges; then suddenly, he changed his tactics, and openly admitted his complicity in the plot. As a result, he was one of the first among us to be brought to trial before the "People's Court," condemned to death, and executed. The attitude in which he went to his death is best attested in the last letter he wrote to his wife, who, with their children, was repeatedly arrested, released, and rearrested. The letter runs:

I have always had the firm impression that you were walking by my side, and this feeling shall remain with me to my last hour. I know that you will always be convinced that I did not wantonly destroy your future, but only because I was serving an idea which I did not believe could allow any considerations of family or private interests.

During these past weeks it has become absolutely clear to me that our every step and our destinies are ultimately guided by God alone. In my own case, too, I have had the feeling that from the beginning everything was taking its course according to God's will. I commend to you, because of its truth, a beautiful verse which often has uplifted me and given me strength: "Do not worry about anything; instead, in all things let your pleas be made known to God in prayer and supplication with thanksgiving." And should our appeals not be answered, we have to realize that God's ways are not our ways. The Christian faith and belief in a "Kingdom of Heaven" are the only help in distress. The road to it, however, seems to lead only to sorrow, and all our old habits must first be removed by force—only then can one become a "new being." In any case, I shall die in this faith without fear or dread. The verse chosen for me at my confirmation: "Watch ye, stand ye fast in the faith, quit ye like men," shall be my guide to the last.

My stubborn denials led to the first coercive measures against me: I was shackled day and night. The chains were especially hard to bear at night, for then they were fastened in a way that forced me to lie on my back throughout the night without being able to move or change my position. Eating with the manacles on demanded considerable dexterity and I need scarcely stress the fact that the food in the Gestapo prison was far below the minimum, both in quality and quantity, a man needs to sustain his strength.

During the interrogations that followed I came to the conclusion that the Gestapo was less interested in getting from me a confession of my own complicity than the names of the other persons involved in the plot. I was to be the instrument through which they would gain information about—and then destroy—as many anti-Nazis as possible. My own confession was to be no more than the first step towards that goal. When I persisted in my denials, a number of names were shown to me. I either denied knowing the persons in question or declared myself completely ignorant of their anti-Hitler opinions and activities. Thus the interrogation soon reached a deadlock.

Judged by the standards of criminal law techniques, the interrogation was conducted in an extremely clumsy fashion. It was not really difficult to withstand the crossfire of questions which often lasted for hours and took place at all hours both day and night. Nor could the rudeness of the interrogating officials shake me. I had learned to endure, without even batting an eye, long hours during which these officials shouted at me and heaped the coarsest and filthiest insults upon me.

The Gestapo agents used a number of different methods in their attempt to play on a prisoner's nerves. One method was to take him out of his cell for questioning, and then let him wait endlessly in an anteroom. If that had no effect, other means of influencing him were employed. Usually three officials worked together. One would threaten the prisoner and shower him with abuse, the second would talk to him in a soothing manner, urging him to calm down and have a cigarette, the third would then try to appeal to the prisoner's code of honor. In this way, the Gestapo provided for three different kinds of temperament in the hope that the prisoner would in the end succumb to one of these approaches or to the combination of all three.

The assumption that my officer's uniform would help protect me against harsher measures soon proved to be an illusion. One day, the Commissioner of the Gestapo who was questioning me switched to violent tactics. Although I was chained and helpless, he hit me in the face. I remained outwardly calm, but observed that such conduct was both vile and illegal. It may be that this only infuriated the Gestapo, for my interrogator now proceeded to try and extort my confession and the names they wanted by employing brute force.

One night I was taken from my cell for questioning. There were four people in the room: the Commissioner; his secretary, a girl of about twenty; a sergeant of the Security Police, in uniform; and an assistant in civilian clothes. I was told that I was being given a last chance to confess. When I persisted in my denials, the Gestapo officials resorted to torture.

This torture was executed in four stages. First, my hands were chained behind my back, and a device which gripped all the fingers separately was fastened to my hands. The inner side of this mechanism was studded with pins whose points pressed against my fingertips. The turning of a screw caused the instrument to contract, thus forcing the pin points into my fingers.

When that did not achieve the desired confession, the second stage followed. I was strapped, face down, on a frame resembling a bedstead, and my head was covered with a blanket. Then cylinders resembling stovepipes studded with nails on the inner surface, were shoved over my bare legs. Here, too, a screw mechanism was used to contract these tubes so that the nails pierced my legs from ankle to thigh.

For the third stage of torture, the "bedstead" itself was the main instrument. I was strapped down as described above, again with a blanket over my head. With the help of a special mechanism this medieval torture rack was then expanded—either in sudden jerks, or gradually—each time stretching my shackled body.

In the fourth and final stage I was tied in a bent position which did not allow me to move even slightly backwards or sideways. Then the Police Commissioner and the Police sergeant together fell on me from behind, and beat me with heavy clubs. Each blow caused me to fall forward, and because my hands were chained behind my back, I crashed with full force on my face.

This first round of tortures ended in my losing consciousness, but none of the brutalities succeeded in getting me to confess a word or to name one of my fellow anti-Nazis. After regaining consciousness I was taken back to my cell. The guards looked at me with undisguised expressions of horror and pity. Completely exhausted and unable to move, I lay on my cot in my bloodstained underwear. The following day, I had a heart attack, even though I had been in the best of health before then. The prison doctor was summoned, and although I was deeply suspicious of his treatment, I had no choice but to submit to it. I was unable to get up and about for several days, and the only result of my recovery was a repetition of the torture.

The Gestapo subjected many of our group—for example, the lawyer Carl Langbehn, Count von Bismarck, and State Secretary Erwin Planck, son of the famed physicist—to similar tortures. I am often asked how we were able to endure these brutalities. There are a number of sources from which a man can draw the strength to carry him through such ordeals. We all made the discovery that we could endure far more than we ever had believed possible. The two great polar forces of human emotions, love and hate, together formed a supporting structure on which we could rely when things became unbearable. Love, the positive force, included our faith in the moral worth of our actions, the knowledge that we had fought for humanity and decency, and the sense of having fulfilled a higher duty. Those among us who had never prayed learned to do so now, and discovered that in a situation such as ours prayer, and prayer alone, is capable of bringing comfort and lending almost superhuman strength. One also finds that love in the form of prayers by relatives and friends on the outside transmits currents of strength.

Hate, the negative force, was just as important in sustaining us in our darkest hours of pain and need. The consuming, unqualified hatred, made up of equal parts of revulsion, contempt, and fury which we felt for the evil of Nazism, was so powerful a force that it helped us endure situations which otherwise would have been intolerable.

After having gone through the second round of tortures, I had to decide upon the tactics I should adopt from then on. There could be no doubt that the Gestapo was determined to continue its brutal treatment and, as the Gestapo Commissioner made quite clear to me, to intensify the torture until it became, in his own words, "horrible." While I was determined not to disclose the name of a single one of my co-conspirators under any circumstance, I had to realize that sooner or later the limit of my physical endurance would be reached, and so I made preparations to take my own life, in spite of my chains. In the midst of my planning and my deliberations a possible way out of my dilemma suddenly occurred to me, though at first I was not aware of its full significance. Following a sudden inspiration, I admitted—seemingly under pressure—that I had known of my dead friend Tresckow's plan to try and induce Hitler to surrender his position to one of the Field Marshals. What followed was completely unexpected: the Gestapo seemed satisfied with this declaration, and for the time being left me alone.

One day I was informed that the so-called "Court of Honor" of the German Reich, under the chairmanship of General Keitel, had expelled me from the Armed Forces on the strength of the Gestapo report. This was done although I had never appeared before this "Court of Honor" to which, among others, Generals Guderian and Rundstedt had been appointed by Hitler.

A few days later, I was informed of a warrant for my

arrest which had been issued by the examining judge of the "People's Court." This judge had never seen or talked to me, but the wording of the warrant made it clear that he considered me sufficiently suspect to be charged with high treason.

A short time afterwards, I was led from my cell, and taken by car to the concentration camp of Sachsenhausen. There I was brought to an area which showed unmistakable signs of having been used as a shooting range. The accompanying Gestapo official pointed this out to me with a sneer, and said: "Well, now you know what is going to happen to you. But first we have other plans for you."

I was then taken to a room which was evidently part of the camp crematory. There stood the coffin of General von Tresckow, which the Gestapo had taken from his grave in Brandenburg. Before my eyes, the coffin was opened. The Gestapo had hoped to extract a confession from me by exhuming Tresckow's coffin and confronting me with its contents, in the belief that the body in the coffin was not his. The sight of Tresckow's remains must have been more of a shock to the official than to me.

To understand this, one must realize that the Gestapo, in the course of their investigation, had come across considerable evidence that Tresckow had secretly evaded many of Hitler's orders. There was, for instance, the unconditional "No Retreat" order. The only exception to this rule was permission to make small tactical adjustments known as "straightening out the front." Tresckow, in a desperate attempt to save as many soldiers' lives as possible, took advantage of that permission, and pulled back the front line the prescribed maximum of ten kilometers. In fact, Tresckow's unit had "straightened out" the front

315

line every day. If one retreats ten kilometers every day, by the end of the month the front line is 300 kilometers away from where it is supposed to be. The troops swore because they had to dig in anew every 24 hours, but they later realized that Tresckow had saved their lives by this strategy.

Such evidence convinced the Gestapo that Tresckow had been a very devious and crafty man, which immediately led them to suspect that his suicide, which had taken place without witnesses in the no man's land between the Russian and German fronts, had also been a trick. They finally came to the conclusion that Tresckow had deserted to the Russians, and that I had placed the body of a Russian soldier in his coffin, and had then taken the coffin for burial on Tresckow's estate. By opening the coffin before my eyes and confronting me with evidence of the fraud, the Gestapo had hoped to force me to confess my part in the conspiracy.

After rallying from the shock of discovering that the Gestapo's assumption had been erroneous, and while we still were standing beside the open coffin, the official urged me in a tone half-threatening, half-imploring to make a full and final confession. When I stuck to my previous denials, the coffin with Tresckow's body was burned before my eyes. Then, contrary to what I had expected after the Gestapo official's earlier remarks, I was taken back to the prison in Berlin.

CHAPTER TWENTY-THREE

Before the

"People's Court"

The moment the Gestapo was sure that I would be condemned to death by the "People's Court," my treatment improved. For example, I was allowed to write letters, to speak occasionally with my relatives, and to receive parcels. Of course only parts of these packages were delivered to me: the guards always levied their toll.

In the second half of December my court-appointed counsel appeared and introduced himself to me. He told me that my case would come up before the "People's Court" in two days, and that judging from my dossier the death sentence could be expected with certainty. As soon as he had finished, I told him that I had been tortured, and explained in what manner. He fully agreed with my decision to deny everything before the Court because of the tortures, but he pointed out that I must be able to prove that the tortures had taken place. He also promised to acquaint the President of the Court and the Chief

Prosecutor with the pertinent facts; otherwise he felt that the objection would probably be brushed aside. I was later able to satisfy myself that my counsel had kept his word.

On December 21, 1944, I appeared with five other defendants before the "People's Court." Not all these cases could be settled in one day, and as I sat in the dock as the last of the accused, I was able to witness the procedure of this so-called "People's Court" in several cases. Roland Freisler, the president, deliberately avoided all judicial objectivity by describing as high treason the smallest offenses against National Socialism. In most cases the sentence was death, usually by hanging.

Freisler did not hesitate to make long-drawn-out, cheap propaganda harangues, delivering them in a voice which would easily have carried through several large court rooms. He had acquired these tactics by studying the performance of Andrei Vishinsky during the Soviet purge trials of the nineteen thirties. Freisler had been a prisoner of war in Russia during the First World War and an ardent Bolshevik before later becoming an ardent Nazi; he had great admiration for the terror methods of the Soviets.

The trials which I witnessed taught me that my only chance was to trap the Gestapo with their own tactics, and invalidate my meager "confession" by charging that it had been extracted by torture. Because my case was not tried that first day in court, I was returned to prison.

During the days that followed, I managed several times to exchange a few words with Goerdeler. The warrant for his arrest was supposed to have been signed on July 17, even before the abortive attempt on Hitler's life. Goerdeler had been warned, and had decided to go into hiding.

After spending a few days in Berlin and Potsdam, he had gone to the country estate of a friend, returned to Berlin and stayed with other friends, and finally had left for East Prussia on August 11. A prize of a million Reichsmark had been offered for his capture or information leading to it. A woman who recognized him spoke to others about having seen Goerdeler, and shortly afterwards he was apprehended.

In prison, Goerdeler and I agreed to pretend that we did not know each other, an agreement which was kept by both of us, although the Gestapo repeatedly accused us of being acquainted and threatened us with confrontation.

Even under the depressing conditions in the Gestapo prison, Goerdeler remained an optimist. In January 1945, he mentioned the military situation and voiced the hope that the collapse of the Third Reich was imminent. But on February 2, both Goerdeler and former Minister of Finance Popitz were taken from their cells in a manner which left no doubt that the last hour had come for them.

Among our fellow prisoners during those days in the Gestapo prison was Dietrich Bonhoeffer, the noted Protestant theologian, who had spent several years in the United States shortly before the war. I first noticed him one night during an air raid as we were taken to the bomb shelter in the prison yard. When I saw him I was alarmed, for I knew that any sign of recognition could only make matters worse for both of us. However, his upright figure and his eyes, which radiated calm and serenity, assured me that the dangerous moment had passed without his having lost his customary self-control.

I learned that Bonhoeffer was in cell No. 19, while I

occupied No. 25. The very next morning we were able to exchange a few words in the washroom, even though the guards were watching us closely to see that prisoners did not talk to each other. My acquaintance with Bonhoeffer dated from before the war, but we had come to know each other more intimately later on.

During that first brief conversation in the prison washroom, he told me that he was determined to resist the Gestapo to the end and that he would reveal nothing.

A few days later, Bonhoeffer was transferred to cell No. 24, and became my neighbor. That gave us an opportunity for daily contacts, during which we usually managed to exchange a few words. Our main chance came in the morning, when we hurried to the washroom, one corner of which had been equipped with showers. In spite of the icy cold water, we made ample use of the showers, for the noise of the running water drowned out our conversations, and for a few minutes we were able to evade the ever-watchful eyes and ears of the guards.

Another chance for talk came in the evening, when we were led to the washroom again. The doors of our cells remained open until all the prisoners had been brought back, and we took advantage of this opportunity to stand in the doorways of our cells and whisper to one another through the cracks of the door hinges. Air raids, which came at all hours of the day and night, occasionally gave us an added minute or two for exchanging information.

In this way I learned from Bonhoeffer about his interrogations by the Gestapo. He told me that he had been threatened with torture the very first time, and that the entire procedure had been based on sheer blackmail. Outwardly, he betrayed no sign of what he had gone through:

he was always in good spirits, always pleasant and considerate to everyone—so much so, in fact, that very soon and to my complete amazement even our guards fell under the spell of his personality.

As far as our relationship was concerned, he was always the hopeful one. He never tired of pointing out that the fight is lost only when you yourself give up. Often he would smuggle a scrap of paper into my hands on which he had written words of comfort or hope from the Bible.

He saw even his own situation from an optimistic point of view. He assured me that the Gestapo had not been able to trace his really important activities, and that he had been able to minimize his acquaintance with Goerdeler. As for his meetings with English bishops, he said—especially those with Lord Bishop Bell of Chichester—his interrogators had evidently failed to realize their true meaning. Bonhoeffer added that if the investigations were to continue at the same slow pace, they could drag on for years.

I shared joy and sorrow with Bonhoeffer during those dark days in the Prinz Albrechtstrasse prison. We divided between us the few possessions we had and the little our relatives were allowed to bring us. With sparkling eyes he told me of the letters from his fiancée and parents whose love and care, he felt, surrounded him even in the Gestapo prison. On Wednesdays, when he had received his weekly package containing clean underwear, and usually cigars, apples, and bread as well, he promptly used the first unobserved moment to share his presents with me, full of happiness that even in prison he was still able to give.

DIETRICH BONHOEFFER

1 9 0 6 — 1 9 4 5

The young and distinguished theologian, son of a noted psychiatrist, was an ardent and uncompromising foe of Hitler and
Nazism. By nature optimistic and filled with a zest for life, he
unflinchingly accepted his fate at the hands of the Gestapo.
Bonhoeffer was hanged by the SS in April, 1945.

On the morning of February 7, 1945, I spoke to Bonhoeffer for the last time. About noon his cell number was called, together with many others. These prisoners were divided into two transports, and the one to which Bonhoeffer belonged was sent to the concentration camp of Buchenwald. I found out later, by questioning his former fellow prisoners, that he was dragged from one concentration camp to another until he finally met his end in the "extermination" camp of Flossenbürg, in southwestern Germany.

To the very end, even in those dark days when the Nazi rule was crumbling, Dietrich Bonhoeffer felt himself the chosen servant of the word of Jesus Christ. By that time the prisons had become so overcrowded that the inmates could no longer be segregated. Bonhoeffer took advantage of this condition by arranging prayer services, consoling those who had lost all hope, and giving them fresh courage. A towering rock of faith, he became a shining example for his fellow prisoners.

Towards the end of January, 1945, my counsel visited me again and told me that my case had become more serious still, for my name had cropped up several times during the trials of other defendants. He said that the Gestapo had apparently overlooked this, but that Freisler would surely remember my name.

Such, then, was my position when I found myself once again before the "People's Court" on February 3, 1945. The case of my friend Ewald von Kleist was being tried before mine. Kleist declared that he had always fought against Hitler with everything he had, that he had never made a secret of his attitude, and that he believed this fight to be in accordance with God's own commandments.

God alone, he said, would be his judge. Anyone who saw Kleist in this moment, proud and undaunted before men but humble before God, could not help but wish to die with the same kind of dignity. For some reason, Freisler interrupted the trial against Kleist, and it was not resumed until the middle of March, when he was condemned to death. My sister later heard through an acquaintance that Kleist had listened to the pronouncement of the death sentence with complete and stoic calm.

Just as my case was being called before the court around noon on February 3, the air raid sirens sounded. The court officials telephoned to find out whether a big attack could be expected. The answer was shocking: huge masses of bombers were approaching Berlin. Hastily the entire court sought shelter in the vaulted cellars of the building. I, too, was taken down to the cellar after having first been manacled.

A terrible bombardment began, probably the worst daylight attack ever launched by American bombers on Berlin. It felt as though the end of the world had come. In the midst of this raging tumult there was a deafening crash which shook the very walls of the cellar. The court building had received a direct hit. It burst into flames, and began to crumble. As part of the ceiling collapsed into the cellar, a heavy beam came crashing down, striking Freisler on the head with full force. A doctor was somehow gotten, and after a brief examination announced that Freisler had suffered a double skull fracture, and was dead. My counsel later told me that in death Freisler had been clutching the files of my case.

The main Gestapo quarters in the Prinz Albrechtstrasse had also been hit and had burned to the ground. The prison in the cellars of the building had remained intact, except for minor damages. However, there was no light, no water, no heat, all of which did not make life easier for the prisoners, especially at that time of the year. Despite these conditions, all the prisoners whose sentences were expected shortly had to remain, while the others—the majority—were moved to other quarters. The few of us who remained behind could now talk with one another occasionally, because of the reduced number of guards.

Shortly before this air raid, which struck Berlin to the very core, a new prisoner had been brought in on a stretcher, his legs paralyzed. He was the former Supreme Court Judge Hans von Dohnanyi, General Oster's close associate and the man who was to have played an important part in the seizure of Berlin by the resistance movement. He suffered unspeakably, dependent upon the assistance of the callous Gestapo guards for all his bodily needs. Dietrich Bonhoeffer, Dohnanyi's brother-in-law, managed to get in touch with him and exchange some information. Dohnanyi, it appeared, had found a way to communicate with his wife. One day, hoping to delay the trial, he swallowed the diptheria bacilli she sent him. The resulting poisoning with its accompanying paralysis, had rendered him incapable of appearing before court for a long time. Dohnanyi was transferred later on to a special bunker in the Sachsenhausen concentration camp. From that time on, all trace of him was lost, but it must be assumed that sometime in April, 1945, during the last frantic days before the final collapse of the Third Reich, Hans von Dohnanyi was carried on a stretcher to the gallows and his remains then destroyed by the SS.

Another one of the prisoners during those days in the

Prinz Albrechtstrasse was Kurt von Plettenberg. When the Gestapo tried to force him, under threat of torture, to disclose the names of other members of the conspiracy, he steadfastly refused. Finally, he was given another twenty-four hours to reconsider.

Early in the morning of the next day I had one last chance to talk with him. He described the situation and said, with a smile: "I shall take my own life before disclosing a single name." Around noon that day, as he was being taken to a room on the fourth floor, he suddenly knocked down the official who was interrogating him, and leaped out of the window. Seconds later his shattered body lay on the pavement of the prison yard.

In the meantime, my trial had been rescheduled for March 16, 1945. The presiding judge was Dr. Krohne, Vice President of the "People's Court." Unlike the late Freisler, Krohne had not heard my name in other trials. Right after the start of the proceedings, I stated that Frederick the Great had abolished torture in Prussia two hundred years before, but that I had been subjected to torture in our day and age. Then I went on to describe in detail the torture. Recalling all the brutalities affected me so much that at one point I had to stop and regain my composure, but I was not interrupted. I had the feeling that the court and all the others present were holding their breath, for one could have heard a pin drop in the room. After a few minutes I regained my composure and was able to finish my statement.

When the court completed questioning me I expected that the Police Commissioner responsible for interrogating and torturing me would be called. But the presiding judge declared that the court had already questioned the

Commissioner in a special session during which neither I nor my counsel had been present, and that this questioning had confirmed my statements. In view of this, the Chief Prosecutor dropped the indictment. The "People's Court" acquitted me and cancelled the warrant of arrest.

I was returned to the Gestapo prison, for there was of course no question of my immediate release and, as I soon found out, no hope of my being released at all. A few days later, there was another air raid alarm. As we prisoners were being taken to the shelter, I heard Gestapo Commissioner Habecker ordering the guards to keep an especially close watch on me. Only a few hours later I was informed that the decision of the "People's Court" had obviously been an error. Although the Gestapo would respect it to the extent of not hanging me, I would be shot instead. An odd sensation overcame me when, to satisfy the regulations of totalitarian bureaucracy, I had to acknowledge this information with my signature.

CHAPTER TWENTY-FOUR

Liberation

Only a few days after my "acquittal," I was awakened around two o'clock in the morning and told to get ready. Several other prisoners and I were loaded into closed trucks and transported to the concentration camp at Flossenbürg, in the southwestern part of Germany.

Flossenbürg was one of the "extermination camps," where those people were murdered who either had never come before the "People's Court," or had been acquitted by it. Dr. Carl Sack, the former Judge Advocate-General of the German Army, Admiral Canaris, and General Oster were hanged at Flossenbürg.

Once again I found myself in solitary confinement and in chains. This time, however, the chain was fastened to one wrist only and was long enough so that I could move in a half circle. By climbing on a stool I was even able to peep out of the small cell window near the ceiling.

One of the large adjoining cells housed a number of British prisoners of war who had attempted to escape from a prison camp, and after recapture had been transfered to Flossenbürg. They were treated quite well in comparison with the German prisoners, and I could frequently hear the sound of English songs coming from their cells.

The fact that Flossenbürg was an "extermination camp" was only too evident. Time and again, around six o'clock in the morning, I could hear prisoners in other cells being awakened. They were forced to undress completely and were taken past our cells to the prison courtyard, where they were either hanged or shot in the back of the head. Occasionally I could see from my cell window the bodies of those who had been murdered being carried down the hillside by other prisoners. Because the camp crematory was out of order at the time, the the bodies were burned on piles of wood out in the open.

By pure coincidence I found out that my friend Dietrich Bonhoeffer was also at Flossenbürg. One night I was awakened and asked for my name. A short while later the guard returned and accused me of having given him the wrong name. He insisted that I must be Bonhoeffer. When I denied this, he left and did not return again.

Any faint hope I might have harbored that the interest shown in finding Bonhoeffer might mean that the SS had received orders to release him were shattered one morning a few days later, when a SS guard told me that, the night before, they had again hanged several men of the counter-intelligence. I questioned him about the identity of these men, and soon found out that Canaris, Oster, Sack, Bonhoeffer, and Gehre had been among them. Much later I heard through another guard that Bonhoeffer had been taken to Flossenbürg on April 8. On April 9, Bonhoeffer's few belongings, consisting mainly of the Holy Bible and a volume of Goethe's works, were deposited in the Guard room of the camp. It can therefore be assumed without a shadow of doubt that Dietrich Bonhoeffer was hanged by the SS at six o'clock in the morning of April 9 at the concentration camp of Flossenbürg.

On April 12 the noise of the rapidly advancing American troops came closer and closer. Even in my cell, I was able to distinguish between the sounds made by the firing and the impact of the artillery shells. Around noon that same day, a guard appeared and ordered me to get ready. There really wasn't too much to get ready with, for I had nothing left except the blue convict's garb I was wearing and a pair of canvas sneakers. After my chains had been unlocked, I was loaded on a truck together with other prisoners and taken to the concentration camp of Dachau. The route led through Munich, thereby giving me my first glimpse of a city that had sustained heavy bombings.

We arrived at Dachau during the night, and were lined up in the camp courtyard for a head count. It was a macabre spectacle: the prisoners, pale-faced and shabby, closely guarded by SS-men with their vicious, snarling police dogs, the entire scene bathed in the cold glare of the camp searchlights.

When the names on the list had been checked off, it was found that mine was missing. This caused the SS guard in charge to fly into a rage, which in return resulted in his heaping me with abuse. It also helped to confirm

331

my suspicion that I was alive merely because of a last-minute oversight, and that I had never been meant to leave Flossenbürg alive.

Whatever the reason, here I was, for the first time in many months without chains, and no longer in solitary confinement. The SS evidently did not have sufficient man-power or organization left to guard the prisoners as strictly as before.

That first night in Dachau, I shared a room with the French bishop of Clermont-Ferrant. It certainly was not an appropriate place for a bishop, for the pictures on the walls were unmistakable evidence that the room had been part of the "recreational" facilities provided for the SS guards in the heyday of the camp. The pictures did not bother me unduly; I was interested only in finding out what kind of conditions we could expect from now on. In the morning I was unable to resist the urge to do a little exploring. Over the anguished protests of the poor bishop, who was deathly afraid of provoking the SS, I cautiously opened the door and looked out. I discovered that there were no guards outside the door of our room; I met some of the other prisoners, and even obtained a razor from one of them and the luxury of a shave.

The prisoners at Dachau, I soon realized, were a motley crew of men and women of many different nationalities. The fact that we were no longer segregated told us that the Third Reich was deteriorating rapidly. Actually this was not much of a consolation, for it increased the danger that the SS, in an attempt to save their own skins and get rid of incriminating witnesses, would simply liquidate us on their own at the first opportunity.

Soon Dachau was no longer safe from the advancing

Americans, and so the trek went on southward through Austria. At the concentration camp at Innsbruck, we picked up more prisoners, among them one in full uniform and even with the Pour le mérite—the highest German decoration for gallantry in World War I—still around his neck. He was General von Falkenhausen, the one man whom even the SS hesitated to abuse. Openly and with the help of a map he had somehow obtained, Falkenhausen pointed out the advance of the Allied armies on all fronts, proving to us that the collapse of the Third Reich was imminent.

Still our southbound journey went on, through Austria and into Tyrol. Our number that time included the former French President Leon Blum, Molotov's nephew Kokorin, the widow of General Hammerstein, and several Greek generals. Our fear that the SS would liquidate us increased daily. We therefore were somewhat relieved when General Thomas, also a member of our group, found an opportunity to speak to a German general whom we met with other German troops retreating from Italy. Thomas managed to persuade the other general, whom he knew quite well, to add a company of soldiers to our caravan. Even though these troops were visibly demoralized—the fact that they carried their rifles pointing downward was an unmistakable sign of that—we felt a little safer now that we were no longer entirely at the mercy of the SS guards.

From that moment on a peculiar situation developed. At times it was not quite clear who was planning to shoot whom: Would the SS shoot the prisoners, would the soldiers shoot the SS, or would the Italian partisans, who were beginning to appear along the ridges and hillsides, shoot the whole lot of us?

In these uncertain circumstances we arrived in the small town of Niedernhausen, in the Puster valley south of the Brenner Pass. Because the camp we were supposed to occupy had been taken over by the staff of a German army unit, we had to wait in pouring rain before we were finally quartered in the city hall, where we slept on the stone floor. More than ever that night we had the feeling that the SS would find an opportunity to liquidate us and then try to make good their own escape. And so, before lying down to sleep we arranged to have several of us take turns standing guard through the night. It was not that we, unarmed as we were, could have done much against the heavily armed SS, but we did not want to be caught unawares and slaughtered in our sleep.

But that night passed quietly and without incident. In the morning the door opened and the SS master sergeant in charge of the guard entered. Bracing ourselves for the worst, we watched him warily, but to our complete surprise the blustering bully had changed—literally overnight. The man who had been heaping abuse on us day after day, for whom "swine" had been one of the milder forms of address to us prisoners, stood before us on that memorable morning, removed his cap, and said: "I wish the arrested gentlemen a good morning." In the ensuing stunned silence, General von Falkenhausen, who was lying next to me, said loud and clear: "Now Hitler has lost his war!"

There followed a scene of confusion. The SS simply disappeared, after having tried—unsuccessfully—to get certificates of good behavior from us. We never saw them again, but I have since heard—although it never has been verified—that they were caught and liquidated by Italian partisans. If this is true, I can only say that the death of these men was not too great a loss to human society.

Finding ourselves stranded and left to our own devices, there was some discussion among us as to what to do next. We knew that the region was full of Italian partisans, who at that time were not too particular about whom they liquidated, which meant that we still were in danger. The British prisoners of war finally decided to take command. From that moment on there was a subtle change in the relationship between them and us, with some of the former strong feeling of comradeship fading.

We were still undecided about our further course of action when, on May 4, American troops suddenly appeared in the town. Within a short time the entire place was crawling with jeeps and young American soldiers in their clean uniforms. An American general came to speak to us and my first thought, as I stood there in my shabby convict's clothes, was how beautifully tailored his uniform was and what an elegant and handsome figure he cut in it.

The general was very polite. It was an odd feeling, after all the months in prisons and concentration camps, to have people in uniform address us as though we were human beings. The American informed us that he would have to take us to Naples, because there was too much danger from Italian partisans where we were. In Naples, he assured us, he could guarantee our safety because it was firmly in American hands. There we could be sorted out and eventually released.

There were some complaints about this decision by members of our group who wanted to go straight home. The general, however, remained firm though always polite. I, for my part, had not the slightest objection to going to

Naples; what counted with me was the still quite incredible and dream-like fact that I had indeed escaped with my life from the nightmare of concentration and extermination camps and was safe at last.

The Americans loaded our crowd into their jeeps—three of us in each car with an American soldier as driver—and took us to Verona. From there we were flown to Naples by an American military plane and quartered in what had formerly been a hotel. The food was good and there was plenty to smoke—two luxuries which I had not known for many months and which I thoroughly enjoyed.

At some point during the trip, the Russians in our group decided to part company with us. They simply disappeared one day; probably they felt some qualms about leaving important persons, such as Molotov's nephew, in Allied hands. We others were soon transferred from Naples to the Hotel Paradiso on the island of Capri. There our treatment at the hands of the Americans was again very correct and polite, but we were not allowed to leave the grounds, which were under tight guard by American police.

From Capri, all the members of our group eventually found their way back to their countries, there to pick up the pieces of their lives as best they could. In the preface to this book, I have already related the special circumstances through which I was able to return to Germany.

The last chapter of my odyssey was written in June, 1945. I had obtained the use of a car from the Americans at Wiesbaden and was on my way to locate my wife and children. After having fled from our home in Pomerania when it became clear that the Red Army would occupy the eastern regions of Germany, they had found refuge in my mother's home in upper Franconia.

On a road not far from the place I was looking for, I saw a woman on a bicycle approaching. It was my wife.

And so, ten months after my arrest, I was finally reunited with my family. I was ready to go about the task of rebuilding my civilian career among the shambles of a shattered, divided, and occupied Germany, which the German anti-Hitler resistance had striven so hard, if unsuccessfully, to save from just such a fate.

Chronology

of the National Socialist Era, 1933–1945

1 9 3 3

January 30	Hindenburg appoints Hitler Reichs Chancellor.
February 2 to October 14	Second International Disarmament Conference.
February 27	The Reichstag Building in Berlin is destroyed by fire.
March 5	Reichstag elections: NSDAP gets 44% of the votes.
March 21	Ceremonial introduction by Hindenburg of Hitler as Reichs Chancellor in the Garrison Church at Potsdam.
March 23	The Reichstag, by a law which alters the constitution, empowers the Hitler government to issue laws without parliamentary approval.
April 1	Boycott of Jewish businesses and professions.
May 2	Labor unions are dissolved.

July 14   Law against the creation of new parties (after the dissolution of all parties except the NSDAP).

July 20   Concordat between the German Reich and the Vatican.

October 14   Germany leaves the Disarmament Conference.

The German Reich announces its withdrawal from the League of Nations.

November 12   Reichstag elections: 93% of the votes are cast for the NSDAP, which constitutes the only party in the parliament.

1 9 3 4

January 26   Non-aggression pact and friendship treaty between Germany and Poland.

January 30   Passage of law for the "reconstruction of the Reich" as a centralized state, and elimination of the provinces as federal states.

June 14   First meeting of Hitler and Mussolini in Venice.

June 30 to July 2   "Roehm Putsch." Under the pretext that Roehm, the top SA leader, was planning a revolt, Hitler has countless of his adversaries shot without trial.

August 2   Death of Hindenburg. Hitler becomes his successor as "Fuehrer and Reichs Chancellor."

Armed Forces take the oath to Hitler.

1 9 3 5

January 13   Plebiscite in the Saar territory; 91% are in favor of the return to the German Reich.

January 17	The council of the League of Nations decides to return the Saar territory to Germany.
March 16	Germany rejects the restrictions on armament of the Versailles Treaty and introduces compulsory military service.
May 21	Hitler's Reichstag speech announcing the "13 points" of his peace program.
June 18	German-British naval treaty.
September 15	Proclamation of the anti-Semitic "Nuremberg laws."

1 9 3 6

March 7	The German Reich abrogates the Locarno Treaty and reinstitutes the full military sovereignty of Germany by occupying (in a breach of the treaty) the demilitarized zone in the Rhineland.
July 11	Agreement with Austria.
October 25	German-Italian treaty founds the "Berlin-Rome Axis."
November 25	Anti-Comintern pact between Germany and Japan.

1 9 3 7

November 6	Italy joins the Anti-Comintern Pact.
November 19	Conference between Lord Halifax and Hitler.

1 9 3 8

February 4	Dismissal of Reichs War Minister von Blomberg and the Commander-in-Chief of the Army, Colonel-General von Fritsch.
	Ribbentrop named Foreign Minister.

341

March 11   Germans march into Austria after Hitler's ultimatum.

March 13   "Anschluss" of Austria to the German Reich.

August 27   Resignation of the Chief of the General Staff of the Army, Colonel-General Beck.

September 15   Conference between Hitler and Chamberlain at Berchtesgaden.

September 22   Conference between Hitler and Chamberlain
to 24   at Bad Godesberg.

September 29   Conference in Munich: Hitler, Mussolini, Chamberlain, Daladier.

                  German-British Non-Aggression Declaration.

October 1   German troops enter the Sudeten-German territories.

November 9   Excesses against the Jews, organized by Goebbels (Crystal Night).

December 6   Non-Aggression Declaration between Germany and France.

1 9 3 9

March 15   German troops march into Bohemia-Moravia (Czechoslovakia).

March 21   German offer to Poland (return of Danzig to Germany, extra-territorial road and railroad through the corridor, long-range guarantee of the German-Polish border).

March 23   German troops enter the Memel territory.

March 26   Poland rejects the German offer of March 21.

May 22   Conclusion of a military treaty (the "Pact of Steel") between Germany and Italy.

May 31 to June 7	Germany concludes non-aggression treaties with Estonia, Latvia, and Denmark.
August 23	Conclusion of the German-Soviet Non-Aggression Pact (with a secret protocol on Poland).
August 25	British-Polish treaty.
September 1	Secret euthanasia order.
	German attack on Poland begins.
September 3	Great Britain and France declare war on Germany.
September 17	Soviet troops enter Poland.
October 6	Hitler's peace offer to the Western Powers.
November 8	Assassination attempt against Hitler in the Buergerbräukeller in Munich.
November 21	British blockade of German exports begins.

1 9 4 0

April 9	German invasion of Denmark and Norway.
May 10	German offensive against Holland, Belgium, Luxembourg, and France.
May 14	Rotterdam capitulates.
May 15	Truce with the Netherlands.
May 17	Occupation of Brussels.
May 18	Germans take Antwerp.
June 4	Germans take Dunkirk.
June 14	Occupation of Paris.
	Breakthrough of the Maginot line south of Saarbruecken.
June 22	Truce with France at Compiègne.
July 10	German air raids on England begin (London, in September; Coventry, in November).

1 9 4 1

February 6	Creation of the German Afrika-Corps under Rommel.
March 2	German troops march into Bulgaria.
March 24	Beginning of the German offensive in Africa from the Gulf of Sidra. Conquest of Cyrenaica. Offensive pushed to the borders of Egypt.
April 6	Campaign against Yugoslavia and Greece begins.
May 20 to June 1	Conquest of Crete.
June 18	German-Turkish Friendship agreement.
June 22	German offensive against the Soviet Union.
August 12	Roosevelt and Churchill announced the Atlantic Charter.
September and October	Victorious German battles at Kiev, Briansk, and Wjasma.
November	German offensive gets bogged down before Moscow.
November 18	British counter-offensive in Africa.
December 7	Japanese sea and air attack against Pearl Harbor.
	Hitler's "Nacht und Nebel" (Night-and-Mist) order.
December 8	Declaration of war on Japan by the United States.
December 10	British free Tobruk, in Africa, from German encirclement.
December 11	Declaration of war on the United States by Germany and Italy.

December 19   Hitler, replacing Brauchitsch, assumes the Supreme Command of the German Army.

1 9 4 2

January 18   Military alliance between the states of the Three-Power Pact.

January 21   German-Italian counter-offensive in Africa at El-Alamein.

June 28   Drive by the German Army toward Stalingrad and the Caucasus.

November 8   Landing of American and British troops in northwest Africa.

1 9 4 3

January 14 to 26   Conference of the Allies in Casablanca. They announce their policy of "unconditional surrender."

January 18   The German siege of Leningrad is broken by the Russians.

February 2   Soviet troops take Stalingrad after month-long battles and force the German 6th Army to capitulate.

April 17 to June 16   Annihilation of the Warsaw ghetto by the SS.

July 10   Allies land in Sicily.

July 25   Mussolini, forced to resign, is arrested.

November 28 to December 1   Roosevelt, Stalin, and Churchill meet at Teheran.

1 9 4 4

January 3   The Red Army reaches the former Polish border.

June 4	The Allies occupy Rome.
June 6	The Allies land in Normandy.
June 22	Beginning of the successful Russian offensive against the Army Group Center.
July 20	Assassination attempt on Hitler by Colonel Count von Stauffenberg at Hitler's Headquarters in East Prussia, and attempt at a coup d'état by the resistance movement in Berlin.
August 1 to October 2	Revolt by the Polish underground movement in Warsaw.
August 23	Arrest of Antonescu and coup d'état in Bucharest.
August 25	General de Gaulle enters Paris.
October 20	Belgrade falls to the Red Army.

1945

January	The Red Army reaches German soil in East Prussia and Silesia.
February 4 to 11	Conference of the Allies in Yalta.
April 12	Death of Roosevelt.
April 13	The Red Army occupies Vienna.
April 27	Allied and Soviet troops meet at Torgau.
April 30	Hitler commits suicide.
May 2	Berlin capitulates.
May 7 to 9	Total capitulation of the German Army.

Index